THE OPTION METHOD

The Myth *of* Unhappiness

The Collected Works of Bruce Di Marsico on The Option Method and Attitude

VOLUME
2

Feelings, Beliefs, and Desires

Emotions

Motivation

Wanting, Doing, and Knowing

Relationships

Believing Yourself

Forms of Unhappiness

Arguments against Happiness

The
OPTION METHOD
The Myth *of* Unhappiness

The Collected Works of Bruce Di Marsico

on

The Option Method and Attitude

VOLUME
2

Edited and with commentary by Aryeh Nielsen

Foreword by Frank Mosca

Introduction by Deborah Mendel

With contributions by Wendy Dolber

DIALOGUES IN SELF DISCOVERY LLC ◆ MONTCLAIR, NEW JERSEY

The Option Method: The Myth of Unhappiness
The Collected Works of Bruce Di Marsico on The Option Method and Attitude
Volume 2

Materials © 2010 by Deborah Mendel
Foreword © 2010 by Frank Mosca
Commentary © 2010 by Aryeh Nielsen
"The Man Who Found Diamonds" © by Wendy Dolber

Dialogues in Self Discovery LLC
P.O. Box 43161, Montclair, NJ 07043
www.DialoguesInSelfDiscovery.com

Disclaimer
The information provided within is not a substitute for professional medical advice and care. If you have specific needs, please see a professional health care provider.

Design by Williams Writing, Editing & Design
www.williamswriting.com

Volume 1
Paperback, ISBN 978-1-934450-01-7

Volume 2
Paperback, ISBN 978-1-934450-02-4

Volume 3
Paperback, ISBN 978-1-934450-03-1

Printed in the United States of America

Listen to your heart,
  for that is where knowledge acts.
Do only what attracts you.
Do what you feel like.
Cor Super Ratio. *The Heart above logic.*

—Bruce Di Marsico

Contents

PART II: EMOTIONS

PART III: WHAT MOVES US

Foreword by Frank Mosca

THE READER OF THESE WORKS IS GOING TO FIND A ROADMAP TO THE vast and varied workings of Bruce Di Marsico's mind. But despite the sometime appearances of complexity, there will be a road sign pointing always, always in one direction: to your happiness. That is the key to remember as you set out on your journey. I know that this is what has sustained and enriched my own journey, one that began decades ago when I was fortunate to come upon Bruce's ideas and then had the great fortune to meet and learn personally from him. This brief introduction is really simply one person's experience of Bruce, of The Option Method and what that has meant in my life.

First at the core, it has meant everything. It has meant ongoing happiness to the degree that I learned to remember my happiness should I forget it. It has meant the disentangling of what seemed to be impossible knots of contradictions, complexities and conundrums that seemed never to yield to whatever I would bring to bear to try and help myself. The image of Bruce like Alexander cutting the Gordian knot of human misery comes to mind. But it was not an act of hubris, but one of immense insight that allowed him to see through the apparent insurmountability of the problem of human happiness. He could then dissolve what stood in the way and open to view that most profound but simple truth: your happiness is always yours; it is in fact what and who you are. Beliefs are the artificial blockages to that direct and incredible knowledge. Questions are the key to removing them.

Like Socrates, from whom he drew some inspiration, Bruce relished the dialogue and the coming to the key "I don't know" moment. The moment when we stand on the edge of two worlds. The one we could now leave behind. The one we have constructed with the aid of culture in all its forms and configurations. Once the veil of our dedication to the pseudo-certainty of what we think we know is rent, we are naked to the possibility of taking that giant step to acknowledging the unshakeable truth of our own happiness now and in every moment we are privileged to allow ourselves to know it.

As you read these volumes it will at times seem that Bruce may be going off in endless tangents of discussions. But these are not tangents at all. Remember, that one blinding truth about happiness is resisted by us in almost endless ways. His students and clients raised doubts and difficulties at every turn as they wrestled with the import of surrendering their beliefs in some apparently necessary miseries, some absolutely irreducible requirements to be unhappy. Remember, our whole world rests upon these assumptions. It is no wonder then that Bruce brought his particular eloquence to elaborate and draw out incredible subtleties of argument, wit, and pure intellectual power to counter these objections and to continue thereby to hold out hope to those who continued to bury themselves in needless labyrinths of their own making. But he was patient; it was his signature strength. He knew what seemed to us to be at stake, and he wanted for all who would to hear that joy that he himself was living.

So, don't hold back in your engagement with Bruce; he will not disappoint you. In all these decades, he has been my constant companion in life and even in death. His words, his vision, his immense verve in being willing to take on your fears and doubts with extraordinary intellectual skill will get you to that place you yearn for. So it has been with me, through so many unexpected turns and twists my life has taken.

Now in my seventies, I am filled with joy at the prospect of his work being made widely available. He has shone a bright, inextinguishable light into the shadows and darkness of the human condition. Do not fear it. It will not consume but will enlighten and elevate. I am so glad you are taking this opportunity to discover this for yourself. Written with deep gratitude,

Frank Mosca
May 5th, 2010
Hampton Bays, New York

Guide to the Collected Works

The Collected Works of Bruce Di Marsico SPAN THREE VOLUMES, which together constitute his explanation of the truth about happiness: that we are already perfectly happy, and unhappiness is merely the belief that we could somehow not be.

These writings are created from lectures and writings created over a period of a quarter century. Bruce taught a number of extended courses on Option, and this book attempts to follow the general order of presentation in his teaching work, and to serve as a course in The Option Method and Attitude for those who were not able to experience Bruce firsthand.

The course progresses in this manner: first, an introductory overview is presented (*Overview of The Option Method*). This is followed by core Option concepts (*Happiness, Unhappiness, Feelings, Beliefs, Desires, Emotions, Motivation, Wanting, Doing, Knowing*).

Next are the most immediate, everyday implications of these teachings (*Relationships, Believing Yourself, Forms of Unhappiness*), more advanced implications (*Arguments against Happiness, Behavior, Myths*), and then the most esoteric implications of Option (*Happiness without Reason, Enjoying Your Happiness, Option Mysticism*).

Only at this point is *Practicing The Option Method* considered. The Option Attitude is the foundation of The Option Method. Just as "technically correct" music empty of emotion is an empty exercise, so is The Option Method practiced without the Option Attitude. Bruce did not cover the practice of The Option Method until well into his courses, so that the fundamental Option Attitude was well-established in those who used the Method. He demonstrated and taught that once the Option attitude is well-understood, the practice of the Method flows organically.

Finally, *Stories and Meditations* and *A Comprehensive Overview* provide a summing up and review of Option teachings.

The material, while presenting an overall arc of argument, has many loopbacks and repetitions. Bruce often said the same thing in many different ways so that everyone would have a chance to understand the implications of knowing that unhappiness cannot happen to us.

The truth of happiness is simple. Why does it take three volumes to explain? Because the belief in unhappiness takes many forms, and is incredibly complex. But to be happy, there is nothing to know. All the medicine contained within these volumes is to help release unhappy beliefs, and as they fall away, they become of no importance. After studying the Collected Works, you will know far less than you did when you started. What you will no longer "know" and believe is that you have to be unhappy. And you will find that, without these beliefs, you will know your own happiness.

The three volumes of
The Collected Works of Bruce Di Marsico

Volume I
An Overview of The Option Method
Happiness
Unhappiness

The first part of Volume I provides an overview of The Option Method, and touches on all aspects of Option, to provide a framework for understanding the details. The remainder of this volume explains happiness and unhappiness: happiness is what you are. Unhappiness is believing that what you are is somehow wrong.

Volume II
Feelings, Beliefs, and Desires
Emotions
Motivation
Wanting, Doing, and Knowing

Relationships
Believing Yourself
Forms of Unhappiness
Arguments against Happiness

Volume II starts by explaining how unhappiness happens. Believing, or predicting the consequences of an event for how you feel, is how emotions happen. Why does unhappiness happen? It is the (unnecessary) use of emotions to motivate your wanting. It also discusses happiness in the context of relationships, how happiness is synonymous with perfect self-trust, and the forms that unhappiness takes. It concludes by dismantling arguments commonly made against happiness.

Volume III
Behavior
Myths
Happiness without Reason
Enjoying Your Happiness
Option Mysticism
Practicing The Option Method
Stories and Meditations
A Comprehensive Overview

Volume III addresses myths: the myths that behavior has anything to do with happiness, and myths such as "the meaning of life." It continues with discussing how we need no reasons to be happy, and then discusses enjoying your happiness, as you get more and more in touch with it (perhaps ultimately manifested as a form of mysticism). It explains how to practice The Option Method to help you or others get more in touch with their happiness. It concludes contemplations on happiness in the form of stories and meditations, and two summaries of Option teachings, one comprehensive and one reductive.

Introduction by Deborah Mendel

*The Option Method takes unhappiness from that vague cloud
of confusion and that which just happens to you and brings it
down to the real dynamics that cause your emotions . . . your
beliefs and your judgments.*

BRUCE DI MARSICO

FUNDAMENTAL TO BRUCE'S OPTION METHOD IS THE NONJUDGMEN-
tal approach to exploring unhappiness. This attitude, combined with
The Option Method questions, unravels the mystery and "cloud of
confusion" that usually surrounds our emotional upsets. The Option Method helps you let go of those beliefs that are fueling your
unhappiness.

Bruce understood that we are our own best experts. We each have
our own individual, specific reasons for becoming unhappy when
we do. The Option Method questions are designed to help us identify
those reasons. Unlike other modalities, The Option Method does not
require you to rethink, memorize, or adopt a new belief or thought
pattern. The Option Method questions present a painless process
that allows us to simply let go of self-defeating beliefs. The Option
Method reveals the beliefs behind our bad feelings and unhappiness.
Through this process we discover it is painless and easy to let go of
the beliefs that cause our unhappiness.

Did you ever notice that when you anticipate getting upset about
something you begin immediately to feel upset? The moment we begin to fear or predict that we are going to feel any way that we don't
want to feel in the future, we have already begun to feel that way
in the present. It is likewise true of our good feelings. When we are
looking forward to feeling good about something, we immediately
feel good and are in a good mood.

I believe that one of the most profound discoveries that Bruce made in his creation of Option is that our current unhappiness is derived from our predictions and imaginings of ourselves as unhappy in some way in the future—more specifically, our *beliefs* about what we will feel in the future. The answer is not to convince ourselves that our future will always be bright. We know from experience that life does not always work out the way we want it to. The Option Method gives us a tool to question our beliefs and realize that, whatever our future holds, we don't have to feel unhappy about it. When we are free from these "future fears," we will naturally be happier.

Deborah Mendel

Notes to the Reader

1. Whenever an entire passage appears in this sans serif font, it is editorial commentary.

2. Bruce developed Option Method in the early years of his psychotherapeutic practice, initially calling it Existential Analysis, Option Psychotherapy and other similar names. At that time, he was teaching mostly to mental health care professionals. He quickly saw that his teachings—concerned specifically with unhappiness and beliefs about unhappiness—really did not fit into the paradigm of the medical or psychotherapeutic model. They had a much wider application to all those interested in personal growth and development. From 1970 on, he used only the name Option Method. It was his intention to make the Method available to as wide a group as possible so those who were trained could carry on the teachings. Early lectures often included the words "therapist" and "patient," which soon gave way to terms like "practitioner" and "client." These terms should be considered to be used interchangeably.

3. The purpose of editorial commentary in this book is twofold: sometimes to clarify areas that Bruce spoke about during many talks, but did not create any central document or lecture on. Other commentary is meant to provide a roadmap to essays or talks that some have found particularly difficult to understand. By reviewing a roadmap of the teaching first, it is hoped the reader will be able to absorb the works more easily.

4. More resources can be found online. In the archives sections of the ChooseHappiness.net website there are many study guides for topics featured in this book, and audio recordings of Bruce's original lectures. **http://www.choosehappiness.net**

PART I

Feelings, Beliefs, and Desires

SECTION I

Introduction to Beliefs

The Body

Believing Is with the Whole Body

Here, Bruce Di Marsico discusses that, since the mind-body split is mythical, beliefs are always held with and as the whole body.

Beliefs aren't just a mental set, an intellectual construct. When we turn something into a belief, it doesn't just exist as some kind of a symbol in the brain, a verbal pattern, but it exists throughout the whole body as an act, which the body can manifest. A belief is not in the so-called brain; a belief is in the mind and the mind is between the top of the scalp and the bottom of the soles of the feet. The whole idea that your mind is in your head is archaic. *Believing* is believing with the whole body.

FROM JANUARY 28, 1974 LECTURE

Although a belief may not ever have been expressed in words or recognized as a personally held assumption, it is nonetheless held in at least a non-verbal way and in all other psycho-physical ways as an aspect of the person, which we refer to as "the personality."

FROM WRITING: "THE CAUSE OF UNHAPPINESS"

Emotions and feeling bad are attitudes. Attitudes are bodily stances—they're the way we hold ourselves in the world.

FROM NOVEMBER 11, 1995 LECTURE

The Body, in Itself, Is Happy

Here, Bruce Di Marsico discusses that the body, in itself, is perfectly happy. Every belief about how the body *should* be both is experienced as unhappiness, and impedes the well-being of the body.

 This does not imply that a happy person will necessarily have a well-functioning body by general cultural standards, but rather that a happy person's body will function as well as it possibly can, and be as comfortable as possible, even in the context of an illness or injury.

To wonder if some manifestation of your body (pain, pus, puke or perspiration) could be caused by unhappiness is the belief that unhappiness can happen to you.

FROM WRITING: "ALL UNHAPPY BELIEFS ARE DERIVED"

BELIEVING is with the body in a certain way. It is actually a destruction of the body. Believing always manifests itself in the body as some kind of a problem, as something uncomfortable. So, the more we believe, the less of our body we will have, and so every belief is a hole in the body. It is a void in the mind because it implies a "not being yet." If I believe something about myself, I am saying I am not being something yet that I want to be.

FROM JANUARY 28, 1974 LECTURE

WHAT we call the experience of feeling happy is the physical phenomenon of the body functioning undisturbed by our beliefs in unhappiness. Whatever causes us to desire happiness would of necessity cause also the desire to sustain whatever function is the feeling of happiness. Certainly, life, in some sense, is part of our experience of happiness. When happy, we feel alive.

FROM WRITING: "WHAT EVERY OPTION THERAPIST KNOWS"

"You" and "Your Body"

Here, Bruce Di Marsico addresses the myth of the mind-body split in more detail, discussing how unhappy beliefs are the cause of this apparent split.

THE will is the name of the relationship between mind and body. The will is the relationship between beliefs and behavior. The will is the process, the act of manifesting, what is unseen but real. The will would not even seem to exist were it not for a disparity (or apparent disparity) between the desire of the heart and the behavior of the body.

FROM WRITING: "THE WILL"

WHY would I want to believe I should do something? It's really only another way of saying I don't want to. If we really believe we should do something, you know psychologically what happens in our bodies? Our bodies believe us, and start acting like we don't want to do it, because what you've told your body is "I wouldn't want to do this in a million years, I just think I should." And your body says, okay, and now acts like you wouldn't want to do it in a million years.

So once you believe you *should* go on a diet, you *should* lose weight, gain weight, anything else, forget it. Your body will obey you. We've got this "unfortunate" relationship with our body: it believes us, and anything we believe, it believes. And if we believe we *should* do something, we have effectively taught ourselves that we don't want to.

FROM NOVEMBER 11, 1995 LECTURE

Words and Attitudes

Beliefs Are Not Inherently Verbal

A belief, whether conscious or not, is an attitude. It is a postulate, presumed to be true, and therefore is an attitude held by a person which determines every aspect of the self that is pertinent to that attitude. Although a belief may not be, or ever have been, expressed in words or recognized as a personally held assumption, it is nonetheless held in at least a non-verbal way, and in all other psycho-physical ways as an aspect of the person; which we refer to as the personality.

From November 11, 1995 lecture

Words as a Sign of an Underlying Attitude

Many words that people will use are just other words for being unhappy, like "stupid."

From "The Practice of Option," 1973

"Perfect happiness is not good for me." That belief can be made self-proving by manipulating the meanings and loading the words so that the terms are mutually exclusive.

From Collected Writings, "Happiness and Safety," February 20, 1974

Romantic love's greatest test is when the beloved needs something contrary to the lover's need. These are the kinds of words that you'll find being used by these kinds of lovers: duty, sacrifice, selfishness, disappointment.

From "Love as Giving," Monday Night Study Group, 1973

On the Meaning Behind Other's Words

The reason we don't use other words besides the client's own language is twofold: first, they will very frequently have a different meaning for another word, and secondly, they will think that your use of another word is some kind of a judgment on the word that they were using, and that you have a reluctance, perhaps, to use the word that they were using. And perhaps you might very well be, if you're avoiding their word and using your own.

FROM "THE PRACTICE OF OPTION," 1973

Beliefs Are Not a Problem

Questioner: *It seems like believing is the problem, that we should not hold any beliefs if we want to be happy.*

In *believing* there are questions. In *knowing*, there are no questions. Believing is a predictive guessing fantasy.

Now the only judgments and beliefs that are really going to affect your happiness are judgments and beliefs that have to do with your happiness. It might not make much of a difference to your happiness for you to make a prediction about where the stock market is going to go, as long as your money, or your lack of it, is not going to be something that you're going to make a judgment that you'll be happy about or not. A person who is really being happy might not make judgments or beliefs about their *happiness*, but they might make them about anything else, knowing that they are only just judgments, they are only just guesses, they're only just beliefs, which they're doing in order to get something or to conduct some business or to negotiate or to relate to someone.

There isn't anything certain about any belief; and the reality of who you really are or what things really are, I needn't know for sure if I know that my happiness is not implicated. So since I needn't know with certainty, I can guess, I can predict, I can believe. Why don't I need to know? Because the only thing I want to be is happy. Only if my happiness is contingent upon my knowing would I need to know; only if my happiness is contingent upon those beliefs about whether the sun will rise, whether the stock market will fall, would I want to get out of beliefs. The only future I'm really concerned to know is my future happiness.

If we were happier, we wouldn't be afraid to predict or foresee the future, and then whatever was in our power to make clear would be clear. What is truly unforeseeable by us is truly unforeseeable by us. But most of us suffer from screwing ourselves by unclear thinking, predicting something that somebody with clear thinking would never predict: getting into a situation, pretty much being able to know what the outcome would be, but fearing to see that—not wanting to see that until it was "too late," so to speak, and then regretting it. And the feeling of stressful thinking that some complain about is maybe a lot of irrelevant things that we search for because we don't feel happier.

There are two ways of looking at happiness: we can consider happiness in itself, or happiness in things, so that if we were seeking happiness in itself, I think we could all agree. If we are seeking happiness in things, some of us believe that what prevents happiness is one thing, and others believe it is another. Some of us believe that what prevents happiness is unclear thinking. Some of us believe it is fear. Some of us believe it is unhappiness.

Questioner: *Do you think it is ever possible to let go of all the fears at once?*

I'd like to answer you in two ways, one directly, and one indirectly. Directly: yes, I think it happens. I myself have experienced it. Now the question that follows for me from that is, if it happens, why doesn't it happen once and for all? Why does it only just happen at times? I definitely know for myself, and you probably all know for yourselves that there have been times when that really has happened—when you've let go of everything and you've really been okay. The second way I'd like to answer is this: even if I thought it were impossible for us to let go of all fears, even if all of us thought it were impossible to do that, who are we? Has our past history given us the competence to make that kind of a judgment, whether it is possible or not? Even if the wisest man in the world, or an angel, were to come to me and say it wasn't possible, I think my feeling would be "I don't care whether it's possible or not, I'm going to try to do it; I'm not going to let something so little as thinking it is impossible stop me." So that whether we will ever really do it once and for all or whether we will do it more and more and more, we're going to try. We want to. That would be the way I'd really like to answer you. Don't let a little thing like impossibility stop you. In fact, how many of us do believe it is impossible, yet we're still wanting to with all our hearts? We walk around really believing that true happiness, real happiness, perfect happiness is impossible, and yet everything we do is geared to that end.

My own experience about the "once and for all" is this: I'm so sure that the freedom and peace is always there, I can kind of walk away and ignore it, because I know it's there, and if ever I wanted it, it'd be there for me. At those times, I'm even aware of that. At those times of being really at peace, I also know I don't have to be at peace. I really don't have to. And maybe it's something like this: you could have a million dollars, but you don't have to sit and look at it; because you know you've got it, you can throw it in the bank, and walk around and act as if you were poor. People can get into giving up everything, and going away somewhere to be a missionary or something. Very frequently, the people who allow themselves to do that have made themselves very secure first and they have that to fall back on. And so they've got a lot of money, and then they'll go off, and they'll live poorly. And somehow, they could live that way for the rest of their life, as long as they just know that their money is in the bank. And you will find people who have sought out money their whole lives, and put it in a shoe box, or in the closet, or some such thing just so that they could live poorly—just in case. Well, I think that I do that with my own peace, because I know I have it, because I know it's mine, I can kind of act crazy. What's the difference?

A lot of people say that perfect happiness means dying. They believe that if they were to achieve that state that they would have to die, that somehow it would just mean the end of them. That it's a kind of suicide, a kind of explosion to the whole universe, and something inside them rebels against that.

We're trying to imagine and see if there's anything that's preventing us from being perfectly happy. Could it be that the reason we're not already happy is because there is something that we think is there that is frightening? The question began as "why are we not already happy?" We see it as somehow not such a good place to be, in some way. Some people see it as a deadly place. I'd like to say, "Why don't you get there, and tell me what it's like?" And then you say "but I don't really know if I want to go there." And that's the inherent contradiction. Where you *don't* want to go is *not* what we are talking about! That would be unhappiness!

We have that fantastic ability of making real happiness equal unhappiness, to imagine that there'd be something about real happiness to be afraid of. Now happiness itself becomes an object of fear, and it's even a contradiction in language, I think by the very fact that we're reasonable, rational, have to have reasons and causes, we can't accept a place where there is no reason to be there. And there really is no *reason* to be happy. We have all kinds of reasons to be unhappy, but we have no reasons to be happy. When I'm really at peace and really happy, I understand those who talk about non-functioning: I see very clearly, there is no reason for me to eat, there is no reason for me to sleep, there is no reason for me to work, and there is no reason for me to do anything anymore; there is no reason whatsoever, and so then I say to myself, "What am I going to do if I have no reasons for doing anything?" What I usually answer myself is "watch, wait and see."

It makes no difference. Why should I go to work? Why not? Why should I stay home? Why not? Why go to work, why stay home? No reason. Okay, what am I going to do? Watch and find out. And I watch myself do these things. And that's a way of living without reasoning and of really being in peace.

Questioner: *If beliefs and fears can go on to anything, why deal in words?*

Because words are where your fears are going onto right now. See, that's what we do, whether it be words or other forms of behavior. Why deal with behavior, even? When you really do see that you don't need to have any beliefs, what are you going to do with your ability to believe? Why should you throw away your ability to believe?

Sometimes we get a gift, and we feel so fantastic, but sometimes there is a tinge of insecurity that goes along with it, because there is also the recognition that somehow happiness is happening to me, I'm not really in control, I just found myself being happy. It was because of something. If we've invested a thing with the magic of making us happy, we get the "magic pebble" and feel happy, but we also know we're playing our game, so there's an insecurity there. What more can you do for the world, to make one more happy person?

We talk about happiness, because happiness is what we say is better, and better is what we call happiness. Happiness and better are kind of equivalent terms. Better is a judgment that we make: "I will benefit from that." I could say "I better be happy" or "it's better to be happy" but that's what happier means.

Questioner: *What if people have inherent imperfections?*

I know that you're happy, whether you admit it or not. By my definition, I can know that you're happy. Because you're really happy, you can do everything you're doing. You could also act unhappy, and you could make believe you're unhappy, and you can make believe you have all kinds of reasons to be unhappy, and you can act as if you are unhappy, because you really are happy. Who or what could possibly disprove that?

Questioner: *How do you know I'm happy?*

Why do you even need to know why I know, if I know, how I know? It's not for your benefit I know; see, my telling you that I know is not keeping you from your benefit.

Just what if you were really innocent? And there wasn't an evil bone in your body, but yet you believed somehow that you weren't? I responded to so many people who think that something is wrong with them, that there is something bad about them, believing that. How will they act, then? As if there was something wrong with them and that there was something bad about them. I've never met a bastard who didn't believe more than I did that he was a bastard.

We want to know that we're not bad. We somehow must be believing that we are, otherwise why would we want to know that we're not? We want to believe we're justified in things. Somehow we're believing we're not justified. So what if you were perfectly happy? Essentially happy, really happy, and the kingdom of God was within you; what if that were really so—but you just didn't believe it? And you believe that it was something you had to strive for or work toward or achieve or accomplish, something that you would get someday. That would be enough to make it as if it weren't true, and its being true would almost be irrelevant. *Almost* irrelevant. And you would then be afraid, which might have nothing to do with the reality of the fact that you are essentially happy, and that the kingdom of God is within you.

You Do Your Own Believing

January 19, 1992

Regarding persuasion ...

THERE's no such thing as me believing for you. You've got to do the believing. If you believe what I believe, then we share the belief, but you have got to agree to believe it—you do your own believing. If you agree to believe something, then *you* agree to believe it.

If I've "made" you believe, then that's not really believing ... I've made you perform, perhaps, with some chemicals, or strings tied around your arms, or whatever.

Oftentimes, what a "persuader" does is initiates. A lot of people want to do all kind of things but don't give themselves permission, so you pay someone to give you permission. What are exercise classes? You can't do those exercises at home? What are college classes? You can't go to the library? So a lot people are willing to pay other people to give them permission to do something they wanted to do, but they needed someone to initiate by giving them permission.

Testing Beliefs

This essay responds to the question "How do I know my beliefs are true?"

MY first answer to your question is don't worry about it. We honestly believe what we honestly believe, because we believe it's true.

If you are believing something is not real, for example, that there is a doorway in that wall, you'll bump up against it. If it's relevant to your reality, then it becomes time to question it. You question it when it becomes uncomfortable, when you notice an incongruity between what you're trying to do and what's happening—something's not working.

Say that you've been believing your gas tank is full, and your car starts to sputter. Then you might look at the gas gauge. Why? It's bringing up the question, "Is my gas tank really full?" You're lighting the match, and the tinder isn't catching on fire. You thought it was dry and was able to be set on fire—that is now in question.

When you trip on it, when you bump into it, when something doesn't work, then it becomes a question.

Ninety percent of your mistaken beliefs will never matter, because you'll never come across any challenge to the beliefs that will be relevant to you. The ones that do matter are the ones that interface with your reality, your life, with the things you are trying to do.

When something you are trying to do just isn't working, and you had every reason to believe it should work, you are coming across some ignorance of your own. There are two possible explanations for why you just don't know. You are believing something that isn't true or you're lacking information. But in *either* case, you are lacking information. So my approach is, look for the information that you need—that will correct any misinformation that you have, and that will correct any mistaken beliefs you have.

If you are not holding onto your beliefs, and you don't need to be right, but want things to work, then you never have to worry about deceiving yourself, because any mistakes, any prejudices and misinformation you have will evaporate in the light of being put to the test. Reality hits us, and now we know the truth. And if they never get put to the test, it doesn't matter.

If you believe that there is a certain tribe of people somewhere in the world who have tails, I can't imagine a situation where it would ever be a problem. If you come across a tribe with no tails, you'll just say, "They're not the ones!"

I wouldn't be concerned about believing things that aren't true. When it's relevant, if you know you're open-minded, and interested in truth, they won't stand the test.

Time and the Truth of Beliefs

August 24, 1975

PEOPLE often experience that they dare not or should not deny their past experience. Past experience is hoped to be a teacher, a guide into the future. Of course, nothing could be further from the truth. The Future is our real guide.

There is simply a question of truth as we learn it or become aware of new things. The past in itself is nothing to deny. It doesn't even exist. Past experience really refers to what I now hold as true, which I *say* I now hold as a residue of the past. It is like: I passed through a town and picked up souvenirs, which I now have as a remembrance of that event which is no longer.

The value or usefulness of the souvenir (or remembrance) is either for direct use in the present or future as a thing in its own right (like a shawl from Spain or math principles from grade school, they may have a present or future use. They are memories perhaps but not valued as souvenirs) or for indirect use.

An indirect use is in associating or relating to other past events. Some things are used essentially to evoke past feelings and as emotional lessons. They are supposed to warn or promise about similar feelings in the future. The only actual result is a desire to avoid that which "caused" (evoked) bad feelings and the desire to repeat those kinds of events that produced (evoked) good feelings. Sufficient to say that one draws from the past whatever one wants. One picks and chooses the so-called lessons to suit the occasion.

The memories reflect a current belief, which may have of course been acquired in the past. The so-called remembrance is a model sought out to support a belief.

The belief came from the past and now seeks out a past event in order to validate itself by evoking feelings of the "truth" of the belief.

For example, the current belief "Death of a loved one is cause for mourning" could be supported by the memory "I cried when my bike broke," or "I felt terrible when I failed geography," or "I was overwrought when my mother died." Therefore the belief is true.

The truth from the past was a product of the beliefs of the past. Since even past experiences (no less than present ones) were subject to the beliefs involved, they would have been the truth of what was believed, but not any truth-in-itself.

There is no reason, I suppose, why those beliefs should change, since inherent in believing them is the belief that they are true. By definition, a belief is held because it is held as truth, and so is the basis for perception of behavior in the future. The real truth is not that truth itself is the basis for perception and determines behavior, but that it is a belief that a belief is truly based on truth itself.

The only way a belief can be changed, modified, replaced or dropped altogether is for it to be questioned or challenged and compared to another alternate belief. The person would then judge which of the two choices are truth. Incidentally, this decision is usually based on that which can't be denied or what one "must" believe rather than on what one would like to believe. For example: I believed that I was a good child and loved my parents and they loved me. Now I am forced to admit that I am not a good and loving child and have made my parents not love me. This new belief is chosen instead of an alternate, which might be quite different: I am a good and loving child and do not want my parents to be unhappy. I did not make them unhappy. I make them happy. They are unhappy for nothing. They punish me for reasons which cannot be reasons to punish me. Or the truth may be: They punished me because they are unhappy after I broke my toy. They are showing me that they want to punish me because I broke my toy.

But it is not necessarily eternal truth that breaking a toy is an event the parent must be unhappy about (except, of course, that they must because of their wonderful other truths!). The parent's unhappiness and consequent behavior (punishment) is an event which the child must believe he caused, or that he believes is proof that he is against himself and his own well-being.

The ultimate truth may be:

They punish me. That is a truth about them. There is no truth that makes them do what they do. It is only true that they do what they do. It is only true that they think they follow truth. They are wrong, mistaken.

A common myth is that "Consensus is truth": what others believe is based somehow on truth or they wouldn't believe it. The most common consensus "truth" is that the search for happiness is necessary and based on a "truth" that happiness is not immanently available and ever-present, since if it were everyone would be happy. If one does not have to do anything to avoid unhappiness then how is it to be avoided?

"Consensus as truth" boils down to: I believe what I believe because of the beliefs of others.

The second most common myth is the unquestioned belief that there is a truth to be known besides the truth I hold, that there are *two* truths: Good and Evil, Past and Future, etc., Dichotomy after Dichotomy.

For a belief to be replaced by a belief that would allow more happiness there must at least be no belief that would prevent the new belief being allowed. For unhappy, "mistaken," or unwanted beliefs to be discarded there cannot be a belief that says that process is not allowed.

Is there a belief that one should not believe what one wants? Any preventive belief would have to be in some way questioned as to whether it is what a person really wants to believe any longer. The rational process of trying to demonstrate the error or accuracy is an exercise doomed by its own premise. People will either believe what they want or they will believe what they believe they must, which is then what they want.

People either believe or they don't.

This is not an unanswerable dilemma. The way out is very simple. Beliefs are not explored or examined or scrutinized or continuously judged. They are simply experienced. Once they are held as true they are forgotten, so to speak, but behavior follows from them.

A belief only needs to be exposed and the person can let themselves know if the belief they are holding is indeed what they really now believe. If it is, it will still provide the basis for action. If not, it is automatically gone.

Since people believe they are not perfectly happy they also will believe that they can have mistaken beliefs and imperfect beliefs. Any behavior that can be seen as a product of a belief will change whether it is desired or not. Any belief that is seen as a belief will be dropped.

People do not believe that they are what they want to be, or have what they want because they believe this to be so, but because they don't know that that is a belief. The unhappiness and dissatisfaction, the yearnings and hopes of all people are based on beliefs (predictions) and it doesn't really change the basic nature of the problem whether the belief is seen to be true or false. The problem is that there is believing. Any belief dissipates when exposed as a past belief. When the belief evaporates, happiness emerges.

By analogy, when the cause of disease is cured, health fills the space left, as beliefs disappear at the sight of knowledge. Symptoms disappear when health returns. Disease ceases when proper functioning takes over. It is not true that disease prevents health and function. Lack of proper function allows disease.

Lack of truth allows superstition. Superstition is not the cause of untruth. It is a product of the absence of truth.

Beliefs are not the antagonists of knowing truth but are only the symptom of its apparent absence. Unhappiness is not the enemy or preventer of self-happiness but rather, is the symptom. Yet it is not true that Truth, Health, Happiness are truly absent. They are hidden, in a sense. They appear to believing people to be absent because they are not being manifested.

Truth is not necessarily a presentation of some abstract concept. Truth manifests itself by letting someone know that such and such is a belief. That is truth. What is left is not truth itself but what is truly there.

Health manifests itself by allowing a person to know that the disease is not there. What the person experiences now is not Health itself as some principle, but *themselves* as truly healthy. In other words they as they are, unencumbered and not distorted by disease.

Happiness is the person coming to know that they are not unhappy. What is left is a happy person.

You are not unhealthy—you are cured. You do not believe any more and you know now—you are not unhappy, you are glad. Beliefs don't argue with knowledge per se but with knowledge that is believed to be believed.

A belief that China is a South American country may argue with the truth that it is an Asian country but will never argue with the truth that its being in South America is a belief.

When we are dealing with things that do not need third-party verification, and are either already within the person or not, it is quite sufficient that they only discard a belief. The truth they have already will take over.

You need never present anyone with the facts about themselves; they already have them and will see them when they know that what they have *been* seeing *instead* are beliefs,

A person who believes she is ugly will not believe she is beautiful unless it fits into other beliefs (like authority says so, consensus, etc). If she sees that the belief she is ugly is really a belief, at least a belief, the truth will out. Immediately you will find that she was not concerned with physiology or even the fact that many people have considered her ugly, but her real concern was what shall she allow for herself? What will she think? How will she act? What is she allowed to want based on the "fact" that she is ugly? When she saw it was a belief, she immediately did not believe it was her belief but merely something she *had* believed. She saw immediately that all questions of ugliness are a matter of opinion, not fact, not a necessary determiner.

Unhappiness does not exist. The belief in it does. The prediction that you may in the future make a prediction (believe in unhappiness) is a prediction. You cannot know that you *may* do anything in particular—you only either *know* that you will or you don't know that you will. You either know you won't or you don't know you won't. You can only believe (predict, guess) that you might. Since you are doing it now you must predict you may again. Since you are predicting what you don't know for sure, you are predicting (guessing).

Unhappiness is predicting what you don't want to predict. It is predicting that you are not really wanting what you want. All unhappiness all comes down to predicting that you will act (behave) as if you knew that *what you couldn't want is what will be.*

You merely *believe* that you will believe and behave in a way that is based on a future you guessed would exist, and by that guess and the behavior based on it you will bring about the very future that you didn't want.

You doing that which is not the way you want is you predicting that you will do what you know you do not want, and acting as if you knew it might come to pass.

You do *not* know that you might not get what you want. You are merely guessing. You don't have to. It makes you make more guesses. They make you make more. You make things happen that you don't want.

You do not want to predict a future of having any feelings or performing any behaviors that you don't want now.

The only unhappiness there is, is not knowing the future and guessing that it might be what you won't want; which is guessing that it might be a future in which you will be unhappy and not getting what you want and are believing (guessing) that it might continue that way. The only unhappiness is believing that the future may not be what you want it to be. You don't know that.

You are guessing that you won't get what you want. You don't like that. You have been believing that is what you wanted to do.

Simply:

You are believing that you might want to know the future. Do you *know* that you will still want to know the future if you stop believing it may not be what you want?

You are guessing that the future may not be what you want for you: a future of future guessing about the future yet to come.

You know you will always do what you want but you were guessing that you may not or could not. When you were guessing you couldn't *know* how open you were.

You don't care what you'll want.

You don't care what you'll do.

You just want to know now that you'll do it.

You know now that you'll do whatever it is. You don't care. You're glad to want to do or want anything.

You never want to guess again. You don't care about right or wrong.

You're so fantastically open to the future. You'll do anything.

In the future, you have being you, and being able to know that even though you don't know anything about the future (and that is a glorious feeling) you know everything about it that you'll ever want to know.

You'll do anything because you'll be with the happiness you have.

Any future will be the future I want as long as I believe that I'll have my happiness, my awareness of myself being there to share it with whatever is happening.

I'm going to the future. Don't miss it.

I'm going to be there. See to it that you come. You wouldn't want to not be there. I'll be there. You can spot me. I'll be the one who is doing his thing, whatever happens.

I want what I want now. I don't know that I'm guessing at what I want. I am not going to guess that I may be guessing. It is not my wanting to guess, I am not guessing that I want my real wanting. I know I want my self to be me. I don't guess my wanting anymore. Here I am, this is me. I don't know what I don't know and I know what I love. I love "being" here. I know who I love thinking of having here with me. I don't know about what I will want except I'll want it.

Believing as a Biological Reality

THE ability to believe (interpret and predict, with concomitant acting, behaving, and feeling) is a biological reality of the living organism.

Believing is the physical act of translating perceived phenomena into the person's biology, whether the phenomena are "consciously" perceived or not.

Believing is the physical act, a bodily change, of translating phenomena into biological structure. Human life, which we have supposed to be individual, could be seen as having many aspects of biological structure arising and manifesting beliefs (predictions about the world) prior to any individual's birth. Having legs predicts a ground to walk on, in the sense that you had legs as a baby in the womb, but as baby in the womb had not yet experienced the ground, and had not yet had any desire to walk. The legs of a baby in the womb are nature's prediction that the organism will one day experience the ground, and desire to walk on it.

The meaning of anything is the awareness and feeling about it as desirable or not. The meaning is "I want it," "I don't want it" or anything that ultimately can be translated as "I feel good" or "I feel bad." Meaning, awareness, feeling, desirability, reality enjoyed or perceived, my life... all are believing. Believing is all that is and all I mean by my being.

"What do I believe?" is the same as "How do I change?" or "What changes me?" What I use to change myself is *me* (as a biological entity, a body) and the manner I use is beliefs. What I believe (predict, model, interpret) I am or do is ultimately the most basic change among changes that occur. What do I believe reality does to me and me to it? Happiness or not?

There is no such thing as unemotional (that is, judgment-free) awareness. All awareness is either "enjoyable" or "unpleasant" or a mixture which defines the person's psychological state, e.g., annoyed to outraged, amused to ecstatic, etc. Awareness is our way of enjoying or hating our life. The perception of reality is one's statement about one's self to one's self. Awareness is a guideline, a taste of life, a set of instructions of how to live and change. Awareness is happy or not. "Reality" and "Life" are perceived as (believed to be) happy or not. These "subjective" impressions of life are really instructions to one's self on how to change (for change one must) amidst apparent changes of other things. Believing is changing what is.

All that *is*, is by definition *known*.

All that *will be* is a *belief*, or will be a product of beliefs that are *now*.

We therefore know all that is and can be known, and believe (act upon to change) what is known. Knowledge is never mistaken but can be transient and outdated from moment to moment. Knowledge that is no longer true is no longer knowledge, but a mistaken knowledge and is in itself now really a manifestation of change.

Unhappiness is confusing reality with how reality changes. It is not enjoying the changes of reality by believing reality itself is the *belief* in reality. Unhappiness is believing that *believing* is reality and does not believe that *knowledge* exists.

Desire and Cause

August 7, 1977

Beliefs Are Predictions

Desires, wants, etc. are just words to describe the feelings (and subsequent reactions to those feelings, like thoughts, gestures, postures, etc.) we give ourselves before we experience what we believe (predict) we will experience. So are fears, sadness, etc. Desires are "good" feelings. Fears are "bad" feelings.

"I desire to eat. I am hungry. I feel like having an apple." These are not a chain of thoughts or reasons or deductions or discoveries. They are expressions of the feeling people give themselves. (Note, the feeling of hunger is not "natural" or "universal." It only seems natural. It is only "natural" because most who don't "feel" that way die, and have died, and are not present to communicate to you how it is not natural for them. It is statistically normal, not "natural" as an inevitable fact of any particular person in time.) The feeling of hunger is simply a prediction that the person is going to move themselves toward the predicted goal of eating.

We predict. It doesn't matter in terms of happiness how or by what means: physically, mentally, perceptually, consciously, unconsciously, or whatever. We may predict our future by something we call experience or learning. We see this and this and this and predict, based on such a similar combination of events in the past, that similar effects will result in the future as they once did. Even gravity and most other "laws of nature" are such prediction. "Laws" means predictable results to those who "know" the law. Those who do believe they "know" the law say the results are certain and inevitable, meaning absolutely (as opposed to usually) predictable. The implication is that the law is known wholly and that certain effects are intrinsically basic, and the same as the Law. Laws are stated in terms of the certainty of the effect or else they are called "hypotheses" and considered a glimpse and usually "workable" aspect of a yet-uncertain law. This is an emotional state of predicting in a particular way called "tentative, hesitant, comfortable, practical, etc."

The "Law" of Cause and Effect

"Certain events cause definite effects" is what a given law means. This concept of law is based on the "law" that there are causes and effects and they exist whether they are known or perceived or discovered or not.

The "law of cause and effect" is based on a prediction of certainty called an axiom. This means it cannot be (should, must, bad to be) denied without absolutely certain results. The law that all that *is*, is caused by something in the past, is a belief that is lived by believers. The belief in cause is a way of observing phenomena, events that occur and are. It extends to feelings that are "caused" by events other than feelings.

The concept of "facts" and "realities," in most people's minds, means "events that were caused, and will be causes of, new events." Certainty is the feeling that believers in this have. All laws purport to be descriptions, but all descriptions are based on values.

Laws are what we use. "The laws of cause and effect" are mere redundancies to believers. That all laws, like good definitions, are self-contained and self-proving, self-defining, etc., is a decision and choice of believers, of people. A law is anything that "convinces" me to stop wanting to know the "cause," that convinces me to stop questioning. It may be "proof" of absolute predictability so that I "feel" that I now "know" and therefore will stop searching; or it may be a "feeling" of indifference which judges the search as valueless, because the so-called results are judged as inconsequential, valueless, or not repeatable, and therefore not desirable or a "fit" matter for predicting: e.g., no one bothers to find the "cause" of countless "little" things that come and go in our lives, like an itch for a second that is relieved, and doesn't reappear.

The Significance of Causality

Some questions:

If indeed there are causes and events that necessarily follow from them,

1. So what?

2. Are all causes prior?
3. Does prior mean in "time" or in "principle"? E.g., the artist's idea causes the painting even if the original (in time) idea is different than the final idea of the painting. The final "idea" is a feeling of "satisfaction" meaning no further action on this painting. Did the original idea cause or allow the final idea?
4. Can cause and effect be contained in the same event (in the same moment) distinct from perceptual illusions of sequence?
5. Does not the very existence of all things rather imply a time when they were not?

If happiness is the understanding of causes that are chosen as values for future use, and "value" means that which makes me happy, then all the relevance of truth, causes, and effects is that it means happiness, or not.

If anything is said of anything, then happiness is what is meant.

All present happiness depends on a belief in the future dependability of happiness. Is unhappiness always said or believed to have a cause because we believe in causes? Is the belief in causes the cause of unhappiness, or does it just allow the possibility to further believe that we will be caused to be what we would not want to be, and that will cause us to "feel" bad? Evil is the name of a double or conflicting cause, i.e., that which causes "good," which is desired but is unattainable, or that which caused that which is "undesirable" but is eventual anyway.

Desire as Cause

This is an assumption that desires (feelings, choices) are caused and are causes, sometimes doomed to frustration (ineffectual) or blessed by success (effective) depending on whether the desire is according to the laws that pertain: "realistic" laws, "moral" laws, etc.

All desires are judged by the eventual happiness or unhappiness they are said to produce when confronted with "reality testing." Desires are said to cause happiness or unhappiness if they succeed or fail. When considered as expectations, they are judged for their "normality," "realism," and so forth, after the "outcome" (sometimes after a specified length of time which is judged to be normal or reasonable). All concepts of hope and despair are time standards that are used to measure the "realism" of an expectation or prediction.

The concept of "mistake" could be seen as long-term or short-term, depending. Some things that are "mistakes" now (failed according to predictions or expectancies) are called fortuitous or lucky when later they are seen as causes of a more valued effect.

To judge a desire (or anything) is to "feel" and believe (feel) it is "about" the thing judged. This fulfills the law of cause and effect. "That" makes me feel good (or bad). "That desire was crazy." (It causes me to feel that I was caused to feel [desire] what now I don't feel [believe] that I should have felt.) I feel that I felt in a way that I now feel that I wouldn't have felt if I knew that I was going to be feeling this way. My past feelings were what they were because I did not know they were not realistic, and I want realistic feelings. I want to succeed at having the feelings I "should" and which will be seen to be "right" in the future. I want to want only what I will get. I must predict accurately or I will feel bad. My future happiness means "I successfully predicted" what I would do and get. I followed the laws of cause and effect, and my desires coincided and used the laws rather than were used by them.

The Accuracy of Predictions

This all assumes that predictions should be correct for some reason. It is accepted as axiomatic that it is better to be right when predicting rather than not, or it's better not to predict. It all amounts to:

 * It is best to predict accurately.
 * It is second best not to predict (if accuracy is not "certain").
 * It is wrong to not predict (or care) if one's accuracy is "reasonable".
 * It is worst to predict inaccurately.

Best, worst, etc., are feelings that are felt to be caused by Nature or the future weighed against the past—but they are feelings. Everything is a feeling. Feelings are judgments because they are chosen to serve as judgments on predictions, which are feelings, too.

Predictions are what we do. Believing about the future, right or wrong, we do it. Thinking is a low-grade feeling, but pervasive. A thought is the total experience of self. From head to toe, it is all we "know." A feeling is part of the thought, a way the thought is conceived and experienced, caused and felt effectively.

Happiness and Prediction

Doing can be seen as predicting. Predicting can be seen as moving, thrusting, creating, pushing into the future or drawn to it. It is not *what* we do or predict that is happiness (that is the same as emotion in general) but *how* we do or predict: happily, or not.

Happiness is a way of predicting; it is not the prediction in itself, since at the "reality" test of outcome one can be happily wrong as well as disappointed.

Happiness is predicting and being glad for the "real" truth if it is otherwise than predicted. Feeling a desire can be happy. We can wish to do something (believe we will somehow) and find we do not (believe we could not) in the way we tried. We can find the result of our trying was other than predicted.

We all try to cause (or allow) results. We all try to cause (or allow) everything. We all try to cause (or allow) the future. That is unhappiness (or happiness) now.

Trying

Trying (not predicting) causes unhappiness. Trying is believing in a law and not *really* believing. It is trying to change what you already believe is a Law of definite certainty. It is trying to fly, while believing it "defies" the laws of gravity and fearing (believing) that truth will win. It is trying to lie. It is not lying. It is believing that truth is unchanging and wanting it different. It is setting oneself up against a god that one set up oneself in the first place.

Trying is being against what *you* say is real. It is denying that you created the concepts of laws, truths, gods that you *try* to change, rather than just simply changing them. It is believing (making yourself feel) that you are supposed to, by a "law" *you* said exists, have, do or be some way that you don't want.

It is believing that what you call truth is imposed on you. It is not realizing that truth is what you decided was true at the time and was imposed only by your decision that you were satisfied, and felt it was Truth, and now you feel there is another truth and you also impose that now.

Our ways of thinking, judging, balancing facts, weighing values, may change, but one thing remains: we do it all. That is what "I" means. The one who decides that the truth is what I need to prevent unhappiness is believing in a new truth, a new decision, insight, desire, prediction, etc. and *trying* to believe in the new truth that you *already* do now believe in.

Unhappiness Is Trying

The state of being unhappy about a desire or prediction is not realizing that something we are wanting to change has already changed. Unhappiness is trying to change a prediction that we have *already* changed. It's trying not to worry when *not* worried. This means it is trying not to care, need, want, change what we already stopped caring about, or wanting, or already stopped changing.

Wanting someone to change is either predicting that they will change or is the unhappiness of fearing that they won't. Wanting another to do anything other than you believe you predict they will or you can make them do is unhappiness. Either you believe you can cause them to be different or you believe you can't. These are predictions about yourself, not them. To *try* to change someone is trying to lie. If you can change them, you can. Do it!

It is impossible to push the wind you blow out of your mouth. Trying to breathe is trying nothing. It is changing the breathing you already do. Trying to change, if it is more than wanting to change, is not realizing that you will change, or you won't, as you choose. Wanting to change, if it is more than expecting to change, is not realizing that you will, or won't, as you now choose. Expecting to change, if it is other than beginning to change, is not realizing that you are, or you are not, changing.

Your Purpose in Living

Beginning to change is joy. Beginning to change, if you do other than realize you are changing, is not realizing that you are as you hope, or want, or choose to be. Your choices are always choices *for* you and changes *of* you.

Realizing happiness is realizing that your desires, predictions, choices, hopes, etc., are your way of changing yourself. They change you because *you* change you that way. Their effect is *your* effect.

The future is your choice. The cause is your happiness, which is *your* doing *yourself* as you go. You are happiness causing itself. All happiness is only your happiness *as* you. Your happiness is uncaused. You do it as you.

Happiness is believing that you already are what you want to be and hoped to be.

It is realizing that as you may do things, you will not change. It is realizing that what you mean by you is what you say of it. All that you want is for you, or not. Yourself is your *own* self, your joy, your best friend. You are all you need for you to have yourself.

You are all that is required by you for the perfect you that you now are. You are what you mean by wisdom. You are heart and mind, body and soul, dreamer and doer, God and creature, thinker and feeler, life and happiness, all the dualities of self. The other dualities of good-evil, wanting, frustrated, thoughts-undone, tired, on guard, nervous, sad, fearful, hopeful-despairing, God-you are a result of not realizing you are all you need for you to enjoy yourself always.

These dual parts of you are not facts, but are not fictions. They are one thing. They are the name of happiness. They are the function and the dynamic of enjoying. If you call it enjoying life, it is *your* life you mean. If it is enjoying reality, it is *your* reality you mean.

You can only refer to your love affair with you. Your unhappiness is ignoring or denying or not realizing you always refer to your love affair with you. You only relate, create, feel, perceive, anything for you. You are only you. You are where you begin and end. That is who you are. You are all you know what you know for. You are your end-all and your purpose for your life. You are the one and only one you are you for. You are you enjoying your awareness, or you are not realizing this.

The duality is your way of doing what you do for you. The duality was your purpose. You already have become what you came to be aware for. You came to be aware; you chose to be aware, means you chose to be aware of yourself as for you. You for you. You in you. You doing you. You feeling you. You to you.

The duality of you is what you did it for. You did yourself, as the knowledge of you, for happiness. Knowing you are your one-and-dual self is what you do.

You are knowing you are you. You did it long ago and have been unhappy by still trying to do it, as if it were not done. You have reached your purpose in living long ago. You have achieved your choice, change, purpose, goal, ideal, etc., and have not enjoyed or realized it. The only thing left to do is to enjoy what you achieved, by allowing the achievement to continue on its own *as* you enjoying whatever this achieved goal continues to do (as you).

Enjoy
that you choose to know
that you choose to be
what you choose as yourself.

SECTION II

Introduction to Desires

Boredom

ALMOST every person I've ever met who's used the word "boring" means "there's something else I should be doing." There's a belief that "there's something else I ought to be wanting to do."

"Well, I want to play basketball—but I should do my homework."

One hundred percent of the people I've ever asked what they meant by boring always meant—they're not free to do anything. All the things that might otherwise make them happy and all the things they might otherwise enjoy, at the times when they're feeling bored they cannot enjoy them. And when I asked them why, it's because there's something else they should be attending to, and for some reason don't want to. And they're sitting on that edge of nowhere. They can't let themselves enjoy anything; they can't let themselves do that because it's like giving themselves permission not to do the other thing that they should do, and that's the feeling of boredom.

If they're bored doing their homework that might simply mean, "I don't like homework. Homework doesn't motivate me to want to do it." If they're having a problem with it apparently they have a value for it or they wouldn't be bringing it up. They want to do the homework because they want to get the grade and they want the advantages of what doing homework does. So why would they say it's boring? Because they're believing there's maybe something else they should be doing. It's quite possible for a young person to believe that they should be socializing, because that would be more important to them for their welfare or their well-being at that time.

All "shoulds" have to do with "my own good," somehow. "I should be doing it for my own good," and "I don't want to do what's for my own good" becomes the feeling, and that's the feeling of boredom. "I don't want to do what I've already judged to be good for me." So for instance, a boy may have judged homework to be really in his own best interests to do it, "and yet I never want to do it, I always want to go out and play. I always want to do this and I always want to do that. Homework really bores me." But yet he's beginning with the proposition that, "It is to my benefit if I do it and I should want to do it." He can't be in touch with wanting to do it because he's believing he should want to do it. He forgets that he made the judgment that doing homework was to his benefit. Everybody else is out at the basketball game and you're in your room doing your homework, you can feel very restless and very bored. It's the feeling that you're not doing what you want to do.

Boring almost always has a feeling of anger in it, always blaming the boring thing for the feeling. And there's a feeling of having to be there, where you are doing what you "have" to do. And then, of course, bored people feel that the solution is to get away, to prove that they don't have to be there.

Attraction

In decision-making, wanting, motivating and all of that come into play. The whole purpose of wanting is motivation. That leads to a decision. We want to be happy so we start this magical process of, "Now I want to be happy but that's not enough. I have to do something." So to make decisions on what I want, I set up a whole bunch of magical things that I'll be happy with and now that gives me something to do. I can work toward them. Toward health, toward wealth, toward power, toward ease of movement—whatever.

The whole idea of having to make decisions is a myth, but since we live with that there are ways of proceeding with it happily and not unhappily.

So let's look at wanting on multiple levels: attraction and wanting and doing. There may be many things that we're attracted to. Attraction is the early stage of wanting. Think of attraction as a question. Attraction is just basically the question or the guess that, "I may be happy with that, that may make me happy. That may contribute to my happiness." So a number of things may attract us. Now we're faced with the question, "Which do we want, though?"

There are a number of things that attract us. For example, some things attract us to sit still, and some things attract us to get up and move. Right now it attracts me to continue talking to you, but it also attracts me to go out and have some coffee. That's no problem, that's just a question. But in order to make that decision I can use fear, or I can not use fear. I could use desire. In order to use desire I have to get in touch with "What do I want more? What do I want this for?" These questions will help me to know why I want them more. Both choices are attractive. Both have consequences and the choosing of one and the not choosing of the other has consequences. And they're parts of a package, they're parts of a path that are different paths and have different constituent parts to them as I go along. And they will lead to perhaps totally different ends and conclusions. Now if

I decide to continue to talk to you, that is going to give me certain advantages or disadvantages in terms of other things. That's the package. If I decide not to continue to talk to you and go have some coffee, that's another package that has its prices and its rewards.

So we use a price-reward system for ourselves in order to make decisions. We can focus on the rewards or we can focus on the prices. Very frequently, through fear, we focus on the price, and all prices become too high. We can focus on rewards and be in touch with, "What do we want more?"

Now, sometimes things become attractive, and in order to guarantee that we do the thing that's most attractive we will frequently say, "I should do it. That's what I should do." Now, there are things that we will want to do, and on that basis decide not to do other things that are attractive, and those other things may even become more and more attractive, and the attraction increases for me. It just means the question is getting louder. A decision isn't being made yet, and just because the question is loud that doesn't mean we'll decide to go where is loudest. We could really be happy in not doing the thing that most attracts us. Why does the question get louder? Because there's more that we want to consider.

Wanting the Whole Package

Now for example, it would really be attractive if all of us right now could be sitting on a beach, or enjoying the breeze in some nice cool woods. That could really be attractive to us, but we simply didn't decide to do that. We can't say we decided against it; we didn't decide to do it because we didn't want that whole package. And what it amounted to is that only part of the package was attractive. The goal is attractive but what we would do to reach that goal may not be as attractive: the money it would cost, the time it would take, the things we wouldn't be doing in place of that, may not all be attractive. And it can really be okay to find that attractive, knowing that it isn't really what I want. I can rest well with that: it's really attractive, very attractive, but it's only part of a package and I don't really want the whole package, and that's my freedom.

Now some people will torture themselves when they find something attractive and think "To make sure now that I don't go running off to the woods of Canada, I've got to drive that thought out of my mind, I've got to keep it from being attractive, I've got to make it repulsive."

Someone told me that somebody offered their daughter a car for a dollar, but she didn't have enough money to pay the insurance on the car or to pay for the gas. And she tortured herself, because part of the package was attractive, but she didn't want the whole package. And she was in the process of torturing herself about, "Why did you have to tell me I could have it? Now I have all these decisions to make." In the end she made the decision that she couldn't really keep the car.

Yes, by the time she was done I bet you she felt very deprived of a car that, up to before it was even offered, she didn't feel deprived of. Why? Well, her fear was that she wasn't being good to herself somehow if she turned it down, she would really be denying herself.

But you see, if you were really in touch that what you really wanted more was other things, and you were really being nice to yourself by not taking that car, who could complain? How could you feel bad? I have the opportunity to have a car for nothing, for $1.00. Well, now if I want the car, to go with it to protect myself I would want the insurance and I'd want to keep it up, etc. What do I want more? Do I want more to spend my money on that whole package, or do I want more to spend my money on something else? And however I decide, I'm deciding that it's really for me and to my benefit what I've decided. It's what I wanted more and I can rest real easy if I decide, "Oh, no. I'd rather not use my money that way. I'd rather use my money another way." I can't feel deprived at all. I can feel like I've treated myself to working toward what I really want more.

The person who seems unable to decide anything, they're forgetting that whatever decision they make is really in their own best interest. People do feel sometimes, "Why am I given these choices? Why do I have to choose? Why can't I have everything?" Since you have such a sense of deprivation you go into the question with a sense of deprivation, feeling that you're always being deprived.

You need so much to have so many things that every time you can't have something, even if it's something you really don't want, you're still feeling deprived because you're not used to seeing (and you're not into seeing) that you are choosing for your benefit.

"Don't tell me it's for my benefit if I can't have this or that," but yet it really is. If I decide not to go that route it's really that I've decided somehow, on some basis, that it was better for me not to. But yet, after having done that, I could still believe the tricks that we play on ourselves, that I wasn't the best thing for myself. And the reverse of that—how many times do we do something that we really have decided we wanted to do with the total feeling that we don't want to be here, or we don't want to do it, that we have to do it somehow? And yet we're the one who decided we wanted to. We could only have possibly done it because we thought it was in our own best interest, and yet we are doing the thing with the feeling that we don't really want to do it.

This whole thing about people being "self-defeating," it's really what they wanted to do. It's really not that they're doing it in order to defeat themselves, they're doing it in order to help themselves.

Wanting Is More Important than Getting

WANTING in itself is much more important than getting. What is it you really want? To be happy. So why go through unhappiness to get what you want in order to be happy? Perhaps by the time we're done you'll see more clearly why any of this has to even be talked about.

Wanting is more important than getting because getting is not guaranteed, and the only key you have to *getting* is to continue wanting. The getting is the goal. Your only hope is to continue wanting.

For instance, I could be married to you and I want us to be closer, and I put us through hell. Before you know it, we stop wanting to be closer and I look at you and you don't seem very attractive. My relationship with you is not as painful. What did I do? The only way out was to stop wanting. I loved somebody, I wanted to be closer, and before you know it I'm not with them anymore.

You can't really stop wanting, exactly. But you can force yourself to where the choice becomes (but only because you coupled the wanting with unhappiness), do you keep up the unhappiness or stop wanting? And sometimes you *do* appear to stop wanting and then start the whole pattern all over again with somebody else.

As prerequisite preparation for what I want, being assured *that* I want is much more important to me than actually getting what I want, because as long as I keep in touch with *that* I want things, and I keep my wanting alive (even though I'm not getting it), I have the hope for getting something "just as good" in the future, then—but I couldn't begin to get *anything* if I didn't start by wanting it.

All of these wants that are used with unhappiness are what we'll "need," for convenience. They start off perhaps purely as a desire, as a want; but once we play the unhappiness game with them, then we're into needs and fear.

What we do to stop needing is to stop wanting, and so we become really afraid of giving up. In a self-defeating situation where my unhappiness is just not getting me what I want, what's really going on is fear of giving up. That's why we use the unhappiness, even though it apparently doesn't pay off, because it *is* paying off in a larger sense: at least I'm not selling myself out. "The hell with you, I'll leave you, but I won't sell out by stopping wanting what I want." I'll screw myself left and right but I will not stop wanting what I want, because if I stop wanting what I wanted I'd even be screwing myself more.

An example: My job requires me to work at things I don't like or with circumstances I don't like. To keep the job, and the money that comes from it, which is the benefit of the job, I must sacrifice other good things. Since it is attractive to me to not give up the other good things, I fear that if I want to keep my job I'm also kind of wanting to give up those good things—which I also want. It looks to me like I'm wanting bad things for myself. I don't like the circumstances of my job, yet I want the money; I'm afraid that I want money more than I want happiness. Sometimes it starts to seem to me that I hate the job, and yet I keep going, and I'm also afraid that I want to quit the job more than I want the money, which I really want to be happy, too.

The more I am tempted to stop wanting what I want *most* (and what I want most is clearly the money, which was my motive for taking the job in the first place) then the more unhappy I become about the conditions that tempt me to quit. Therefore I become afraid of my desire to give up wanting the money as much as I do, and afraid of my desire to give up wanting better conditions as much as I do, because either one would relieve my pain. If I could just give up wanting the money I could quit and I wouldn't have any more pain. If I could give up saying, "I want better conditions," that would be okay too, and I would have no more pain. But I *want* to want what I want, and I can't give up my wanting, so I have to have pain, I believe.

I become more unhappy and eventually drive myself away from the whole situation. Since I *want* to keep wanting money, I want all the help I can get to motivate myself to go to work to get that money, and I resent anything in my job that decreases my motivation: lousy coworkers, long hours, traffic, whatever. I'm unhappy about anything that would make it easier for me to not want what I want. The reason I resent the things that go on in my job, and I hate them so much, is because they're making it very easy for me to stop wanting that job, and I'm scared of not wanting what I *do* want.

My degree of unhappiness will be in proportion to my temptation to stop wanting. The more there is that motivates me away from my greater want, the more repellant factors there are connected to my goal, the more I fear I will give up my goal in order to counteract the repellant factors. My unhappiness will be in proportion to what I think is required to counteract the other unhappiness I use to want or not want the other factors associated with the greater desire. This associated unhappiness is what is meant by, and constitutes, the temptation to give up the greater desire.

More specifically: I don't like traveling to work in the morning. The distance, the time, the traffic, etc. are things I'm unhappy about. I otherwise like my job and the money inducement. The traveling factor constitutes a temptation to not go to work. In order to assure myself that I keep wanting to go to work, I become afraid of what will happen if I don't go to work. Now I institute another fear to counteract it: I become afraid of losing my job, I become afraid of poverty in order to get me out of bed in the morning, to go through that traffic that I hate, in order to get to my job. And I only go through the fear, and I only start fearing losing my job, because I've started tempting myself to quit it, because I've gotten unhappy.

The whole idea of not traveling in traffic, that's a temptation, a slight one maybe, but nonetheless it is removing some of my motivation to go to work, and we're beginning with the premise here that what I'm most scared of is giving up wanting what I want more than anything. And the commute is eroding my desire; it is eroding my wanting to go to work. So in order to assure that I'll keep on wanting to go to work, I become afraid of what will happen if I don't go to work, for instance, by means of a fear of poverty.

Staying in Touch with
What We Want More

WHAT you are scared of is that you would lose your wanting, like you lost your getting. That's what you won't let happen, that's why you keep your unhappiness alive.

And here's what I mean by the traffic jam making it easier for me to not want my job: it is something I'm unhappy about, and it's connected and associated with my job so that's one of the factors of my job. What I'm unhappy about could, of course, be another factor at work, such as my boss.

In order to stop the pain, we stop wanting. In the example that I just gave you, it becomes so painful that a way out is to just give up the wanting. In terms of a job, you can make it so miserable that when we get fired or when we quit, we say, "Whew, at least I don't have to go through that traffic anymore." And I can stop wanting the job.

We're starting with the premise that I want the job more than I want to quit it. Now, if I want to quit it more than I want to keep it, then there's no problem, and that's not our example—that's a nice calm, easy way: "The job is not worth it, so I'm not taking it," or "I quit." One doesn't go through a whole lot. That solves it. I'm staying in touch with what I want more.

The idea is to stay in touch with what you want more. That's what the unhappiness is all about: to make sure that we keep wanting what we want *more*, that we won't go ahead and want *less*.

Any time there is a fear, there is a corresponding wanting of something that looks very similar to the thing that is feared, or almost as good, or almost as attractive. The *desire* to quit work is very similar to the *fear* of quitting work and the *fear* of losing the job and the *fear* of poverty. In order to keep the desire to quit work from overriding your desire for money, you used the fear of poverty.

If a good thing, for instance a job, requires giving up, for example, the conveniences of traveling, in order to have the job I will have to want to give up those conveniences, and I fear that I won't want to do that. I fear that I may just not want to go through all that traffic. And so I have a desire to stop wanting my job, a building, growing desire; every day when I go to work I have more of the desire to not want the job that I really do want. I fear that I'll stop wanting what I really want and that's a horrible thing to feel, and it is a horrible place to be, because I do want it.

This is similar to a lover getting angry at the loved one because they might leave. It is a fear that I'll stop wanting what I really want. I want you to be closer to me, and I'm afraid I'll stop wanting that.

Desires and Wanting

January 10, 1980

I DON'T like some things. I dislike some things. I like other things more than that something. There are various ways of experiencing our desires or lack of them.

The desire for pleasure may be experienced as a desire to avoid or heal a pain. Our desire for wealth may be experienced as a "lack" of very strong feelings about a "little" money. We may take some things for granted (not necessarily ignore them) because, as good as they are, they are not as good as something we are comparing them to. This doesn't mean we are unnecessarily denigrating or berating the lesser thing. It simply is what it is (and has its value) and by comparison it is lesser. It's not so good comparatively, and vice versa.

In certain circumstances of my life there are things I will disdain that I might have otherwise valued if my circumstances were different. There is no reason (now) that I should feel or think better of the thing than I do.

When I was friendless I may have welcomed even rude friends, (not the rudeness, but the minimal "friendliness" of being open to relating). Now I may want more.

48

COMMENTARIES

by Aryeh Nielsen on

"Feelings, Beliefs, and Desires"

Truth, Belief, and Verification

This commentary represents the editor's synthesis of ideas Bruce Di Marsico expressed only in fragments.

OUR truth is what we accept as the unquestioned ground and framework for living our life. Are some things absolutely true, for example that the sun rises every day? It matters not, because we have experienced the sun rising every day very consistently, enough for us to take the sun's daily rise as an unquestioned ground of our life. We have no reason to believe this will change in our lifetime. If it ever does, then that change can be dealt with then.

That there is no absolute truth outside our own experience does NOT mean that truth is infinitely mutable. The truth of our beliefs is subject to verification. For example, we may know as true that there is a key hidden under a rock in our garden. When we turn over the rock, we do not see a key. Then, what we hold as true becomes suspect to revision, expansion, or disbelief. Because much of our activity in life is social, we submit our beliefs to shared verification. If I tell you there is a key under the rock, and you turn it over and say that there is not, I may very well simply accept that what I held as true was not. Truth is always situated in the lived experience of a person or a community.

Truth is plastic; it changes and drifts, as our values shift, the world changes, and our understanding of the world changes. How the truth changes and how fast it changes may or may not be within our control in any given domain. Truths about human nature are more mutable than truths about physics, and truths about the appearance of clouds in the sky are highly mutable . . . but not infinitely so. For example, take "the law of gravity." It is true enough for everyday life. But in some contexts, such as interplanetary spaceflight, it is not true enough, and quantum physics is truer. The force of gravity was quite possibly an infinitely small amount different billions of years ago, but within our lifetime, we have reasons to predict sufficient constancy that the question of the absolute truth of "the law of gravity" has no relevance.

Beliefs are experienced by their holders as true. But beliefs are not experienced as beliefs by the person who holds them until they start to be experienced as possibly not true (that is, possibly not universally necessary). Much of what are called by people "their beliefs" are perhaps more properly called "the beliefs they aspire to." To the true believer, only the truth is experienced. Only when doubt begins does what is experienced as true become what is experienced as a belief. On the other hand, to an outside observer, if they do not hold the same truths, then what is true for a person is considered a belief by an outside observer. This happens even to a single individual when they wake from a dream: in the dream, they knew the truth of what was going on; on waking up and remembering the dream, what was the truth is now considered to be what they believed.

In summary, truth is contextual, situational, and subject to verification (personal or communal). Truth is neither something absolute and eternal, nor is it something that can be whimsically created in any form possible, but something in between, part and parcel of our experience of everyday life as neither perfectly static nor infinitely changeable.

Beliefs, Feelings, Truth

This commentary represents the editor's synthesis of ideas Bruce Di Marsico expressed only in fragments.

A BELIEF is an embodied and operative causal prediction. Some beliefs explicitly state causality, in the form If . . . Then, for example, "If I release an apple from my hand, then it will fall to the floor." Beliefs in the form of so-called "facts" have no meaning unless they have relevance to your life and actions, and all "facts" carry with them many implicit causal predictions relevant to each of our lives. For example, "Paris is in France" may, for a given person, have the causal prediction that if I want to experience the charms of Paris then I will need to arrange an airplane flight to France. Some beliefs—for example, how the organism may utilize gravity and oxygen and nourishment—are biological realities of the body itself.

Truth is what we call beliefs that are operative for us. Every belief we have is perfectly true for us, until it is not. We say it is "true" that the sun rises approximately every 24 hours. We believe (predict) that the sun rises approximately every 24 hours. This is true, for us, until, perhaps, one day it is not (as an interplanetary collision throws the earth out of its orbit, perhaps).

Feelings are whole-body organizations, and the most global organization of the organism. "Feelings" are what we call the most fundamental physical attitude the organism is taking. Feelings are what an organism does to best prepare itself for enjoying, utilizing, or responding to what is expected (predicted, believed) by the organism to be happening, and happening next.

The only beliefs that are relevant to happiness are beliefs about our feelings. An unhappy belief is a belief (prediction) that we will have a feeling (attitude) that is *not* best for our enjoying, utilizing, or responding to what is expected (predicted, believed) by the organism to be happening, and happening next.

Since the organism organizes itself according to its beliefs (predictions), the belief that we will not have the best feelings (attitudes) for us actually causes the organism to not have the best feelings (attitudes) for itself. Such a belief is both a self-fulfilling prophecy and self-defeating (in the sense that it is not what is best for the organism).

The experience of unhappiness is what it feels like to believe (predict) that you will not have the feelings you want (the best attitude for yourself). And, this will indeed happen, but the only cause of these feelings (attitudes) is the *prediction* of these feelings!

There is always a "best attitude for yourself that you *can* have." To predict that you *will* not have that attitude, when by definition you *can*, and want to, is inherently false. That is why unhappiness is a lie.

The Option Understanding of Beliefs

This commentary is a synopsis of ideas that Bruce Di Marsico expressed in many writings or talks, but did not express summarily in a single writing or talk.

Beliefs

In Option, the word "belief" is used in the tradition of Pragmatism and Functional Psychology: it means a prediction that is the basis for action. The vast majority of our beliefs have no bearing on our happiness, for example, "a knife is good for cutting," or "The plane arrives at 5:30."

Objective Knowledge as Beliefs

Many beliefs we have are also held by other people, and seem consistent over time. We all may look at a thermostat and agree that it is 70 degrees outside. My knowledge is objective in the sense that someone besides me has the same understanding as I do. That a belief is "objective" means that a community has the same belief. What is universally acknowledged is, nonetheless, a belief—that is, a prediction that is the basis for action.

Beliefs that we hold most fundamentally, we call "knowledge." To the extent that we become aware that our knowledge may be tentative or incorrect, we become aware of our knowledge as a belief.

For example, I may look at a thermostat, and know that the temperature outside is 70 degrees Fahrenheit. Reading temperatures off of thermostats has served me well for decades. I may even step outside and believe that my experience indeed confirms this. Someone could then note that my thermostat is broken, that it is only 55 degrees, and that I have a fever, which is why I experience the temperature as warmer. To the extent that I become convinced that their understanding of the temperature is more useful than my understanding, I start becoming aware that my knowledge is a belief.

What is widely known as objective knowledge shifts over the course of history. For example, in the nineteenth century, scientists researched the nature of "the ether," the substance that light travels through. Then, a new wave of scientists formed new beliefs about the nature of light, which required no ether. The nature of shifts in what is considered objective knowledge is often described as "scientific revolutions," or the overturning of "scientific paradigms."

Nature as Beliefs

In the Option understanding, beliefs are not limited to humans or to human cognition, but can properly refer to any organism's predictive basis for action. For example, the growth of a baby in the womb is a prediction by the organism of birth and the circumstance outside the womb. There is no need for lungs or legs in the womb; rather, they are a prediction that the baby will be born into an atmosphere, and there will be a ground to walk on. And this may not happen.

Similarly, animal reflexes are also beliefs. The tongue of a frog moves quickly toward a speck, predicting (sometimes incorrectly), that the speck is a fly. There is a continuum of beliefs from biological, to instinctual, to cognitive. The common thread among them is that an organism takes action based on a prediction of the outcome of that action.

Beliefs about Feelings

Option is fundamentally concerned with only a small subset of beliefs: the beliefs an organism has about their own emotional state, whether directly, or indirectly through a chain of linked beliefs (for example, "I believe X, which implies Y, which implies Z, which implies I have to feel bad"). Only beliefs about an organism's own feelings ultimately have any relevance to happiness.

Beliefs about the Necessity of Feeling a Certain Way

In particular, ultimately only beliefs about the *necessity* of feeling a certain way impact happiness. For example, "That makes me angry" is the belief that "If such-and-such happens, I will *have* to feel anger." The belief in the *necessity* of feeling a way you don't want to feel actually *causes* feeling a way you don't want to feel. Without the belief, one of two things would occur: 1) you wouldn't feel the way you don't want to feel, or 2), you would feel the exact same way, and recognize that it is exactly the way you *do* want to feel.

Aspirational Beliefs

There is a large literature that uses the word "beliefs" very differently from the Option understanding of beliefs, defining beliefs as a way of thinking, not as the predictive basis of action. These are perhaps well-described as "aspirational beliefs." For example, someone who believes (in the Option sense) that eating vegetables is good for them will demonstrate this belief effortlessly by eating vegetables. If someone says "I believe that eating vegetables is good for me," and they do not eat vegetables, they are speaking of an aspiration, a belief they want to have. The "Positive Thinking" community, for example, commonly uses the term "beliefs" this way.

Rhetorical Beliefs

An example of using the term "belief" that is even more distant from the Option sense of the term is a rhetorical statement by a politician that is completely incongruent with the politician's actions, such as "I believe that every citizen in this country needs to pay more taxes," while simultaneously reducing the amount of taxes they pay personally. Many uses of the phrase "I believe" in political discourse have no relationship whatsoever to the actions of the speaker, and thus, from an Option sense, are in no way actual beliefs.

"Choosing Beliefs"

There is a practical sense that beliefs can be chosen: by considering that a belief *might* be useful, and acting as if it was, we may come to *actually* believe it. For example, we may have believed that peas taste funny. We then may aspire to believe that vegetables are delicious. On the basis of this aspiration, we may try peas, and conclude that they are indeed delicious. From the Option point of view, we do not believe that peas are delicious when we start telling ourselves "I believe that peas are delicious," but only when we actually are acting on the basis of our personal knowledge that, to us, they are indeed delicious.

Conclusion

In the Option understanding of beliefs, beliefs are not merely statements or affirmations of how we aspire to view the world, but beliefs are our actual understandings that underlie our actions. Since our understanding is always based on what has happened up until now, and the basis of our actions from now on, our understandings underlying our actions are inherently predictive, using the past to predict the best action in the present, in order to affect our future.

There Are No Unhappy Emotions

This commentary is a synopsis of ideas that Bruce Di Marsico expressed in many writings or talks, but did not express summarily in a single writing or talk.

COMMONLY, unwanted emotions are presumed to be inherently unhappy; "I am afraid, angry, sorrowful" are used as synonyms for "I am unhappy."

But what makes the emotions *unhappy* is that they are *unwanted*, not that there is anything inherently problematic about experiencing them. If a bear leaps out of the woods at you, and you fearfully flee, you might not describe the fear as *unwanted* fear.

Why do *unwanted* emotions happen? The root cause of unwanted emotions is a belief that it is necessary to feel a particular emotion instead of another one. This can take two forms: first, a person can believe it is necessary to feel the emotion they are feeling (such as anxiety about a business presentation), but also be aware that if they did not believe it was necessary to feel that emotion, they would feel a different one (such as a relaxed calm). Second, a person can believe that they should feel a different emotion than they actually do feel, and believe that they are thereby impairing their happiness (for example, feeling mildly sad at a funeral, and feeling they should feel overwhelmed with grief).

The first case can be summarized as feeling an emotion only because it is believed necessary. The second case can be summarized as not feeling the emotion you believe you should.

In both cases, the emotions are unwanted. In the first case, the emotion felt is unwanted in itself. In the second case, the emotion is unwanted only because it is believed another emotion would be better to have.

In the absence of any belief about the necessity of having any particular emotional feeling, then the emotion felt *is* (and can only be) perfectly congruent with the emotion that is *wanted*. What is felt as unhappiness is that the emotion is *unwanted*.

In some cultures, certain emotions are universally proscribed; for example, because of cultural beliefs that it is always wrong to feel angry, someone who experiences anger will never want it, believing that another emotion should be experienced instead, and that experiencing anger as always unhappy. Without any beliefs about the necessity of not being angry, the person may still be angry, but happily so, or they may find that without their belief that it is wrong to be angry, they are no longer angry. They will find out what is true for them when they no longer have beliefs about the necessity of having particular emotional feelings. This could be described as emotional motility, the free movement of emotion in congruence with desire.

Unhappiness is the feeling of *unwanted* emotions, which is caused by beliefs in the *necessity* of having particular emotions in particular circumstances. Emotions are the circumstance of unhappiness, but the feeling of necessity is the unhappiness in itself. In the words of Bruce Di Marsico, "Happiness is freedom to the nth degree."

PART II
Emotions

SECTION I

Our Role in Emotions

Option Method Scientific Behavioral Model

Stimulus	*Belief*	*Response*

Event ⟶ { Good ⟶ Happy
Bad ⟶ Unhappy
Neither Good nor Bad ⟶ Okay

Two Kinds of Motivation (Desire)

Wanting: Happy if I get or avoid it
Needing: Unhappy if I don't get it or don't avoid it

Kinds of Being

Beliefs
a. Needing to become (happy): Non-being
b. Wanting to become (happy): Becoming

No Beliefs
c. Knowing being (   ): Being. (Knowing being is when happiness is no longer a question, represented by the empty parentheses. This is discussed more in Volume 3, *No Beliefs Are Necessary*.)

Emotional Dynamics Scientific Model Comparison

MODEL	STIMULUS	ORGANISM	RESPONSE
Biophysical	Light	Photosynthesis	Chlorophyll
	Food	Digestion	Growth
"Psychological" According to Option Method	Stimulus event *or* Perception of event	Organism's belief *or* Person's judgment	Emotional response *or* Behavior
psycho-dynamics	Perceived experience (real or imagined)	Good Not good/Not bad Bad	Happy Okay Unhappy

Unhappy Concepts

Various kinds of "bad" judgment or beliefs:
Should (not)
(not) supposed to
need (not) to
ought (not)
have to
must (not)
wrong
bad
evil
can't be happy
makes unhappiness

Justifications for Unhappiness

"By feeling bad I keep in touch with what I want. As I believe I need this which I want, I ignore my other wants. The more I need, the less I want. Depriving myself of other good things keeps me aware of what I want. If I am not unhappy, I fear that I will ignore that I want what I want."

The question is "Why do I choose to be unhappy in order to want whatever I want in order to be happier?"

Why do you choose to be unhappy (instead of just keeping wanting)?

Nothing Can Make You Unhappy

PEOPLE believed they would be happy by getting what they want. They believed their natural state was one kind of unhappiness or another, one lack or another, which they believed getting what they want (need) would cure. "Something was wrong with them."

Belief: I am unhappy because I don't have what I need to be happy. I don't have what I want. Getting what I want will stop my unhappiness (bad feelings).

Truth: Nothing makes you unhappy, or can. You only believed you were supposed to be. You don't have to believe anymore that not getting what you want can make you feel bad.

Be happy (not unhappy) and be glad to get what you want. Do whatever you want knowing nothing can or will make you unhappy again.

Unhappiness is unnecessary.

What Is The Option Method?

November 11, 1995

THE Option Method has not been created to force anyone to be happy. Nothing can force anyone to be happy; not even God. If God could make people happy he would have done it already.

The Option Method is the second-best method I know of for being happy. The first-best method is simply to be happy. What The Option Method is for is to help people examine why they believe they need to be unhappy.

The Option Method is based on this rationale: that people are only unhappy when they believe they need to be unhappy. So starting with that principle The Option Method now has a rationale why it would work, and why there'd be any purpose to even using it. We can question why people believe they need to be unhappy.

If unhappiness is merely a belief then we can question that belief, and we can see with hindsight that it is merely a belief. While you're believing, you're believing that what you're believing is true. So you don't believe that you are believing, you believe you *know* something.

We would never describe ourselves as merely believing that we have to be unhappy; because the moment we did that someone would say, "Well, don't be silly." Because everybody has an opinion about what we should be unhappy about and what we shouldn't be unhappy about.

How Unhappiness Happens
November 11, 1995

ALL people in all societies—all people in all societies and anyone that I knew of, and certainly anyone you've ever known—have always believed it was necessary to be unhappy in some way, even the most brilliant among us: Buddha, Jesus, Freud, all have believed it was necessary to be unhappy.

What was questioned was, what was the right thing to be unhappy about? What's the wrong thing to be unhappy about? How much should you be unhappy about it?

The Option Method has shown us that people are unhappy to the degree to which they believe they need to be unhappy. For instance, if they believe that there's something to be very unhappy about, they'll be very unhappy about it. If they believe it's something to be only slightly unhappy about, they'll be slightly unhappy about it.

Stimulus	*Belief*	*Response*
Event ⟶	⎧ Good ⟶	Happy
	⎨ Bad ⟶	Unhappy
	⎩ Neither Good nor Bad ⟶	Okay

This diagram shows how human emotions are created. Maybe you've heard that they were created by choice, or maybe you've always believed that they just happened to you.

This is how human emotions are really created: there is an event (stimulus). There's the organism which experiences the stimulus—in this case, a human being. After the event happens, the human being judges them as good, bad or neither good nor bad, and all human emotions are based on that.

If you believe an event is good, you feel happy or as we often say, feel good. If you believe an event is bad, you feel bad or unhappy. And if you feel it's neither good nor bad, you feel neither.

A human emotion does not exist separate from the judgment, and the event can even be illusory. It could be mythical. It could be a dream. It doesn't even have to be real, but if you feel you need to judge it in any one of those three ways you're going to get any one of those three results.

Even if you find out later that the event was only a bad dream, while you believed that dream was bad, you felt bad. When you learned it was a dream you then decided it was a nothing.

The whole point of The Option Method is to help people see that their emotions don't just happen to them. That's the only thing that it's meant to show. It can be used to help people be happy, but that isn't its goal.

The goal of The Option Method is just simply to show people that they are not wandering souls being abused by the universe. That they just get unhappy about this and about that, unhappy about China and unhappy about taxes and unhappy about their boyfriend or girlfriend.

It is to explain why they have the kind of emotions that they have and that they're not victims—that these unhappy emotions don't just happen to them. They are definitely a product of a judgment, without exception.

If there is something that looks like unhappiness, but it's not a result of a judgment, then it's not unhappiness. Then you ate something bad or something like that. But if it's not a result of a judgment, it's not an emotion.

If it's a feeling in your body, it's a feeling in your body. There are all kinds of feelings in your body. The only reason unhappiness produces something called a bad emotion is because you wouldn't be satisfied if you didn't identify that emotion as a bad feeling.

In other words, after you judged something as bad and you didn't get a knot in your stomach, what good is your judgment? So if you don't get a knot in your stomach and you don't get a lump in your throat or you don't get a headache or you don't get tightness, you wouldn't call it unhappiness.

It has to be believable to you. Believing is everything. So for it to be unhappy it has to be believable. Once you realize that, you can realize that even so-called bad feelings are merely feelings that you use in your own body. You created them in your own body and they're your own feelings and you did them to yourself, and they are not inherently any problem.

Once you see you do them to yourself, then you can do one of two things. "I created this in order to experience feeling bad and I'm not into that" and decide that you know better; or you could say, "Hmm, I only do this if I believe I'm feeling bad about something, so I can look at that and see if I am feeling bad about it or not and be done with the feeling bad or not.'"

But in either case what happens is that most people are afraid of what they went and made themselves feel. For example, I'm a child and I decide that something that happened is something I don't want. I've seen models of how people react to crying and I've seen what it's like when my mommy's upset and my daddy's upset or something and I know certain kinds of vocabulary of unhappiness. My point of view is that I can't be happy without this or without that or without the other thing.

I've rarely met a child who was worried about the starvation in China. It's usually more to do with their diaper or their own toys or something like that. It's usually very egocentric to start, because it wouldn't make any sense otherwise.

You can't go from worrying about your diaper to worrying about the world without something like that to use as a model.

So if you're creating the illusion of unhappiness, or the make-believe of unhappiness, or acting out unhappiness, all it takes is that you get good at it. You get good at feeling bad when you don't get what you want and you just simply get so good at it you're no longer talking about the learning process that was involved.

Any unhappiness is learned. In one way or another you've learned, before you ever heard there was a choice, that there are things to be unhappy about and you learned to be unhappy about them.

Actually you learned the kind of symptoms—you have symptoms that only Americans have; those of you who are American-born.

There are symptoms of other cultures that you would never conceive of. We culturally learn to be unhappy and then we learn *how* to be unhappy. Then there are subcultures. There's your region where you live. There's your family heritage. There's the way on your block and in your school. There's the way your friends do it. There's the way your family does it. The things they get unhappy about.

Then there's certainly aspiration to sophistication. So you start getting unhappy about the same thing as the *New York Times*' critics get unhappy about and things like that.

The smarter you get, the finer you hone it. By the time you've got your master's or Ph.D. you should be able to be unhappy about anything in the world—even a Rembrandt, because it's cool or it's smart to be unhappy about that.

There are lots of myths that perpetuate unhappiness; that it's good for you, that it helps you, that it makes you stay on your toes, that it keeps you in touch with reality, and so on. We'll talk about how those things are mythical later, but unhappiness is still constantly being supported by those beliefs.

The Option Method starts with that realization that these *are* beliefs: the belief that something is good, the belief that something is bad. I call it a judgment because it affects our emotions.

If it doesn't affect your emotions, for instance, if you believe a knife is good for cutting there is no reason to feel anything about that. That's not an emotional judgment. That's meant to be a factual judgment and insofar as you make factual judgments you don't have emotions, except if you're glad that you have a sharp knife to cut with.

But to say knives are evil or guns are evil is like saying, "you mean a knife that my surgeon uses is evil? The scalpel that he uses to save lives is evil?" No. Calling things bad and evil tends to be a moral judgment; overall judgments that just mean they're bad if they exist.

Why Are People Unhappy?

THERE is a connotation to bad and evil that has to do with a more fundamental, theological, religious, psychological sense. In those senses as it's used in psychology, anthropology, philosophy and theology it means this: that which makes you unhappy against your will.

For instance, the only "evil" in the devil is that the devil has the power to make a person unhappy against their will. The only "evil" in cancer is that it has the power, supposedly, to make people unhappy against their will.

That's the only evil in a boyfriend or girlfriend breaking up with you: because they have the power to make you unhappy against your will. Being fired has the power to make you unhappy against your will. And so on. We go all the way down from all the greater evils to all the lesser evils.

Your country being at war can send you into terror. Terror is just simply a belief in the greatest of all evils, that this evil, whatever it is, is so insurmountable that you're afraid that it will and shall overcome you. That's the kind of terror that often can lead to suicide. That's the kind of terror that leads to people running mad, taking all their clothes off, running mad down the street begging, begging, begging somehow to be saved.

So evil and bad by definition are things that make you feel bad against your will, without your consent. If it wasn't, if you didn't believe that about it, you wouldn't have ever called it bad, felt bad about it or called it evil. Anything you've ever felt bad about, you felt bad about because you thought it could make you feel bad without your consent.

I'm not going jump into people's lives and say, "Nothing ever made you feel bad without your consent. You wanted it. You loved it. You asked for it. You wanted to be unhappy." That's not true.

Nobody wakes up in the morning and says "I think I'll be unhappy about six things today" and starts choosing them as the day goes on.

People don't choose to be unhappy; people don't choose to be happy. I use "choose" only to say something else: unhappiness doesn't happen to you. It isn't happening to you. You're creating it. You're doing it. It's a feeling in your own body that only you can create.

I'm using the word choice in a way it was never used before. I'm using it because I'm at a loss for words, because I don't really want to say people want to be unhappy, because they universally describe unhappiness as a feeling they don't want. That's why it gets that name. I mean, it doesn't matter what the feeling is, even if it's not your unhappiness, it's their unhappiness and they mean the feeling they don't want or they wouldn't call it unhappiness.

So I don't want to say that they want it and I don't want to say anything like that—that they delight in it or that they enjoy it or that you delight in it and you enjoy it if you get unhappy. That's the whole point of unhappiness. And it's supposed to feel like it happens to you. Otherwise it won't be unhappiness.

So if you've ever felt unhappy and you didn't feel like it was happening to you then I don't know what you're talking about because for it to be unhappy you've got to feel like a victim and you've got to feel like it's happening, even if it's from some demon inside you. You've got to feel like it's happening to you.

But there is a sense in which we choose it, and only if you understand that sense right can you use the word choice. The sense in which we choose it is in the sense that we don't want it, but we believe it's necessary. We believe we have to be unhappy. We believe we have to feel it.

Where do our beliefs come from except by a choice? So indirectly, we choose it. Our beliefs are chosen. I have to agree that a belief is a worthy belief. I have to say yes, that's true in order for me to believe something.

Remember, I'm not talking about merely an opinion, because nobody gets unhappy that way. It's more that, as soon as I *really* think it *could* make me unhappy—oops—I'm already unhappy, because I just thought "that is something that could make me unhappy, or that is something that I would get unhappy about, or that it's something that I should get unhappy about, or I need to get unhappy about, or it's just simply something that makes somebody like me unhappy."

As soon as you think somebody like you gets unhappy about something, you will get it, can get it, can catch it, can remember it, can stumble into it, cannot resist it, can't keep it away. You're unhappy already. Why?

If you believe it's yours, it's yours. That can be called a choice, because that's not forced on you. Now, you don't feel like you chose it and you don't feel like you merely believe it. You just thought that's the truth. So anything that you believe that's true between you and something called unhappiness, it's done; because that's the way emotions work. That's the way all human emotions really work.

If you believe that you're the one who's going to get woozy, dizzy, sleepy, you're the one who does. "Oh no, I saw this coming, " is called panic, because people know sometimes that they've set it in motion by something that they thought and believed.

The problem is that they fear themselves, that they would do that to themselves. The person believes that they tripped the wire that set off their bad feelings; for example, that they went and thought of their dead mother again. And they're afraid they set off the wire and that they're torturing themselves.

So there's a whole cluster of unhappinesses that people believe are ones they set off for themselves. But nonetheless, they're still victims and they're afraid that they're victims to some kind of evil force within them—whatever you call that, insanity, usually, neurosis, psychosis; something like that.

But you're afraid of it, and that "it" was what? Your belief that you're going to have to feel that way. Sometimes "that way" may be nothing more than a slight feeling of exhilaration, which is entirely frightening to some people. And they just felt a little exhilaration because they're very afraid of that particular kind of feeling because they remember what they've done with that, what has happened with it, some superstitious connection they've made—their dog died as soon as they felt that, or something.

What makes "that feeling" a bad feeling? Say the feeling itself is a slight feeling of exhilaration. What makes it a bad feeling is that the person is scared of it.

How are we ever going to know that? Well, that's where The Option Method comes in. The Option Method is starting off with the principle that those feelings may come from beliefs and insofar as those feelings come from beliefs, and then the person has beliefs about them, there can be feelings about feelings.

People have feelings about feelings, because after they have these feelings and these results, then they make judgments on those feelings. A lot of people seem to have asked questions like, "Well, we've been taught that feeling unhappy is bad." Well, not lately you haven't. If you're not unhappy at proper times, you're wrong. If you're unhappy at improper times, you're wrong. So there were always times when it was wrong to be unhappy. For instance, it was always wrong for you to be angry at somebody. Do you have anybody that you were ever angry at who agreed with you that you were right to be angry at them?

In fact, when you're trying to express your anger you're saying to somebody, 'you're making me have a bad feeling, and I want you to stop, or else I'll have a worse feeling and I'm not accountable" or something like that.

People have always told other people that they were wrong to be unhappy with them. So it's not new to any of you to hear that you're wrong to be unhappy.

I don't think you like believing it's wrong to be *anything* you are, do you?

The Perceived Locus of Unhappiness

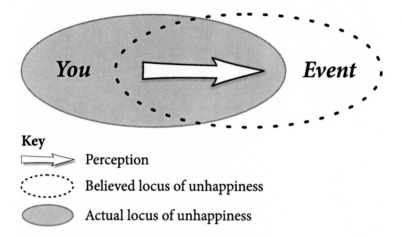

Key

 Perception

Believed locus of unhappiness

Actual locus of unhappiness

An unhappy person believes their bad feelings are within the event they are unhappy about.

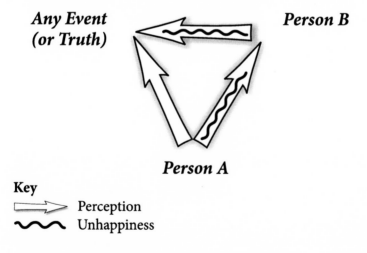

Key

Perception

Unhappiness

A person can be unhappy about an event directly, or they might be happy about an event in itself, yet unhappy that someone else is unhappy about it.

SECTION II

How We Create Emotions

Comparative Consistency

THE degree of unhappiness is proportionate to the importance of the desired thing. For example, I'll be more unhappy if I lose $100.00 than if I lose a penny. I'll be more unhappy if I don't get any food than if I don't get a seven-course meal. I'll be more unhappy if I don't get love than if I merely don't suffer. Somehow it is all in proportion.

What determines the importance of a desired thing? Two factors are present: comparative judgment and consistency in judgment, or what I call "Comparative consistency." For example, if it is bad to lose a little of something then, in comparison, it is worse to lose more.

I make the comparison: if I decide it is bad not get a *lot* of something, then it is worse to not even get a *little* of it. That's how I determine what's important to me. I'm exploring with you how we determine what's important, because that's what our unhappiness feeds on: the idea that some things are more important than other things.

In my comparison I have to be consistent. So for instance, if I find that I feel a *little* bad when you rip my shirt, I'd feel worse if you ripped three of my shirts.

Now this comparative consistency is the way we do it all the time. For example, if it is a pain in the neck to travel 10 miles, it is going to be more of a pain in the neck to travel 20. If I hate getting up at 7:00 I'm going to hate getting up at 6:00 more.

If it is lousy to get up at 7:00 in order to go to a job, it'd be worse to get up at 6:00 in order to go to a job. But it might not be worse to get up at 6:00 in order to go camping. That's not inconsistent. That's consistent with another comparison, that it is better to get up earlier for the things that I want, than for the things that I don't want.

Another example: if someone thinks it is really bad not to have that $100,000 in the bank, they'll think it is much worse to not even have $10 in the bank. And if you think you need $100,000 and you don't even have $10 you'll feel worse off.

Sometimes people won't put any money in the bank because they can only put in $10 a week. "If I could only save $10 a week what's the sense? I won't bother." If I allow myself to keep wanting, and if I want money, I'm going to be pained at the fact that I'm not getting as much as I want, and so therefore I'll just stop wanting to save altogether.

Prerequisite Preparation

PREREQUISITE preparation is a function of choosing something that in some way we believe leads to more good things—it is a prerequisite, a preparation for more of other things. And that is another way that we decide what's more important.

So in other words, given one domain of choice, in that domain alone we decide in terms of more bad, less bad—that is comparative consistency. But now, when you're comparing two different domains, apples to oranges, how do you do it?

It is good to have a lot of oranges, so it is worse to have less. If I stayed with oranges I know how to decide. But when I compare apples to oranges, now how do I decide which is more important? Prerequisite preparation. In summary: if I believe I can become more, or get more, or function better, with, for example, approval than with money, then I will say therefore that approval is more important to me. If I think that I can become more, or get more, or function better with money than approval, then I'll say money is more important to me.

My question to myself is, what is best for my wanting?

So the whole concept of prerequisite preparation is, "I want the thing that will enable me to get more. Period." When I furnished this room, I bought a chair before I bought a painting. Why is a chair more important than a painting? And in many ways I could protest it is not. They're two different things but the benefit of one enables me to get the benefit of the other in some way. By having the chair and having a place to relax, only then it would make sense to get the painting after, to then relax with the painting. The chair is a prerequisite for the painting—why have a painting if you can't even sit and relax with it?

Let's say you want to prepare something the next day, and you have a choice between working late on something, or going to sleep. Which is the better preparation for the next day? They're two separate things, but if I look at them in terms of preparation *for the rest of my life* it is easy to compare them.

And so we're always going to be looking at things in terms of comparative consistency and in terms of prerequisite preparation, or how they prepare us for other things that we want. That unhappiness is proportionate to importance is only apparently different from that unhappiness is in proportion to the temptation to give up, but they can be seen to be the same. For instance, the more important it is, the more I want it, but it is important *because* with it I can get more of what I want. So things are important and become more important because somehow we judge that with them, we can get more of what we want and that's how we decide what's more important than others.

What I want is *more*, and what will give me the ability to get more. So since I've become unhappy to assure that I get it, it follows then that I must become unhappy also to make sure I don't forget that I want to get it. In this frame of mind it is a prime prerequisite that I never forget that I want more and more. And since I use unhappiness as a cause of remembering, I use unhappiness in order to remind myself—which is exactly the very reason why I want might want to *stop* wanting more and more.

This is all because I believe that I want more *in order* to be happier. Since happiness is *really* what I want more and more of, then I'm tempted to give up wanting more and more when I've coupled it with unhappiness or pain.

Using Unhappiness to Motivate Others

Unhappiness is also used as a way to motivate others to give me or help me get what I want; and, remember, what I want is more. What I always will want is more, more, more. More happiness basically, but since we're into unhappiness here, we're wanting more to *make* us happy. Unhappiness is also used as a way to motivate others to give to me or to help me get what I want. One of the reasons people want love is that because love helps them get the help they need to get what they want. Someone I love makes the environment around me happy. They cater to me perhaps, so then I'm free to now use more of my own potential.

You clean my house; I'll go out to work. Or I'll clean your house, you go out to work and then you'll give me money for clothing, stuff like that—somehow we're helping each other.

If you believe others use unhappiness to motivate themselves, you will use it against them as a way of getting what you want.

If I believe you're into using unhappiness yourself I'll use it against you, and if I can threaten you that somehow my unhappiness threatens to stand in the way of what you want, you'll try to prevent me from being unhappy—at least, that's the ploy. So I'll get angry at you or whatever. It's a kind of blackmail. Since you use unhappiness and I want something from you that you won't give me, I'll use the whole principle of unhappiness against you.

Since I believe that, being another human, you probably are unhappy about some things, and I think I know what they are, and if one of the things that you seem to need is my approval, then if I threaten to be unhappy, you'll start worrying about not getting my approval, and you're going to make yourself unhappy if you don't get my approval. So to prevent your own unhappiness you'll give me what I want.

There is an underlying fear which is disclosed by The Option Method. It sounds something like this: if I don't get unhappy it means that I don't really want it enough to try to get it, it couldn't mean that much to me. If I don't get unhappy that's almost like saying, "It'd be okay with me if I don't get it." If I don't get unhappy, that's tantamount to not wanting what I want. This belies the fear that I will want *less* rather than *more*, and that I just might not naturally want what is more important.

Example: Honesty vs. Approval

Another example is: I want to disagree with you, but also be honest about what I feel, yet I don't want you to dislike me for being disagreeable. So I've got those two wants. I'm going to have to decide which one is more important, right? So let's say I've decided that your approval is better preparation for getting more of what I want; that it is more important for me to get approval in this case than to be honest.

Now, since honesty is very attractive, and is tempting me away from the approval, I'm afraid I may seek honesty, which is less important to me right now than approval. Since I'm afraid I may seek honesty, I become unhappy and start becoming afraid of your disapproval in order to reassure myself that that's what I want *more*.

I started off by wanting two things: your approval and my honest expression. I've made the judgment that your approval gets me more than my honest expression. That can be a fine, nice decision, and doesn't have to be a problem. But I'm afraid that I'm going to have a real temptation to be honest. Honesty is attractive, and so I'm afraid I might do it just because it is attractive, and I might forget that what I want is your approval more than I want to be honest.

If I'm into unhappiness to motivate myself, the fear is that I'll screw myself, the fear is that I'll forget that I want your approval and wind up being honest. I'm afraid that if I don't keep the fear of disapproval in my mind I'll blurt out something honest—which *is* something I want, but not at the expense of your approval, which is something I want *more*.

I'm afraid I'll get one thing I want and defeat myself and not get the things I want even more, because I noticed that I want both these things. And especially, the more I want the honesty, the closer I get to being honest, the more afraid I'll become that I'll get overcome by that and that'll overcome my desire for what I really want most, if I'm into using fear to motivate myself. If I'm just confidently knowing that I'm going to do what's best for me, then I'm just going to try to get the approval if that's what I want, and I will have no temptation to be honest.

COMMENTARIES

by Aryeh Nielsen on

"Emotions"

Children Are Self-Created

This commentary is a synopsis of ideas that Bruce Di Marsico expressed in many writings or talks, but did not express summarily in a single writing or talk.

DURING the twentieth century, there were many popular strands of psychology that claimed that unhappiness arose from early childhood experience. There are two ways to investigate this claim: empirically (is there evidence of this?), and logically (is the proposition at least not self-contradictory?).

Empirically, if children could be taught values, then there would not be the universal experience of parents that children do not behave as they would like them to. In both children and adults, offerings of values are made by so-called "teachers." The "student" decides what to accept and reject, based on which values they find sympathetic resonance with. The role of teacher can, at best, be an offering of opportunities for the student to learn. But teaching, as somehow making a student change via the methods or techniques of the teacher, is fictional.

Behavioral compliance is not a sign that a child has learned values. As with adults, compliance is the behavior of acting differently than one would behave if there wasn't a carrot to reward or stick to punish. Compliance is "I value what I value, *and* I find it useful to act as if I value something else in order to gain a reward or avoid punishment."

Logically, the idea that unhappiness arises from early childhood experience is merely a special case of the existentially false claim that events "make" people unhappy.

Nothing has ever been proved that one value is better than another to anybody. Rather, some decide to be convinced. If proofs were possible, then all would be convinced. Instead, we find that those who choose to be convinced by an argument to change their values are convinced by the argument as long as they choose to be, and no longer.

Specifically, a parent cannot "teach a child to be unhappy" by any action. If the child finds it useful to behave in an angry, sad, or fearful manner, they may do so. If later on, the child believes that they are angry, sad, or fearful against their will, they are simply mistaken. They are choosing to believe that they didn't create their own beliefs because they find it useful in some way.

Children are entirely self-created. They have never been and can never have been taught values. They have only chosen to learn values that they have been offered.

Symptoms vs. Emotions

This commentary is a synopsis of ideas that Bruce Di Marsico expressed in many writings or talks, but did not express summarily in a single writing or talk.

O NE way in which people feel bad is to only feel bad because they've *deduced* (reasoned to the conclusion) that they must be unhappy, based on symptoms.

To elaborate:

The symptoms of fear can be such bodily signs as a tight gut, fast heartbeat, and hyper-alertness.

The symptoms of anger can be such bodily signs as tense muscles, broad and fast movement, and a loud voice.

The symptoms of sorrow can be such bodily signs as limp muscles, tightness in the chest, and tears.

The symptoms of depression can be such bodily signs as low energy, lack of appetite, and desire to sleep more than usual.

All these bodily signs can arise from non-emotional causes; for example, a fast heartbeat can be caused by exercise, low energy can be caused by an illness, tears can be caused by onions.

All these bodily signs can arise from emotions that don't feel bad; for example, hyper-alertness can be caused by fascination, broad and fast movement can arise from excitement, desire to sleep more than usual can be caused by great satisfaction.

All these bodily signs can arise from past habits of emotions, not currently operative; for example, a pattern of being afraid of dogs may habituate the body to take on the bodily attitude of fear when a dog is seen, even if there is no fear in the present.

All these bodily signs can arise for reasons you don't know, or can't know or don't understand, or can't understand.

These symptoms can be used as reasons to be unhappy. This happens when someone reasons that they must be unhappy, because they are feeling bodily signs that are similar to the symptoms caused by unhappiness, i.e., they are deducing that they are unhappy.

Additionally, others may deduce that your visible bodily signs mean you must be unhappy; they may tell you that you're unhappy, or ask you why you're unhappy, or what you're unhappy about. And you're not unhappy. Bruce Di Marsico gives examples such as: you are sitting, relaxed, at an active party, and someone deduces that you are depressed because you are not active like the other partygoers; you are excited about a contrary opinion you are offering, and someone deduces that you are angry because you have a high energy level.

In these cases, Bruce Di Marsico notes that the simplest thing to do is merely correct the misapprehension: "No, I'm not depressed, I'm relaxing"; "No, I'm not angry, I'm excited."

Bruce Di Marsico sometimes called the mistaking of symptoms for unhappiness the attitude of the "psychological hypochondriac." When questioning your unhappiness, one of the first things to find out is if you are actually unhappy, as opposed to merely deducing that you are unhappy based on symptoms, and using that deduction as a reason for unhappiness. You can simply ask yourself, when you think you might be unhappy, "Am I actually unhappy about something, or am I just presuming that I am?"

PART III

What Moves Us

SECTION I

Motivation from Happiness

Wanting Is Sufficient

Fear of Not Needing Something You Want

When a person fears losing something, what they are fearing is realizing that they do not need it to be happy and will get along without it. They are fearing that when they realize they don't need it, that they might not want it, and since it is an apparently good thing to have that thing, they fear not wanting it. It is the fear that they will not want what is good for them; this can be a terrifying realization for someone.

Example: In Childhood

Let me illustrate the underlying dynamic that's behind all of that: as a child grows up and begins to see that they really do not need their parents as they used to, they often become very afraid of their parents' dying. Most of their wanting of their parents, up to that point, has been based on needing them. Even simple wants are often expressed as needs in their relationship. "I need you to feed me. I need you to allow me to go out to play, to stay up late"; parents encourage and reward this belief that they are needed for just about everything.

When a child begins to realize that they don't need their parents, that is tantamount to no longer having any excuse for wanting anything from them. A child has been almost incapable of wanting something from the parent that hasn't actually been only the domain of the parent to grant, and so it's easy to see the parent as needed for the thing you want, and therefore, needed for your happiness.

When a person fears losing something, what they're fearing is realizing that they don't need it. So that when the child fears losing his parents, what they're afraid of is realizing that they really do not need their parents in order to be happy and they don't want to believe that they don't need their parents.

Parents also want to encourage the belief that they're needed for just about everything. And parents don't want to believe that they don't need their children, either. The parents are afraid that once the children lose their need for them, and the parents lose control of the children, they, as parents, will have lost everything. When you're afraid of losing something, it's because you're afraid of knowing that you could be happy without it, and they don't want to know that they could be happy without control.

In the extreme, just about every time the child wants something that they perceive that they can only receive from their parents, they will choose to need it and express it as a need, even a new toy that they were perfectly happy without a moment ago. The child will act as if they need the new toy. The child will cry and thereby, by crying, they're acknowledging the parent's belief that they are needed by the child. And that their denial is capable of making the child unhappy.

The child has well learned that unless he plays the game with his parents and continues to encourage them to believe that he needs that, what is liable to happen? If you live with people who will not give you anything unless they believe you need it, what are you going to do? If you're an infant and you wet your diaper, do you think anybody would care if you didn't cry? And if you were hungry, do you think anybody would care if you didn't make a stink about it?

You quickly come to perceive that nobody really cares about you, except that you bother them. It doesn't take much for a child to come to that realization. Originally, the sound of the cry is just simply one of communication. In subsequent months of the infant's existence, that cry changes and becomes a cry of pain and a cry of need, which wasn't there in the first place.

A parent assumes that if a child is crying, the child is unhappy. They're not unhappy. What are they going to do? Write you a letter? How else do they tell you that they want to eat? Type it out on a typewriter? Whistle? They do what they're biologically capable of doing and that's making sounds from their mouths that we call crying.

Can you imagine a child that asks for a toy and the parent said, "No," and they just walked away happily? Do you think that kid would ever get another toy, knowing most parents? Hardly. He doesn't need toys. And, to the degree that the parent needs to be needed, every time a child cries, the parent has got to feel glad to be needed. It was one of their motives, in fact, in having a child. They wanted somebody to need them.

Feeling happy that your child is crying can be seen to be a contradiction to some people. A parent who doesn't feel much of that joy could really be very firm in their denial. And they can see it as a rational and suitable thing. No, you cannot play with matches. And no, you cannot play with the razor blades. And no, you cannot go out and play in the street. They'll feel really okay about that, and there's no secret joy in the child's crying.

Apparently the worst thing any parent can say to a child is "you're being childish." You just simply accuse them of being who they are, and that's the biggest put-down somehow. So you can berate the child for being a child, for being childish, or you can even acquiesce and give the child everything it asks for because you want to be needed as a loving parent, because you really need to be seen as a loving parent.

So that's the dynamic of being afraid of not needing something you want, in childhood.

Using "Need" to Order Life

If you fear losing a friend, what you're really fearing is finding out that you don't need that friend in order to be happy. If you fear losing money, if you fear being poor, what you fear is realizing that you don't need things that money buys you to be happy. You can be afraid of losing your health because you don't want to know that if you were not healthy, you could still be happy. You could be afraid of being stupid, because you don't want to know that you could be happy without being smart.

In other words, I'm afraid of not being loved because I believe I need it to be happy. But I believe I need it to be happy because I'm afraid that if I don't need it, then I might not want it. And I'm afraid of not wanting it because I do want it.

Deep down inside, I know I don't need it in order to be happy. So there must be something wrong with me for needing something I don't need. Now if I could need something I don't need, I could also want something I don't want. Or not want something I do want because I really don't need it. And so since I don't really need anything, I could want what I don't want, not want what I do want. Want it, not want it. My God, I could go crazy!

If I don't need anything, how do I order my life? How do I justify my wants?

What's Wrong with Me?

If I could be happy not having what I want, I might not want it enough to get it, and there would really be something wrong with me. What's wrong with me is that I don't have enough freedom, that's what's wrong me, that's why I'm unhappy. What's wrong with me is that I don't have enough mobility. What's wrong with me is that I don't have enough success. What's wrong with me is that I don't have enough money. What's wrong with me is that I'm stupid, I'm thick. I don't learn very well. I don't change very easily. That's what's wrong with me. What's wrong with me is that I'm lazy. What's wrong with me is I'm unkind. I'm unloving. I'm selfish. That's what's wrong with me.

I know what's wrong with me, I'm not loved. I'm afraid of being alone. What's wrong with me is that I'm weak willed. I don't want to know that this is not what is wrong with me, that I could be happy without some personality attribute. When I fear losing something, what I'm really fearing is realizing that I don't need it to be happy.

If you fear a thing enough, you run headlong into it in order to relieve the fear or to relieve the anxiety. You're somehow wanting to prove that you don't need it in order to be happy. And at the same time, you are afraid of seeing that you don't need it in order to be happy, and believing that the only way to see that you don't need it in order to be happy is to actually make it happen and deprive yourself and then live through it, knowing that you'll get over it eventually. And then, of course, since you're doing it with that fear, you live through it miserably and unhappily, too.

What If I Stop Caring about My Health?

My only answer to those of you, who are afraid you will give up your wanting to be healthy, is that although you say that you know you wanted to be healthy, I say to you that because you're unhappy, you're lying. That an unhappy person lies even when you're telling the truth. Sure you want to be healthy but you are more concerned with being unhappy than about being unhealthy. You're more concerned with being afraid of being unhealthy, and you're thinking that's the same as wanting to be healthy. So to the degree that you're unhappy, to that degree you may be considering and believing that wanting not to be unhealthy is the same as wanting to be healthy.

We will turn to things that, even though they destroy our health, will make us happier. How do you account for drug addicts and alcoholics? When you're in touch with wanting to be healthy, you are becoming healthier. You are tending toward health. When you're wanting to be healthy, you're not going to do things to be unhealthy. You can only do things that would be unhealthy when you're wanting something else and, perhaps at the same time, not wanting to be unhealthy.

Wanting is only in terms of when there's still a question about it; it's only in response to that questioning that you could not want it. How can it always keep coming to be a question, "Do I want to be healthy?" Because my unhappiness has led me away from it, that something that I have wanted has been exactly opposite to it.

So if you're not tending towards your health, when you're realizing that you're wanting to, that's all you need to do. And that's it. Now you want to again. That never will be contradicted until you actually contradict it. That will continue to be so until you contradict it by wanting something else when you want not to be unhappy.

And if there's something you want in order not to be unhappy that contradicts your health, you'll choose that if you believe you need it not to be unhappy, to save you from your unhappiness—drugs for example.

Your Wanting

I Want What I Want

I just want what I want. It's okay for me to want it; I don't need it to be happier. If I'm unhappy, I believe I need it to be happy. We say we need things when we're unhappy, but we really know we don't need whatever it is to be happier.

Whatever it is, I don't need to want it. I don't need *not* to want it. I don't need *not to want* to want it. And I don't need *to want* to want it. I don't need anything. I just want whatever I want. I feel good wanting. Let yourself get in touch with the truth of this for yourself. I feel good wanting.

I feel good not wanting. I just feel good. I want whatever I know about. Some things I want more than others. The things I don't think of, I don't want. All I think of, I want. I dis-want nothing. There isn't anything that I dis-want. There are just things I want more. What do I mean by dis-want? Things I'm against wanting.

There's nothing you really dis-want. There's just lots of things you want more. You don't dis-want cancer. You want health more. Given the choice between having cancer and something else you considered more unhealthy, you'd want cancer. So it's not that you don't want any of those things. You want each thing, but some things you want more. You'd want disease if that was all that you could have or if that was the best you could have. You'd want that. It's just that you want other things more. You want health more.

If by wanting one thing now, it turns out that I can't have another thing I want more, that's okay. I don't need either of them anyway. If I know that somehow by wanting the lesser, that would prevent my having what I want more, I will not do anything that I know will prevent me from having the thing I want more. It's impossible.

If I know there's one thing I want more and another thing I want less, I cannot do the lesser thing. I can only do for the thing I want more. I can't do anything that I know would stand in the way of what I want more. For example, I want a new car and I want a vaca-

104

tion. And I can't have both now, for example, because I do not have enough money. I will want one of them more. That's all. I will want one more than the other. Not that I won't want one and will want the other. It's just one I would want more. And if they're equal in my mind, any little desire could tip the balance in either direction.

If I want the car now more, I will not go on the vacation, and if I want the vacation more, I will not buy the car. It's impossible for me to go against what I want more. To think of anything is to tend toward it and to want it. If you're unhappy, you might fear that you couldn't want a particular thing. If you're unhappy, you might fear that you would want something. Another way of saying it is that if you fear wanting, you would be unhappy. If you're afraid of wanting, you'll be unhappy. *Old belief – When I want Things I am bad / Wanting things gets you in Trouble*

Your experience is that if you are unhappy, you can fear that you could not want something or another. There might be something I just can't want, because I'm unhappy. The truth of the matter is that if you feared wanting it, that's *why* you would be unhappy. Just because you don't seem to know why you want what you want, that doesn't mean it's wrong or that wanting it could make you unhappy.

Some things you want, you don't worry about that you want them; you don't seem to need to know why you want them, just that you want them—they seem natural, like food, air, shoes. You can give yourself some kind of a reason that tells yourself you need them—for example, that your body needs them or your life needs them—and then it's okay to want them.

There are other things that you want, for what seems to be no reason or for a bad reason. In other words, it came from your fear or unhappiness or need, and you disapprove of your wanting. You call that wanting bad and evil and try not to want what you believe you shouldn't want, or to want what you believe you should want. And that's unhappy. If you're angry and want someone dead or frightened and need someone possessively, you disapprove of those desires because you really want something else more. For example, what you really want more is, the person you wanted dead, you really more would like them to live. And the person you feel possessive of, you really *more* want them to love you freely. So you want them dead but you *more* want them to live. You want to have them possessively but you *more* want them to love you freely.

"Bad" Means Wanted for Unhappy Reasons

"Bad" comes from when you realize you want something that you have unhappy reasons for wanting. That is why everybody says that sex and death and money are bad—because you have unhappy reasons for wanting them. There's nothing wrong with wanting sex, death, money, whatever. There are other things you may want more when you realize that what you thought you needed, you don't really need but only want.

You may fear that that wanting of these still means you need them. You fear wanting because you know there is no real reason to want them. You wonder why would you want anything and why would you want one thing more than anything else, since your happiness doesn't depend on anything you've already got, especially something you've only ever wanted out of unhappiness, like sex or money. Since you know they are of no real use to your happiness, you wonder why you could want them. They don't seem natural, like wanting air and water and sleep.

Something causes you to want what you want. But it isn't reasons. All you could do with reasons is to have reasons not to want things. You want everything you think of. So it isn't reasons that give you the wanting. All reasons do is to give you reasons not to want them. First you tend toward a thing and you want it. Then you make up the reason for it.

First, all you become aware of is that you're moving toward it, that you're wanting it. It came into your mind and you're tending toward it. Then you make up a reason to explain why you're tending toward it, why you want it. This same something, which is a cause but not a reason, is the cause for your wanting anything and everything. Reasons are not the true cause for your wanting. Even if you want to protest right now that you really do want air and water for a reason, the only reason you can come up with, ultimately, is that you want to live. But then is that really a reason? Do you or can you have a reason for wanting to live?

There is a cause for your wanting to live. But not a reason. Are you wanting to live? Or are you breathing *and* living? And if you thought that you were wanting to live and if you thought there was a reason, you would make up a name for that reason. You'd say, "I know the reason why I want to live. I really want to live in order to be happier." And that's your made-up reason for wanting to live. You say that wanting to be happier is a reason for everything, including life. Is wanting to be happier really a reason for everything, including your life? Since you know that nothing makes you happy or unhappy, or happier, you wonder why you really want everything.

No Reasons Are Necessary

There are no reasons, but there are causes. You know you want to be happier, and that is even a reason why you get unhappy. You know you really feel the wanting to be happier. What is the reason? You can make up some. That only leads in circles: "If I was happier, I would be healthier and kinder." "If I was happier, I'd be more loving." "If I was happier, I'd be more efficient," etcetera. But I want those qualities because I believe that with them, I would be happier.

There is a cause for wanting to be happier and for wanting everything we want. There is no reason unless you want there to be. Reasons are made up. All you know is that you want. You don't really have a reason. You make up a reason. What's your reason for wanting to be happier? Everything you say you want, you tell me "the reason I want that is because I believe it will make me happier." What's your reason for wanting to be happier? No reason. You just want it. And so everything you're doing just comes to that.

You know the cause for wanting to be happier: because you want to be. Because there's no way not to be. There's no way not to want to be, because that's *you*, because it is in you, because it has always been in you. It's the whole goal of your existence. You can give that a name, any name you want. But you'd only be giving it a name, but that wouldn't explain it.

Your reasons and your rules don't hold in this universe. You make up your reasons. They have nothing to do with what *is*. Your rules of "what is possible" are irrelevant.

If You've Been Waiting to Be Loved…

Your greatest fear is that you might not do what you always wanted to do, be happy. That somehow there'd be something wrong with you. Who thinks that they're never really able to be happy, that they're never really able to reach happiness?

You'll be happy because you want to be. All you have to know is that you can love. That's all you've ever wanted to know. You don't need to know that you're loved. You have always said, "I need to know first that I'm loved before I can love." Now you know you are loved. So all you need to do is let yourself know that you really are loving. And you can know that you're loving by being glad, feeling grateful for what you have. Whenever you feel you are unloving, you're only *feeling* you're unloving—you are not actually unloving.

If you're doing what you think is best, just ask yourself, "Why do you think you have to be unhappy, just because there's no reason to be happy?"

Believing that Unhappiness Is
Necessary to Motivate Ourselves

W<small>E</small> want our wanting to be clear, with no alternative choices, conflicts or temptations.

The way we make it clearer is by increasing fear. Why do we ever begin that? Where did it ever start? Why do we use unhappiness at all? Why do we use unhappiness in any particular incident? Because we believe in it.

Why do we keep being afraid we won't have enough motivation? Because we've given up in the past. It's a cycle. I've proven to myself that I don't have motivation because I've made things very painful, and then stopped because it was so painful. For example, I wanted to be closer to you, and I made that painful, so I gave up on you and went to somebody else. That was my proof to myself that I do give up on what I want.

If events change and what we are doing becomes not worth it, that's fine. But usually events don't change; *we* start changing: We become more unhappy about the traffic, and now it becomes less and less worth it to go to work—but maybe the traffic didn't get worse, it might even have gotten better.

It wasn't that we just simply decided it wasn't worth it. It was because we've been giving ourselves fear and we sold out. It was not that it *really* wasn't worth it, it is just that I made it so painful that it became not worth it. So I'll start the same thing all over again with somebody else or in another circumstance because I know that I'm the villain in this. If it *really* was not worth it I wouldn't keep doing that sort of thing.

It is fear of being distracted from what you really want more; and in the example that I gave, the fear was that I'll be distracted from wanting your approval into wanting to be honest, when what I want even more is your approval.

This is all under the heading of "motivating myself to continue wanting." I become afraid that I will want less rather than more. A corollary fear to this is that somehow I won't know what is more important, all based on fear that I won't continue wanting what is more important.

When you think you're not going to do what you want to do, you call it evil, or unhappiness. You're using the whole belief in unhappiness to motivate yourself, which is based on a lack of self-confidence. The fact that you would dare to think that you might not do what you want to do, you're using that to make sure that you keep wanting to do it. You're giving yourself an extra motivation that you don't need, but you don't know that because you believe you'll give up.

Fear of Making the Wrong Decision

The corollary fear is that I somehow won't know what is more important. "Important" is that which will lead to getting more, that which will be a better preparation for our future life. And therefore, I'm afraid that I will choose the less important thing, the "wrong" thing, and I use this fear to ensure that I keep wanting the "better" thing. And it is not as important that I get what is better in this case, but that if I don't get it, at least it is not a result of my not wanting it. If I don't know the best thing to want at a given moment—in other words, the way of getting more, ultimately—then what becomes the most important thing is that at least I keep wanting to know what are the best things to want, so that if I can't know right now what the best things are to want at least I must keep alive the desire to know what the best things are, because otherwise without that, I'll *never* know what the best things are.

This is the fear of making the wrong decision. I become afraid that even if I knew what the better choice was I wouldn't choose it, that I wouldn't do what is more important.

I don't know what will lead to more. I don't know what's the best thing to want. I just don't know the future. I don't know with the facts that I have got which will lead to *more* for me, what choice would be the better prerequisite preparation for my happiness. Since I don't know, I become unhappy in order to decide. I fear that in the future I may believe that the other choice, whichever one I didn't choose, would have led to getting me more happiness, and I'm afraid that I might regret my choice. I use the fear to help me. I'm afraid that in the future I'll say, "I should have known better."

In order to reassure myself that I really want whatever is *more*, I must rack my brain and become afraid so that I will be able to say, "I couldn't have known better, I did the best I could have possibly done at the time." I want to assure myself that I don't want to be self-defeating. In case the future comes and it turns out that the other choice would have been the better choice, I want to be able to say, "It wasn't because I screwed myself."

So I use fear of not knowing what is more important to *decide* what is more important, to assure myself that I don't want to be self-defeating, and that I take my wanting *more* very seriously. I am afraid that I only made the wrong decision because I really didn't *want* to know what the better thing was for me. I'm afraid of seeing that I'm really a self-defeating son-of-a-bitch.

Having Reasons to Be Unhappy

I'll believe there must be a reason why I'm unhappy, because I will always want more, and if there is no reason to be unhappy, if I don't conjure up a reason, then there seems to be no way to make certain that I keep wanting more. That's why everybody's got a reason why they're unhappy—but it is all bull. When I am conducting a session, I allow for each person's integrity and never push them, and everybody's got their own reason. The ultimate reason is that, even if there wasn't a reason they want there to be one. And many, many times, always in my practice we've come down to: "I don't know, I don't have the reason, but there must be one. There is no reason to be unhappy about this, but I'm unhappy about this"—coming up with a good reason that is never really a good reason when they explore it.

Always looking for a reason to be unhappy, always wanting to believe that there's a reason to be unhappy. That way I can reassure myself that I want better, because I'm afraid that I won't keep wanting what is better unless I fear.

The two important things that we want in general: the most important is that at least I assure myself *that* I want. Secondly, my unhappiness at least keeps my wanting alive. Then if I keep my wanting alive, at least then maybe I can know what I want. This is more important than, for instance, a particular thing. A particular thing would be to want a cigarette, to want a drink, to want to walk, to want clothing, to want anything in particular. I'll give up any of those, in fact. I'll screw myself left and right. I'll give up everything. I'll even give up life as long as I keep on wanting—I won't give up wanting.

Unhappiness Is a Motivator for Achieving Happiness

I want what I want and I want to keep my wanting alive. It becomes obvious in many cases that this is so painful when there is a deep depression, where a person just doesn't want anything. They're scared to death of wanting, because what they want so much, and what we all want so much, is happiness. Ultimately, unhappiness is a motivator toward achieving happiness. What's beyond all these wantings is the wanting of happiness, and that really can conflict with wanting when you're using unhappiness as a motivator for achieving happiness.

I gave you a model of all the various ways how we use unhappiness to motivate ourselves and others. We use it to motivate ourselves to either get what we want or at least to keep the wanting alive. In my continuing to keep wanting alive, the most important thing is that I keep wanting, so what I'll use will be the fear of giving up wanting. Another way of keeping my wanting alive is to keep the importance of the desired thing in my mind, to decide that that thing I want is important. I create that by one of two ways: by comparative consistency or by prerequisite preparation.

Happy people do that too; but this is the way, in unhappiness, we pervert these against us. Certainly, in happiness we can invert things: good is not losing a little, better is to not lose more.

So now make this become real for you. Pick anything, anything that anybody might be unhappy about, and I mean anything. Find out how it is used as a motivator. If you do that right now you'll find out that you're practicing The Option Method. You will all be inventing The Option Method right now for yourself without ever having been told what it is all about. If you just try to find out how unhappiness is used as a motivator—pick any unhappiness, try to find out how it is used as a motivator—you will be creating The Option Method.

Say to yourself, "How do I use unhappiness to motivate myself?" And you say, "Here's an example" and you give an example. And get really deep into that experience.

The idea is, "I use unhappiness to motivate myself."

"Oh, really? How? How am I using it now?"

Wanting to Be Unhappy to the Right Degree

November 11, 1995

Anything you're unhappy about, you believe is worth being unhappy about, so why would you want that changed?

Why does anybody want to have their unhappiness changed? Only because at some point in your life you're not so sure. You always thought your unhappiness was based on a kind of wisdom. And now you're experiencing some unhappiness and you're not so sure it's so wise. Usually people believe they know the right things to be unhappy about, but they've gone too far. They find themselves having symptoms. They have uncontrollable rage or tears or sadness or something, and their real problem is not that they're unhappy but they're afraid they've gone too far. So when I ask you, "Why would a person not want to be unhappy about what they're unhappy about?" I don't know anyone who doesn't want to be unhappy about what they're unhappy about. I've only known people who've thought maybe they've gone too far and maybe it's causing them to not have right judgment or be the right kind of person that they ought to be. And they're not so sure about its footing and its foundation, and that's what they would like to explore.

So they would like you to tell them, if you're a therapist of any sort, that either it's normal or it's not normal or there's something we can do about it. Everybody who goes for therapy of any sort is going because they're unhappy. But why are they going? Because they're afraid they've gone too far, that their unhappiness has taken a turn that is not good for them. That unhappiness is not all it's cracked up to be.

Unhappiness is supposed to be good for me. And now I find myself lonely or penniless or frightened or without a job or sick. And I have gotten this way by being a miserable cuss or a frightened person, but not because I didn't want to be unhappy. I want to be unhappy but the *right* way.

Wanting vs. Needing

November 11, 1995

THE difference between wanting and needing is a difference in belief. It's called wanting when you know that you'll be happy if you get what you want or you avoid what you don't want. You'll be happy if you don't get killed going home, and you'll be happy if you get home by a certain time, etcetera. That's called "wanting." That's wanting to get home safely and wanting to get home enjoyably.

Needing to get home safely is the feeling that you'll be unhappy if you don't get home on time or if you don't get home safely, if you don't get home the way you want. That causes the feeling called need. Now you need to have those things to not be unhappy. Because, see, you threatened yourself, you've believed in being unhappy if these things didn't happen or they weren't avoided. If you say, "Boy, if I got into an accident I'd be a mess, mentally somehow, emotionally," now you need to stay safe and not get into an accident to keep yourself from not being unhappy. All you are is worried. That's unhappiness. That's called need. You're not just simply wanting to get home safely, which is the only thing that's really going to work anyway. If it was true that worrying would work or needing could work, what would make it true? What would set it into motion? It would be already you knowing what you wanted. In other words, a person doesn't bother putting themselves through the pain of needing, except to achieve what they already knew they wanted. So why do you need the needing? The wanting is the only effective part in there. The fact that you're ever going to do any of those things to get you where you want to be is only going to be because you've been wanting it. You've been wanting to succeed. You've been wanting to be healthy. You've been wanting to get what you want. And the fact that you use need in order to motivate yourself is just simply nothing. It just has nothing to do with anything and it won't work. But it'll make you feel like you need it. You'll feel according to what you think you ought to feel, and if you think you need to feel need, that's what you'll feel. But it won't make it true, in fact.

Not Knowing What You Want
November 11, 1995

YOU'RE always doing what you think is best. *Now* what do you want, is really the only point. Let's say you've been unhappy every day of your life up 'til now. So what? What do you want *now*? You know what you don't want, lots of times in life. And then you ask yourself, "Well, what *do* I want?"

"But I don't know what I want." What do you want when you don't know what you want? "I want to go to sleep" or "I want to watch television" or "I want to eat," or the human things, the family things, stuff like that. Usually the feeling of not knowing what to do is not knowing what you're supposed to do or what you should do, because you don't *have* to know what you want to do.

Don't do anything and see what happens. You'll do something. It won't be too long before you get up and go to the bathroom, or you'll be at the refrigerator or on the phone or picking up a magazine or writing a note or something. You can always treat yourself very lightly, very gently. Not as a serious undertaking but sort of like a flower that you nurture and let grow and bloom and blossom.

And if some things are in your way, insofar as you can get rid of them, get rid of them. And if there's more that you'd like just because you like it, want it. You want more sunlight? Then want more sunlight. Warmer climate? Want it. There is nothing that was written on your birth certificate about what you are supposed to do after you were born. It just says your name, weight, things like that. And it doesn't say "supposed to be a great success or will be rich, supposed to forgive people."

Shame

One of the greatest problems with unhappiness, when we're trying to help people be happy, is for them to learn how to forgive themselves. There's a saying we have in Option: "True forgiveness is knowing that there's nothing to forgive." You've never done anything ever in your whole lives to be ashamed of. You just believed you have. You've never done anything in your life to be ashamed of. You have merely believed you have. Things like that become axioms when you start exploring and you find out that it's always true.

We never find real shame. We only find people who believe they ought to be ashamed. If you look at your life you can't find anything that you really ought to be ashamed of, only what you believed you ought to be ashamed of. You really, probably could see pretty easily that there are no obstacles to your being really happy, if you are willing to look. And I think one of the glories of The Option Method is that it frees you up to realize that. Since you're not at fault and you quickly come to know you're not at fault, you can start to see this. So the whole point of The Option Method is to bring us to understand that it's not a mystery that we get unhappy, not to learn that we are at fault for our unhappiness or that we *should* be happy.

Getting Happier

If you believe you should be unhappy, you will be. If you believe you should be happy, that means you're going to be unhappy. And when you believe you should be anything, you already are unhappy. And the only question is: is that necessary for you to achieve what you want?

And you'll find a very beautiful thing happens: as a person works on their unhappiness as they see fit, according to what they want to deal with, they actually physically change and get happier and happier and happier. Nobody has to tell them what they ought to deal with or what they should deal with. If they have nothing to deal with, oh boy, then real work can be done. Then that's lots of fun.

SECTION II

Motivation from Unhappiness

Why We Use Unhappiness

Wanting Is More Important to Us than Getting

An example: I get angry at you for not wanting to be with me more. That becomes patently self-defeating. The more angry I get, the less you want to be with me, yet my anger is to assure me that I *really* want you. Even if it doesn't work, I have the assurance that it isn't for lack of my wanting. I feel that it is bad not to get what I want, but it is worse not to even *want* what I want—so my anger, my unhappiness, is to reassure myself that I really do want what I want: it is a protest.

Unhappiness in this case is my protest to myself that I will *never* give up wanting. Just wanting in itself is much more important to me than getting what I want—this is obvious in an example like anger.

In situations like the above, apparently the need to keep in touch with my wants is stronger than the need to get what I want. How could that be? Why does that come about? One reason why I may need to protest that I will never give up wanting is that so often in the past, after causing myself so much pain in similar situations, the only way I believed I could relieve the pain was to do exactly that: to stop wanting it, and by believing that it wasn't really important to me somehow. And my desire to give up is strong, so I protest.

There were others in the past that I wanted to be closer too, and remembering the context, I get angry at you for not wanting to be with me more, for not wanting to be closer with me. Yet the more angry I get, the further away you go. Why do I do that? To protest that I really want to be with you. Why do I do that? Because I need to keep in touch with my wanting. I'm scared. I have to get angry so I won't lose sight of what I want. Here's why: There were others in the past that I wanted to be closer to. I used so much unhappiness, and when I didn't get the closeness that I wanted, the way out of the pain was that I stopped wanting to be closer to that person, and then I sought a less painful relationship with someone else. Eventually I stopped having the original relationship that I wanted so much.

I'm very aware that it is attractive to stop wanting in order to stop the unhappiness that I use in order to make sure that I keep wanting. I get angry at you for not wanting to be closer to me even though that drives you away. I keep reassuring myself that I want you to be closer, and keep protesting it so that I won't give up wanting, because in the past and in similar situations I said, "Okay, you don't want to be closer to me, I give up. I'll go to another relationship." To give up the pain, I have given up what I wanted, and now I'm beginning to see that I'm going to have to do that again, and that has been more and more painful to me. The more I foresee that it is going to be painful to me, the more I protest, the more I get angry. The more that I see that you're going to go away from me, in fact, the further away you go, the angrier I'm going to get, because as it becomes easier to give up my wanting, it becomes all the more important for me to keep my wanting alive.

Being Tempted to Give Up Wanting

My anger is all to motivate me to continue wanting. This dilemma is caused by instituting in the first place the belief that I will be unhappy unless I get what I want. The degree of unhappiness is in proportion to the temptation to give up wanting—to the fear of giving up wanting. This is why the more I believe I have to use unhappiness to get what I want, the more and more the choice becomes between giving it up all together, just forgetting the whole thing, or becoming more and more unhappy.

Now, since I've coupled "I want more" and "I'm going to be more unhappy if I don't get it," the choice I am apparently faced with is either to be more unhappy, or to want less.

Since I want it, and need to remind myself that I want it, I must increase my fear of giving up wanting. I must not be persuaded to not be angry, I must remain angry. I must be unhappy until I get what I want, or give up. I cannot stop being unhappy unless I stop wanting. And that's a horrible choice. I don't want to give up wanting, I want this. I want you to be closer; I want you to love more. I don't want to stop wanting that, damn it!

And so if getting this good thing requires this unhappiness or a sacrifice in order to get it, I'll have to then want to make a sacrifice, and there's a fear of not wanting to go through the hell of making a sacrifice, there's a very strong temptation to not bother to go through all that unhappiness. And so there is the desire to stop wanting it in order to avoid having to pay the price.

Your other alternative is to stop wanting it, but you don't want to at this point. It was something you started out by wanting, and you won't stop wanting it unless you're really pushed to the wire, when it becomes really painful.

We know that to stop wanting is not the way out. The unhappiness doesn't work, except in the sense that we become so unhappy that we stop wanting. But that is working against ourselves, because we started off by wanting.

Unhappiness works to keep us wanting. Unhappiness motivates me to get what I want, and if it just got me what I wanted, well then there's no problem. In the example I'm referring to, anger at wanting someone to be closer, it doesn't. It gets me just the opposite of what I'd want. And this is the sticky problem.

Negative Judgments Are Not Necessary

Everything Is Good

So everything that *is*, is not bad. Bad would *not* be a quality of anything that exists. Things don't have intrinsic qualities. An object is what it is, and we invest in its qualities. Now, rather than seeing them as neutral, we can see them all as good.

Everything is good, in the sense that it's not bad. We use judgments very frequently in order to help make these decisions about whether a thing is good or bad, and I would like to talk about the whole nature of judging at all.

Judgments Masquerading as Observations

Judgments are often subtle and try to pass for objective observation. Very frequently, we'll be making a judgment and we'll try to palm it off on ourselves and on others as an objective observation. But, insofar as they *are* judgments, they will cause unhappiness. Some examples of judgments that kind of try to pass for observations:

Somebody was told that their daughter was immature. She said "That's a judgment." The reply was "No, no, that's a fact." So it depends. One could say immature and not mean it as a judgment, if you were referring to a biological fact: she hasn't hit puberty. But there's a good chance that what a person means is that there's something not particularly good about being "immature." To say someone is talkative, why would that be pointed out if it wasn't some kind of a judgment? It isn't an objective observation. And yet it is an objective observation, in the sense that, if somebody is talking, then they are talking. But to say that they're talkative implies some constant state of being, and that there's some other way one could or should be. Why would that even be mentioned as something else you could be? Why do we go around saying to people anything that would imply there's something else you could be, if we weren't making a judgment, as if you're not good enough yet?

You're tall. You're angry. All of these things that I'm saying could, in themselves, be observations, but almost always they're judgments trying to pass as observations. You're very quiet. You're fat. Why would you tell someone that they were tall or fat unless you were a doctor somehow trying to tell somebody something that you didn't think they knew? These are often judgments trying to pass themselves off as simple observations. "Oh, I'm only stating a fact." The question, of course, that comes up is, why even make an observation? We make judgments on the value of things in order to make a decision. And that would also be why you would make observations.

In order to make a decision, we needn't have our frame of reference be good or bad. So what kind of judgment is being made if you're making a judgment on somebody that they're fat? Various people mean different things by it. One of the judgments that might be made on somebody being fat is that that is bad. But another judgment may be, no, that's not bad, but it is better not to be fat. That may be more the judgment. So there would still be some kind of judgment involved. And we want to look at the nature of the judgment; very frequently by good and bad, what we're really talking about is our happiness.

Judging Things as Good or Bad for Happiness

When we make judgments on things—on people, especially, but on anything—we're often saying something like: "This thing is helpful versus destructive to my happiness." Things are constantly being judged as whether they help our happiness or they destroy our happiness or prevent our happiness or affect our happiness in any way. And, of course, the obvious middle judgment is that they have nothing to do with our happiness, which is what most people would see. So we could improve on that by having another system, which would be something like, "Well, it's not helpful to my happiness or it is helpful to my happiness or it's more helpful than something else." There isn't a negative implied there, a negative judgment, which then leads us to saying it's bad and feeling bad about its occurrence. We could just say it from where I'm at; "It's not helpful for my happiness." That wouldn't necessarily be anything to feel bad about. To say certain things are not helpful to our happiness doesn't make us feel bad unless we believe they ought to be. Then, if we believe they ought to be, we're not really saying that they're not helpful. We're saying that they're destructive, or that the absence of them is destructive to our happiness, and the fear of losing our happiness *is* unhappiness.

So if I believe there ought to be something here right now and there isn't, I could say its not being here is not helpful to my happiness. But what I really mean is that its not being here is preventing me from being happy. If you don't have negative judgments, everything is either going to be helpful, more helpful, or irrelevant to your happiness.

Nothing Ever Needs to Be Decided Against

If nothing *makes* me unhappy, then why shouldn't I do it or allow it to be done? For example, somebody might ask you for something, and it wouldn't make you unhappy to give it to them. Perhaps you're not into making those kinds of feelings for yourself, making yourself feel bad. But very frequently, what happens is "if I don't have a negative reason for not doing something, then I *must* do it."

We're bypassing the whole question of our desires when we jump to, "if I don't have a reason not to do it then I should do it." Because we're so used to doing things and not doing things because they're bad and using unhappiness as the rationale, that when the unhappiness is gone we forget, in a way, that there are other reasons for doing things.

Example: Giving Money

I may really have some reason for desiring not to give you money. You may ask me for $10, and I would not be unhappy to give you $10—and then I could play a game with myself, which says, "Therefore, I should give you $10." In that case, what I really have noticed is that there was a slight desire in me to do it for a reason—for instance, that you thought it would make you happy. The reason is that you wanted it and that would make you happy and that would make me happy.

But we bypass that reason and it becomes totally ignored. And we can't even decide on whether that reason is a good enough reason or not for us. Then we come up with guilt feelings. "I should do it and I'm bad if I don't, because I'm not going to be unhappy without it."

And that doesn't only extend, of course, to giving money. It extends to love-making, to sex. It extends to sharing something. It extends to being honest. "It wouldn't make me unhappy to be honest. So, therefore, I *should* be honest," and so you have people who let it all hang out everywhere.

Example: Sex

People may find that in sexual liberation, for instance, they struggle to be free of all of their "should nots." They struggle to be free of all their ideas that sex is dirty and is wrong, all of which they try very hard to see as illogical, nonsensical, irrational. And they try to tell themselves that it's not true that sex is dirty.

After struggling with that for a long time, they have tried to throw out every reason that might possibly prevent them from having sex if they wanted to—and what very frequently would be overlooked by a person who has strived so hard to overcome fear, is the "I *want* to" part! So now they feel "I *must* have sex whenever there's no reason *not* to." That "I ought to have sex because otherwise, it would be like saying it was dirty. It would be like making up a phony reason for not having it, like I used to do. And so, therefore, if someone wants to have sex or it occurs to me that I might want to have sex, I should, therefore, have it, because if I don't have it I'd be playing into my sex-is-dirty game."

See, we're forgetting that we believed that the only reason not to have sex is because it was dirty. That was the only reason we ever used because, well, once you have that, you don't need other reasons not to have it. That *could* suffice, although there could be lots and lots of other reasons for not having sex. But when the one predominate reason is taken away, we think, "Well, now there's no good reason not to anymore because that was the only reason that ever mattered."

Such questions as disease, such questions as "I want to go to sleep instead," such questions as "there are other things that I want in a relationship"; all of those somehow just can't be seen for the fear that they will be a cop-out, that we'll be playing back into our own fear and using these reasons as an excuse. What is being overlooked again is that, perhaps, just perhaps, nothing ever has to be decided *against*. And that we do not have to make judgments ever *against* anything. That really what could be going on is that we will make judgments *for* things, *for* other things than what we used to decide *against*.

Example: Dessert

For example, a person is eating a meal and is finished and they feel satisfied, and they've enjoyed the meal. Someone says to them, "would you like some dessert?" "I couldn't," becomes the expression. "I couldn't eat another bite." All kinds of negative reasons would have to come up against having the dessert. Rather than just simply, "dessert would be nice, but I *more* want where I'm at now, and that there needn't be anything bad about having dessert." It could be a judgment *for* where we're at, a choice or a preference for what we're doing, rather than for making the change, and not a choice *against* making the change.

One does not have to decide *against* chocolate ice cream in order to have vanilla ice cream. One does not have to decide against *anything.* So you don't even have to decide *against* sickness because really, what's the decision? The decision is really *for* health. And if you look at it, you'll find that all negative decisions and all negative judgments are always secondary. They always come second because somewhere there was a preference for something else first, which we never used to feel free to express the desire for, when we were unhappy people.

The only possible reason you ever could have to decide against anything is because you already decided for something else. You would only decide *against* being uncomfortable because somehow you've made the decision *for* being comfortable. After you've already decided *for* something, you are, in effect, pretending that you're deciding *against* something, as if you needed that additional reason in order to follow through with what you've decided for.

You could fool yourself into thinking that you've been deciding against all these other things and then see yourself as somehow good for yourself; then we have to come up with reasons: if I'm going to decide for something, then somehow I have to give a reason for deciding against the other thing. And if you notice, the reason is never that I decided *for* this, it's got to be some other made-up reason.

So if I decide for vanilla, I have to make up a reason for not wanting chocolate: "I had it last week," as if you had to explain why you didn't choose chocolate to yourself, or to anybody. Once we don't admit that we've decided already, we have to find reasons for deciding against another alternative. We have really made a positive decision, but we're pretending that we're using negative reasons.

Decisions against *Are Decisions* for *Something Else*

I'm not talking about avoidance behavior. I'm talking about negative decisions. Decisions *against* things are really decisions *for* something else. If I touch something hot and I withdraw, I am aware that I could *not* withdraw if I wanted to—I could keep my hand on the flame. But there is a mechanism whereby my body will constantly try to return to its equilibrium and its health, and what looks like avoidance is a desire to return to a desired physical state.

Chocolate or vanilla? Without a rationale, who's to say what you would have gone for? You could transcend all of that and behave without reasons at all, whatsoever. Then there would be another rationale but it would hardly be rational in the sense of intellectual. You just do what you do.

For the unhappy, without a prerequisite belief you wouldn't act a certain way, but with that belief you can. An angry person may say that the anger just happened. But why is it that anybody who I've ever seen angry, was angry for a reason? Maybe the reasons were concocted, and angry was just what they were destined to be at that moment, maybe not.

Choices are always *for.*

The major point that I wanted to make was the way we use judgments. And that we use judgments. And that frequently we fool ourselves into thinking that we're deciding against.

And we can be much freer and much more happy if we realize that there really is no such thing as deciding against. That's an afterthought. That really what's happening is that we're deciding for something. And that's good. It doesn't have to be defended. It doesn't have to be justified that we're deciding for something. And that is good. We've decided for that, yes, but in effect, we haven't only decided against one thing, we've decided against the whole infinite universe of things when we decide for one thing. And who wants to be in that position? I assure you, when I make a decision, I'm not deciding against the whole universe because I'm deciding for one thing.

How often do we then believe we have to live up to our decision against something? For instance, if I say I don't want chocolate because it's too sweet, I can never have chocolate again because it's going to always be too sweet, if it's the same chocolate somehow.

"No, I don't want to lend you $10." Or really, "I want to keep my $10," is the decision. Somehow it's implied I could never lend it to you again. You could never ask me again. I have a reason for not giving it to you *now* that will always be a reason for not giving it to you, which is not true. There may not always be a reason for keeping it.

So there's a choice *for* something always. There was another principle operating rather than, you hate this, you dislike that, and that is: there's something else you like better.

No Reasons Are Necessary

You don't have to desire anything if you're already doing it. You only desire it as a reason to do it. Ultimately, you just do what you do. Very frequently, we view ourselves with a teleological approach. We say that roses need thorns for their existence and protection. It's just not so. It's just that the roses with thorns are the ones that have survived. Roses without thorns didn't survive in an evolutionary sense. No rose made a judgment that it's better to survive.

The Only Thing to Know
Is What We Want

June 4, 1975

THERE is only one thing to believe and know about: what we are wanting. Whether it be what we are wanting to "do" or "be" or "have," etc., the only thing to know is that it *is* what we want.

If we ask if it is "good" or "bad" to want, or whether it will get us what we want, these are just questions for us because we haven't decided that we want it.

When such questions such as "What if my wanting is different from yours?" or "Others may not want what I want!" arise, it is because we have not decided that we want what we think we may want.

We may think that in order to decide that what we want is *truly* what we want, we have to answer "absolutely unchangeably, yes." We can change. It doesn't have to be an unconditional decision. It doesn't have to be "No matter what happens in the next moment, I will want this which I am wanting now!" It doesn't have to be "No matter what anyone says or does, I will still want what I now decide I want."

It may be that our wanting will not change in some ways, but we don't have to try to justify wanting our present desire by "strength" or "determination" or "bravery" or "stubbornness."

It is enough for us to want what we want now. We can know that we will be glad to change our minds if we want to. That will be our wanting too. We can never "give up" our wanting or "lose" our desire. We will just be wanting our wanting anew, afresh, but always ours.

No child feels he is losing his tricycle when he gets a new bicycle. No girl feels she is "losing" her desire for her dolls when she finds her desire for a boyfriend.

When you feel like eating supper, you don't regret that you don't feel like eating breakfast. Your wanting will always be experienced as yours no matter how it changes. You will be just as possessed by your future desires as you are now by your current ones.

The question of whether what you want is good or not is an *apparently* useful one. It would seem that by deciding that what you want is "good," it will free you to love and follow your wanting. But then, will you not always be implying the opposite question? If what you are wanting is not "good," then what? What alternatives do we have? What does "good" mean? It usually means that our wanting will not screw us. But what if it did? What alternatives do we have? To not do what we want? To pick another want? Fine, but is *that* one good? What if it screws us, too? "Can I screw myself?" then, is the question. Does it have to be? Do we like such questions?

I can only be me (as I am). We can only be us (as we are). You can only be you (as you are). What are the other options?

Should we trust our wantings? Why is that a question? What will we do with the answer? If we are wanting our wantings to bring us where we want to be, then, that is what we want.

If we want to "trust" our wantings, then that is what we want. Do I want to believe or want to "trust" because it justifies my wanting and relieves my fears or explains anything, or do I just want to trust because I *want* to?

Do we want to believe that our wanting comes from and leads us to God, because then that sanctifies and justifies what would then otherwise be "bad" or frightening or insecure? Or do we want to believe that our wanting is good, God-given, etc., because now we are wanting to believe that or because we need to believe that?

Even if we believe our wanting comes from and goes to God (God: all that is good; all that we want; the cause of our future; the joy of our now) because we want to, will we question that *that* wanting (for our wanting to be from God) is good or not?

In other words, if we believe we can want what we want because our wanting is good, is that a good thing to believe? Do I want to?

COMMENTARIES

by Aryeh Nielsen on

"What Moves Us"

"Negative" Emotions

This commentary represents the editor's synthesis of ideas Bruce Di Marsico expressed only in fragments.

"NEGATIVE" emotions, such as anger, sadness, fear, and depression, are generally a combination of doing what you want to do, and feeling bad while doing it.

"Negative" emotions are the emotions we choose when we do not get what we want, when we believe that if we do not get what we want, we will have to feel a way we don't like:

* wanting safety, and *anticipating* not getting it, we choose anxiety;
* wanting safety, and *experiencing* not getting it, we choose fear;
* wanting an object or relationship, and *experiencing* not getting the object, or the loss of the relationship, we choose sorrow;
* wanting an object or relationship, and *believing* that others may take it away from us, we choose anger.

The feeling bad that is associated with "negative" emotions is what we feel because we mistakenly believe that if we do not get what we want, we will have to feel a way we don't like.

Without this mistaken belief, we may make choices that, behaviorally, look almost identical to the actions of an unhappy person but are free of unhappiness:

* wanting safety, and anticipating not getting it, we choose *caution* (practical accommodation of estimated risk);
* wanting safety, and experiencing not getting it, we choose *avoiding* (practical reduction of risk);
* wanting an object or relationship, and experiencing not getting or losing the object, or the loss of the relationship, we choose
  * *release* of the bodily orientation toward the object or relationship (often in the form of shaking or crying);
  * *retreat* (as in "going on a retreat"), in the sense of withdrawal

from usual activities, for the sake of contemplating what we most want to do given our new circumstances;

- *reaching out* for connection with others who can assist us in our new life without the support of the lost object or relationship;

✳ wanting an object or relationship, and believing that others may take them away from us, we choose to be *forceful* in our pursuit of what we want.

Examples:

✳ Being anxious to not have a car accident vs. being cautious in our driving (anxiety is: cautious *and* feeling bad):

✳ Being afraid of a wild animal vs. avoiding the threat of a wild animal; for example, by turning around and running like the wind (fear is: avoiding *and* feeling bad);

✳ Being sad that someone we loved has died vs. crying, retreating, and reaching out for support (sad is: releasing, retreating, reaching out, *and* feeling bad);

✳ Being angry that someone is trying to take your money vs. being forceful in acting against someone trying to take your money. (angry is: being forceful *and* feeling bad).

In every case, feeling bad tends to diminish both the effectiveness and aesthetic beauty of the emotions we would choose if we did not believe we had to feel bad about not getting what we want. Often, the primary function of feeling bad is to let ourselves know that "indeed, I want other than what has happened, or other that what is happening." Instead, we can simply stay in touch with our not wanting what is happening, or that we did not want what has occurred.

Perhaps most dramatically, when someone you love has died, a happy response may be to be in touch with your knowing that you did not want them to die, crying and shaking for days as bodily orientation toward life with the loved one is released, retreating into a private circumstance to contemplate the future, and reaching out for support of friends and family—and all this without a single moment of feeling any way you don't want to.

Making How You Feel Wrong

OFTEN, people new to Option make themselves "wrong" for not being "happy" when they believe they "should know better." "Happy" is in quotes, because "happy" is commonly used to mean: "the way I believe I would feel if I got what I wanted" (which is the unhappy imagination of what it would be like to be happy), instead of the Option use of "happiness," which means "feeling the way I want to feel."

The two issues of "There's something wrong with me" and "What I want vs. what I really want" often combine when it comes to "negative" emotions.

Bruce Di Marsico's Example: Depression

Often, a "depressed" person believes they should want to be cheerful and vivacious. What they really want is to just stay in bed. The only "problem" is that they believe that "there's something wrong with them" to want to stay in bed. And if you ask them, "What do you want to do?" they will tell you that they want to be cheerful and vivacious—but that is only because they mistakenly believe they should be cheerful and vivacious. If they knew that they were truly allowed to, they might choose to stay in bed.

Feeling What You Want to Feel, to the Exact Degree that You Want to Feel It

Oftentimes, when people come for help—when they are sad, for example—the issue is that they do not feel they are sad to the exact degree they would like to be: someone they love died yesterday, and they feel "cold," because they do not feel as sad as they would like to, or someone they love died twenty years ago, and they feel caught in an endless drama because they feel just as sad today as they did when they first heard the news.

People can feel tampered with when they want help in feeling what they want to feel to the exact degree they want to feel it, and someone tries to make them feel the way they "should"; for example, they want to feel less sad, and someone tries to help them feel not sad at all, or they feel as if they are emotionally cold and want to feel a *little* more sad, and someone tries to help them have "cathartic" experience of "ultimate" sadness.

Bruce Di Marsico did not make the distinction between positive and negative emotions, but between wanted and unwanted emotions. "Happiness is feeling however you want to feel, and not believing that anything makes that wrong."

PART IV
Wanting, Doing, and Knowing

SECTION I

Staying in Touch with Wanting

Staying in Touch with Wanting

Paragraphs of editorial commentary are entirely in this font.

W HAT is "wanting"? Wanting is just simply, *moving toward*. We often say that we use wanting as a motivation. But wanting is the same thing as motivation.

FROM MONDAY NIGHT STUDY GROUP, 1973

We often use unhappiness to stay in touch with our wanting. What are we trying to achieve with our unhappiness?

- To stay in touch with what we want *more*.
- To stay in touch with preconditions to wanting.
- To stay in touch with the wanting that motivates intermediate steps.

To stay in touch with what we want *more*

We often want two things that are not practically compatible: for example, to be honest in a conversation, and to be agreeable. Then we might get unhappy that "we have to act agreeable towards you" in order to *ensure* we act agreeable (which is what we wanted *more* than to be honest), and to ensure we don't fall "victim" to the "temptation" to be honest.

T HE idea is to stay in touch with what you want *more*. That's what this is all about. To make sure that we keep wanting what we want more, that we won't go ahead and want less.

This dilemma is caused by instituting in the first place the belief that I will be unhappy unless I get what I want. The degree of unhappiness is in proportion to the temptation to give up wanting.

FROM MONDAY NIGHT STUDY GROUP, 1973

143

To stay in touch with preconditions on what is wanted

This form of unhappiness often arises as the dilemma, "I have to decide . . . but I can't decide."

THE simple fact is that we know exactly what we want, but there are other things wanted as part of that wanting. For example, I want to go to that party (and I want to bring a friend, or I want it to start earlier, etc.). In other words, I want something like what you propose but not *exactly* as proposed.

Why not realize that we want whatever we want *and* we want to wait to act? What else can we do? Become numb or paralyzed? We can if we want to.

FROM WRITING, JUNE 1975: WHEN SOMEONE SAYS
THEY DO NOT KNOW WHAT THEY WANT.

To stay in touch with the wanting that motivates intermediate steps

For example, we don't want a job in itself; we want the benefits that money brings. We use unhappiness in the form of "I have to go to work" in order to stay in touch that we *do* want to go to work, as an intermediate step towards the benefits we want that money brings.

RIGHT now it attracts me to continue talking to you, but it also attracts me to go out and have some coffee. That's not a problem, that's just a question. But in order to make that decision I can use fear, or I could use desire. In order to use desire I have to get in touch with, "What do I want these actions for?"

Both actions are attractive. The choosing of one and the not choosing of the other has consequences. Each will, perhaps, lead to totally different ends and conclusions. If I decide to continue to talk to you, that is going to give me certain advantages or disadvantages in terms of other things. That's the package. If I decide not to continue to talk to you and go have some coffee, that's another package that has its prices and its rewards.

FROM MONDAY NIGHT STUDY GROUP, 1973

Notice, in each case, there is a choice: happy wanting or unhappy restriction on our freedom.

- "I want this *more*" becomes "I have to do this;"
- "I want *that* only if *this* is included" becomes "I have to make a choice I don't like;"
- "I want *this* for the sake of *that*" becomes "I have to do this."

What Do I Want Most?

August 19, 1979

WHAT do I want most?
Whatever I want at the moment. What do I want now? I want to do what is best for me!

Some things are wanted when the relevance of them is questioned, others when they are threatened, others when they are offered.

Not everything is wanted at once; but because at a given moment something trivial *is* wanted that does not mean more important things are not *also* wanted. If the more important things are offered or threatened or the desire for them becomes relevant, then awareness of wanting them will arise.

Do you want health, wealth, love? When asked, you would probably say yes. Did you want them while you were reading the above paragraphs? Yes, but only in the sense that you were not refusing them; but no in the sense that you were wanting to understand what you were reading and were not actively aware of wanting much else.

When it is relevant, you will desire new things. If you get uncomfortable sitting the way you are now, you might want to shift to a more comfortable position. Being comfortable while reading might be a relatively minor desire compared to wanting safety if a fire broke out while you were reading this. But since your safety is not being noticeably threatened, you can turn your attention and awareness to otherwise less important considerations.

If you are afraid that you are ignoring important issues you desire achievement in, if you are afraid that you are neglecting serious problems, it is because you do not understand your processes of wanting.

The relative importance of things changes slightly or greatly according to how other desires change. You are aware of all the shifts and adjust your consciousness accordingly. For example: you are out of work and want to have an income and a job (if that is a desirable way to make money) in order to pay for what you want. The basic desire is to have those things you want which would seem to be threatened by being out of work.

You might not seem to yourself to really want to do what it takes to get a job. Then you become afraid that your values are self-defeating. What is happening is you are realizing that you want what a job can get, but not necessarily a job. You may consider living off savings, borrowing from friends, getting support from family, unemployment benefits, cutting down on luxuries, etc.

If you are bothered that you are considering these real alternatives, you are not appreciating your intelligence. All you are noticing is that these options approximate what a job can give you but they are not really (according to your values) sufficiently equivalent in satisfying all the benefits of a job.

On the one hand, you don't especially like most forms of employment that are possibly available to you, but on the other hand, you don't like being without the financial and other rewards that these possible jobs offer.

The relevant importance of things changes as circumstances and other desires change. When you had a job, you could afford to be aware of the aspects of it you didn't like because more important desires were being fulfilled. When you were receiving a salary, etc., you then might notice that the boss was unkind or the other workers were uncooperative with you, but at least you had a salary.

Now, without the job, you are aware that another job may not be very pleasant, but the value of a pleasant job shifts downward when there is the alternative of no job at all. You are worried about your values because you are afraid that there is something wrong with you for not looking forward to an unpleasant job. You are afraid that you will not look forward to working enough to do something about it.

The truth is, again, that you do not want a job, but what a job can get you. There is nothing wrong with that. That is the basic desire that will lead most people to getting a job. Your mistake is believing you *should* want a job. It is not natural to want anything (and certainly not a mixed bag of good and bad, like a job, or marriage, or friends, or school, etc.) unless it is seen as the best means for what else you want, which includes many other desires.

While you are torn, in conflict between two desires (to find a job or not), it is simply because you are not sure which is best for you.

That is all. And what you now believe is best is not to decide yet. Even if you were to believe that it is best to decide which to choose, you would still be subject to your own perceptions of your own best interests and would not be able to feel like getting a job until you believed it was better than what you are doing now (which you may believe is in some ways beneficial toward finding a better job later).

The belief that you *should* be wanting to get a job is not appreciating that you do not yet believe it really is best for you (but may at any moment). Yet you are painfully aware that not to do so is in some ways undesirable and bad for other things you want (mostly money).

This example brings us around full circle to the first question:

What do I want? I want to do what is best for me!

What is best to do now? I do not know!

What is best is not to want to know what you want to want (you already do), but to want to know what is best to get what you want. Stick with that.

You still do not know for sure what is best. But now you know what the real problem is.

If you can't get want you want, you don't have to for happiness. This is certain.

And even if you can get what you want, you don't have to for happiness. This, too, is certain.

When Someone Says They Do Not Know What They Want

June 1975

There is no such thing as "I don't know" my wanting.

When someone says that they do not know what they want, they really mean that they do not know whether what they want will help them get whatever else they may want.

Everyone knows exactly they want now. Only when we question whether it will get us what else we want will we have to re-evaluate our present desire.

If we believe it truly will prevent more of what we also want, we will no longer want it. If we believe it will surely contribute, we will want it without further question. If we don't know, we can want our present wanting to be part of our total wanting. We can also want whatever we want, and want to wait to act. When someone asks us if we want something, sometimes we want something like what was proposed, but not exactly.

For example, you are invited to a party. Beneath the feeling of "I don't know if I want to go to the party" is one of these wantings:

Wanting if conditions are met: I want to go to the party *if* some other condition is met; for example, that I can bring my friend.

Wanting to not let you know my wanting: I don't want to go to the party and I want you to not be insulted. So perhaps I will accept, and then later make up a trivial excuse.

Wanting to wait to decide: I want to have more information before deciding to go to the party tonight. For example, I want to wait to see if I am feeling sociable immediately before the party and only go if I am.

Not Knowing Wants

When someone says that they do not know what they want (want to do, or want to have, or want to feel), they really mean that they do not know whether what they want will help them get whatever other things they may want in the future.

Everyone knows exactly what they want now. Only when we question whether it will get us what else we want will we have to reevaluate our present desire.

That can be simple.

If we believe that what we want now will prevent more of what else we also want, we will no longer want it. If we believe that what we want now will surely contribute to what else we want, we will want it without further question.

If we don't know to our satisfaction whether what we want now will contribute to what else we want, or not (which is usually the only reason the question arises), we can just simply know that we want our present wanting to be part of our total wanting.

What else can we do? Become numb or paralyzed? We can if we want to. Then we will have the question of whether paralysis contributes to our answering the original question of whether our present wanting contributes to our total wanting.

Sometimes the answer can never be seen as certain. Wanting to wait for certainty is usually based on the fear that a negative outcome will cause unhappiness. Why not realize that we want whatever we want and we want to wait to act?

Something we think of doing seems attractive (wanted), but I am not ready to prepare to do it in any active way other than by wanting to do it. For example, I am asked. "Do you want to come to my party tomorrow?" I like the idea of my being there but at the moment I am not going to say yes. If you want an answer now, then perhaps I'll decline the invitation. Or perhaps I'll accept the invitation, knowing interiorly that I am free to change my mind.

The simple fact is that we are knowing exactly what we want, but there are other things wanted as part of that wanting. For example, I want to go to that party and I want to bring a friend, or I want it to start earlier, etc. In other words, I want something like what you propose but not exactly as proposed.

If we make a modified proposal when we experience this "not knowing what we want," we can easily decide. When we become aware of the additional condition of what we are wanting to do, we may even realize that we don't want to propose the modification. We may then just know "yes" or "no" to what we want to question.

We did not become aware of what we fully wanted because we stuck with the question of whether our wanting can screw us. The only answer is: "I want what I want to contribute to whatever else I want." Then, wanting all you want, do whatever you chose to do (or say) freely, happily. What else can you do? Everything else is based on the belief that what you want may screw you, rather than on the equal desire that your wanting will contribute to your other wanting.

A dilemma only arises when someone knows exactly what they want but fears their wanting not contributing to their other wanting, rather than desiring their wanting to contribute to their other wanting.

Say yes or no gladly. You can also change your mind if you want to. There is no such thing as "I don't know" my wanting.

Fear of Not Knowing Wanting
March 12, 1975

Some are afraid they will not or cannot be sure of what they want. They fear that what they think they might want might not be what they want. Of course, they're right. They "might" want anything. They become acutely aware of the arbitrariness of choice and free will. They are aware they can "choose" anything to do, or say, and even say they want it. But do they *really want it* is their question.

How can I know what I really want?

How can I know that what others suggest I want is really *my* wanting?

This can all be summed up as:

"I need to know what I want because if I don't know for sure that it is my real wanting, then I may do what I don't want, or not do what I do want, and if that happens, I will have to be unhappy."

This is summed up as:

"I must (ought, should) do what I want. If I don't, then that will be the cause of my unhappiness."

This, of course, is the belief that happiness depends on something.

People usually have well accepted that they don't have to be unhappy if they don't get what they want from others, from fate, from the world, but they believe that it is intolerable if *they* are the cause of not getting what they want.

They see that the only way that they could be responsible for not getting what they want is by not knowing what they want.

This is still based on a version of "I will or should be unhappy if I don't get or do what I want."

It is interpreted as: "My happiness depends, at least, on my doing what I want, and that depends on my knowing for sure that what it seems I want, *is* what I want."

The question is: Do you want to believe that your happiness depends on anything? Do you want to believe that not doing what you want is the cause of your unhappiness or would you rather believe that your "fear" (any fear) is the cause of unhappiness and incidentally also the cause of feeling you don't know what you want?

Do you want to believe that the cause of unhappiness in this universe, in your world, in your life, is not doing what you want (if that were possible for someone not fearing the feeling) or fearing that you won't do what you want?

Do you have any reason to believe that you wouldn't do what you wanted better and better, more and more, if you didn't fear that you wouldn't naturally do what you want?

Do you believe that the only reason you or anyone would not know or do what they wanted would only have to be because of fear?

If it isn't fear of not doing what you want that is the cause of that feeling, what is? Is this true: Not doing what we want is irrelevant to being happy? The only reason I would be not doing what I want is that I am already unhappy—probably because I fear not doing what I want.

I might want to know what I want.

I might want to act on what I want.

I might want to begin working toward what I want.

I might want to be happier.

But I don't have to.

I don't have to be happy or happier. (Incidentally, they demand that no one be unhappy with them or their unhappiness. They will hate (fear) anyone they believe is telling them that they should be happy—and, by extension that they should want, do, etc., anything they themselves want of themselves but are afraid they won't do.)

I don't have to know what I want to be happy.

I don't have to want to be happy to be happy.

I just will be happy. I will just want to be. I will want to be happy, and *be* happy as long as I am not afraid that I won't be, or believe I should be happy.

Basically, people are afraid of being unhappy or staying unhappy, and believe they should be happy instead of trusting that they will naturally find a way and be happy.

SECTION II

Where Wanting Comes From

Your Wanting Is a Favor to God

December 12, 1992

Wanting and becoming—I'll just describe it frankly and simply. I'll speak plainly to you.

When you know what I know, I could say to you, "what do you want," and your only answer would be, "anything, nothing. I don't care. I'll want anything. I'll want nothing." And that's the truth because you already have everything you want. And you'll know you have everything—I mean everything. I don't mean everything but tomorrow's meal. I don't mean everything "but" anything. I mean, you have every single thing you want.

Now, when you have everything you want, you can act like that. Because wanting from then on is a favor you're doing for God. It's like, "Okay, I'll still be around. I'll still choose to live. And I'll choose to want things. But believe me, I don't take it seriously. I'll want this, or I'll want that, or I'll want the next thing. But that's not the same wanting [as needful want]. That's wanting from someone who wants nothing—or anything. So if it takes wanting to live, I'll want. I'll kind of like do God the favor of wanting things if that's what it takes."

When you have everything, and you know you have everything you want, there's a whole other way of being.

This is your life—now. Since you have now, do what you choose. Nothing can happen to you; you're free, totally free. You can count on it. No unhappiness can befall you; it'll never happen. You're invulnerable. Nothing can make you unhappy. There's not a single arrow of unhappiness that can pierce you, because you're ghosts to the arrows of unhappiness; they just don't exist, you're invulnerable to them.

Not Believing Yourself

January 19, 1992

FEAR is—you don't believe yourself. That's what all unhappiness is—you don't believe yourself. What have we shown that people would be afraid of if they weren't unhappy? It would mean that they don't love what they love, or that they don't want what they want, because if I'm not unhappy not having it, how do I know I want it? If I'm not unhappy about having lost it, how do I know I loved it?

You don't believe yourself.

There are people who, if they came face-to-face with God, and knew for a fact that it was God, would say, "It can't be. I can't believe myself."

Denying Self-Creation

What's the advantage, the benefit, the payoff for people denying that they create themselves? It's only so that they can blame others for what they consider bad about themselves—so the only problem is that they've *already* considered something bad about themselves, that there is something wrong with them, something evil, and now they can blame others.

But you wouldn't be interested in claiming that you don't create yourself if everything you did was good and wonderful.

Everyone who has been a parent knows that people don't believe the way you want them to believe, and people don't feel the way you want them to feel—they know it from their own child. If you could make your child feel the way you want them to feel, would they ever feel any way you didn't like? Yet we turn to a peer and say "they've made me feel this way" or "I've made them feel that way," and take the blame or the credit for how other people feel.

Can someone be grounded in reality if they believe that people make people feel things?

Being Aware of Wanting

We are only aware of our wanting when it changes.

The only thing one could or might care to be aware of regarding their wanting is when it changes. There is no desire to be aware of wanting what we know we want, or desire to be aware of wanting what we're having or doing.

The only purpose for awareness would be to let ourselves know when our wanting changes.

For example, without awareness, I'm still wanting to breathe, sit, etc. and there is no purpose for me to be aware right now of wanting to be here and doing those things.

The only awareness I want is to know when I want to leave here, not whether I want to stay. The question "Am I wanting or still wanting what I have been doing?" always has an answer: yes, unless we know the answer is absolutely no. The tacit answer is "I am not aware of a different and new wanting."

SECTION III

Forming and Changing Desires

Attraction

August 23, 1975

THERE is no such thing, strictly speaking, as "being attractive" or "being attracted," insofar as that implies a power that originates within the Attractor to be the sole cause of the attraction.

The power of the Attractor, if any, might be said to be the ability to come into the perceptions of the Perceiver. For example, if the Attractor is a person, he or she might walk past someone, and say "Excuse me, do you know what time it is?"; in other words, use whatever ability he or she possesses to get attention (we might even say "attract" attention). This ability is not even an absolute choice of the Attractor. It will not attract by screaming at a deaf person, or walking past a preoccupied person, etc. The power of the Attractor to attract is simply the ability to meet the prerequisites of being perceived. Generally speaking, we can say that this is done merely by being, and then entering the perceptions of the Perceiver, if it is possible.

Now that the Attractor has succeeded in being perceived, the next requirement for being "attractive" has to be met. The Attractor must be experienced as desirable. Desire-ability is not a quality per se of the Attractor. Nor is it an instantaneous choice of the Attracted. It is the response of the potentially Attracted as a result of their current state.

A person's state or behavioral set or attitude at the moment has many levels. Depending on which level is going to respond to the Attractor, the intensity/ignorability factor comes into play. Some attitudes are deep and sensitive and are ever-present, lying in wait below the apparent surface attitudes, as other more minor transient states are seemingly acted out.

For example, a person at a cocktail party may seem to want another drink (a transient attitude) but will forgo it for a while to be polite (deeper, less transient) and may forgo both the drink and the politeness for an important business phone call (deeper yet, more pervasive attitude) and again may forgo all three if his hair caught on fire (deepest yet of all desires—a most pervasive ever-present attitude desiring life, even though it was not apparent until stimulated).

It follows that, in various situations it depends on which level of desire is to be engaged as to whether there will be an attraction response, so that for something to be more attractive than what is going on at the moment, the Attractor must be a stimulus of a deeper desire or need.

Desire deflection—or, properly speaking, perception deflection—can take place so that what is being truly desired can be ignored (intensely, even) even though there is a strong attraction response; for example a "forbidden" desire. If, within the attitudes of a person, there exist conflicting desires or states, the person will feel "bothered," annoyed or angry with the "forbidden" stimulus' desirability. This can even feel like terror or extreme restlessness and the desire to get away from the offending stimulus. The general term is "feeling uncomfortable." This is classically illustrated by the extremely "uptight" person's "distaste" for those they find highly sexually attractive, which is converted into talk of "evil temptresses."

At this point, it would be good to review just what is meant by attraction for the Attracted:

Attraction is the natural response of feeling glad, enjoying and moving toward (physically) and beginning to grasp and possess (physically, intellectually or both; and emotionally) in a useful and meaningful way for the Attractor.

The usefulness (and hence its meaning) lies in the future relationship with it. Many things are attractive because they can be used to acquire more attractive things. The most useful, and therefore the most attractive, would be that which could be used for everything possible that would be wanted now or ever. If such a thing existed, it would be called God.

The most useful is that which would make Perfect Happiness possible. In other words, the most attractive thing would be one's self becoming or being Perfectly Happy.

If there is something that is so attractive, it would have to be able to change the "Attracted" into everything they wanted. It would have to appeal to the deepest attitude and desire to be happy.

This is happiness, of course, meaning being fully oneself. Being fully one's self meaning, being glad to know God.

What Is Interesting?

May 4, 1979

THE concept of "attention span" as a biological-psychological function is perhaps a misnomer of another much more understandable phenomenon; values-interest.

The so-called short attention span of a child in general is more likely a product of the simple lack of desire in the child to spend more time investigating (playing with, observing, listening to, etc.) anything of which the perceived value is limited.

When a child is young, it is also non-persuaded (or not informed, if you will) of the values (functions, uses, etc.) of certain objects and phenomena. It will investigate an object cursorily or intensely according to the curiosity satisfaction the presented event or object gives (hereinafter I will refer to this object, person, lesson, phenomenon, etc. as the present or presentation).

Curiosity satisfaction is the factor intrinsic in the term "desire to investigate or learn." An object attracts because it promises to reveal more than is statically apparent.

Curiosity is the desire to see if the promise will be fulfilled, and therefore we can refer to curiosity as being fulfilled or satisfied. What is to be satisfied in curiosity is the desire for change, whether it be change in appearance, direction, motion, application of uses or changes in the understanding of the nature of the presentation or present.

A child may only be interested in something if it offers the promise of change.

Children love (i.e., are intensely investigative, curious, absorbed by, attentive to) and have long "attention spans" to fast-changing presentations, such as magic, cartoons, frenetic slapstick, or just about anything that changes quickly and grossly and predictably so. If a child no longer can predict quick gross changes, it loses "interest." In other words, it decides that the investigation is over, the present has exhausted its repertoire, the show is over, the case is closed and now it is time to look for new changes. This is, of course, obvious to parents and teachers, if not to psychologists and biologists who don't regard their own childhoods (and current modes of interest) as valid for human understanding.

Children are bored by (i.e., have short attention spans for) anything that does not meet the value-expectation that it can do more or be more than it seems, both quickly and grossly, e.g., a still photograph, an incomprehensible lesson that does not promise to become comprehensible or useful.

In fact, it can be observed here that parents and others reward or punish children by intuitively grasping this observation.

To reward a child, one must offer a reward that meets the above requirements. A gift must be interesting to the child. A punishment must be boring and predictably so, such as staying in a room, a chair, after school, etc. All forms of "staying" are punishment. Staying a long time while visiting adults is torturous to most children. Corporal punishment is psychological punishment precisely because it is boring, i.e., it is perceived as useless, dead-end, uninteresting pain imposed for its nonsense value.

Physical accidental pain in and of itself would not necessarily be frightening to children, and usually is not. But threatened intended pain (whether a doctor's "shot" or a mother's whack) is feared. The anger or love behind the pain is of no concern to the child, although when anger seems to be feared, it is because it often threatens punishment. When it does not, it is ignored as an empty threat. Mere tones of voice mean nothing except in context. Mere pain means nothing except in context. The context is the promise of boredom or change.

Punishments of children are usually devised to deprive the child of an interesting time. In this regard, corporal punishment need not be viewed as having an essentially different quality in its torture. In fact, if any dread is held by adults in the physical abuse of children, it is in the dread of physical destruction that leaves the child incapacitated or victimized in such a way as to predict long-term or unending deprivation of the ability to escape boredom. Defective infants are pitied in regard to this deeply feared factor: it is feared that they will grow up to be bored and depressed adults, incapable of having interesting and satisfying lives.

Children experiment. Attention span is simply the length of the experiment. An experiment with limited results gets short shrift by honest children. Only adults force themselves into continuously repeating unrewarding experiments. But even then only with the hope that the promise of success will eventually show itself and vindicate the patience of repeated failure (called "hope").

The difference between children and adults in the question of attention span is the difference between the child's demand of quick and gross change (sometimes referred to as the "instant-gratification need") and the adult's patient experiment for slow and subtle results. In astronomy or Hollywood, it is considered a "great" discovery to find one new star in a cast of millions (or billions). No child would ever care about these discoveries. The question of values grows sophisticated, and as a child grows, it "learns" that things of great value are not necessarily things of great obviousness. As the child learns that the potential for gross results is often "hidden" deeper than we suspect, long trials and subtle clues and changes are endured with patience. The child is "maturing" into an adult. The underlying desire is identical. There is the desire in both the child and the adult explorer for dramatic change (often mistaken for "progress") in the secrets of the environs and presents.

The shortness of a child's attention span is no shorter than any adult's who is invited to be involved with something it perceives as useless or exhausted of further value.

Brilliant scientists and successful businessmen fall asleep at concerts of "subtly" changing sounds and can dread retirement or even vacations from their engrossing work.

There are, of course, gradations on a continuum from the happy, peaceful, contemplative mystic to the frantic adventurer-explorer-producer in many endeavors (such as sports, carpentry, science, business, housework). These degrees of difference may only be superficial expressions of the same basic quest. The contemplative explores by being "open" for change to happen and the active explores by "opening" the events. Both work or wait for secrets that are around the corner or under the surface of reality. One believes the good secrets "come to those who wait" and others believe that "time and tide wait for no man."

Peace is the satisfaction of a curiosity fulfilled and joy is the intense involvement with a wondrous unfolding.

Fear of Our Changing Desires

FEAR of persuading yourself out of what you want or like to think, believe, do not do, etc.

Fear of changing and fear of not changing your mind.

Fear of not being *able* to change or keep your mind when you believe it is best.

If we see that a fear is unnecessary we will give it up automatically. Seeing it is knowing it is no longer a fear. You have the fear that you desire unhappiness more than happiness. That is proof that you desire happiness more.

Happy and Wanting Change

April 29, 1976

W E are glad and happy, and find that we want things or people different. We are grateful for what we have and have had, and we want a change.

Feeling bad about wanting or not wanting is believing we are ungrateful (unglad for what we were glad for), unhappy for what we were happy with.

We believe we may be unhappy (ungrateful, forgetful of the truth, throwing away happiness by ignoring or no longer wanting, etc.) if we want someone to change or if we want differently than someone we love has wanted (or has seemed to want) up till now.

We fear that wanting or not wanting is ungrateful and therefore untrue and therefore unwanted and therefore unhappy.

If we believe that wanting may mean differently or other than we want it to mean (implying or reflecting an undesirable but "honest" truth), then we will feel bad about that desire.

If we believe that desire for change implies we don't love what we still love, etc., we will believe we are unhappy now.

In other words, if we think wanting change (or not) contradicts truth, we will feel bad.

Some truths that seem to be contradicted but really aren't: I used to love something and was happy with it; now I don't value it any longer, and I want something else. I was glad for it and still am glad I had it. I am glad to change now.

I used to think I was happy and loved the way it was. I now know I was afraid and unhappy and felt relief and consolation. It was not what I wanted. I now want what I want. I am glad to know now. I am not glad for my fear. Insofar as it was a mixed experience, my reaction is mixed. I am glad for what I am glad for. I am not for what I am not.

My values and desires change. The truth is still true. What I may have once disliked, I may now be glad to have had happened and vice versa. What I wanted from my fear, I am glad to leave behind. What I never wanted, I am glad to forget. What I wanted and didn't get doesn't matter now, I am glad for what I am glad for.

My new desires could seem to contradict my past "happiness" (they may) but they only contradict what I want them to, no more. They do not contradict me now.

Persisting

April 12, 1981

A conversation between H, an advocate of happiness, and U, an advocate of unhappiness.

H: I am trying to achieve a goal—find a way to get what I want. I have not gotten it yet. It has been some time.

U: You may never get it.

H: But I may. Perhaps I can.

U: You don't know.

H: Maybe I do know but have forgotten or overlooked the implications of what I know.

U: You don't know if you know, or can know, so you don't know.

H: But "I may. Perhaps I can." And this means nothing except to answer the proposal that I may not.

U: You may never get what you want.

H: You may never stop saying that I may never get it. I am trying to get it.

U: It has been some time. You're wasting your time trying.

H: I am wasting my time talking to you, explaining nothing. Nothing is happening. It is just that I don't have what I want. So what? I would love to try to get it and not despair.

U: Do you need my encouragement?

H: Your what?

U: My permission?

H: Your what?

U: My help?

H: You are trying to help me to stop wasting my efforts.

U: How do you know you'll find a way?

H: Do I want to? Why do you ask me?

U: Why do I ask you? Because you know you can't find a way.

H: I haven't found it *yet*.

U: And if you never do?

H: When is never?

U: After a long time of trying.

H: It is always a moment since the last failure. Trying again or hoping again is not "after trying a long time" but only after the last try. So what? When shall I give up if I can't know that I'll never get what I want? I don't know.

U: So when will you give up?

H: Whenever I want to. I want to try but I don't care about when I don't want to try, whenever that is.

U: When will it be over, your desire?

H: I can come and go as I wish in pursuing my goal.

U: You may never get it. You risk for nothing. You may never get what you want and you should be prepared for that, and if you are not you should give up trying.

H: I am prepared not to have it now, and I do not have it now. There is no being prepared to not have it ever. There is only giving up whenever I want, or finally achieving.

U: You will give up when you see that you can never have it!

H: Of course I will, if indeed that is what I see.

U: You contradict yourself.

H: There is not now being prepared to never have it. If there *is* me believing that I cannot have it, then I will give up trying to get it.

U: When will that be? How much does it take?

H: Whenever I see that I cannot have it, if I see that I cannot have it. It takes no time. It takes believing.

U: Then you believe you can get it.

H: No, I don't believe I can't.

U: That means you believe you can or at least may.

H: I mean I want to. You want to discuss if it may happen by saying it may not and I must prove it may. I do not know what "may" or "may not" means. I do *not* know that I *can't* have it. There are some things we all do because we do not know we can't. All hope begins with "I may be able to get what I want.

U: But you may never get what you hope for, I know. Do you know better?

H: You only say "may" in order to be allowed to want. I don't *know* that I can't have what I want, or I would give up. I don't know to be prepared to not get what I want. I don't "know better" than that.

U: Do you even know if what you want does or could exist?

H: It would be wonderful to have.

U: You want something wonderful. Is that it?

H: Yes. That's it. That's what it was, just something wonderful.

U: Are you sure it is wonderful?

H: No matter. This is it. Or better. I always want that.

Beliefs Are Known as the Truth
September 21, 1975

WHEN we have a belief, we believe it is knowledge: true, undoubted, certain, and based on fact.

When we realize it is a belief, we automatically mean "merely" a belief or no more than a belief. It means uncertain, doubtful and possibly not true.

Unless we have proof or knowledge, we do not have to believe "it was merely a belief" if we don't want to.

SECTION IV

Trying and Doing

Trying

August 1975

TRYING is not believing that if I can do something, and I want to do something, I will do it (naturally, with no greater motivation needed).

Trying is believing that that which I can *only* do by wanting, I *can't* do by only wanting. I must exert more effort than I want to. The exertion of effort cancels and nullifies the natural ease of the movement that wanting would produce. The harder I try, the more impossible the movement.

Trying is the same as fearing that you might not do what *only* your wanting can do.

This applies to all bodily and emotional activities; for example, only your wanting to go to sleep can lead you to sleep. *Trying* to go to sleep tends to move you away from sleep, and the harder (with more effort) you try, the farther from sleep you will tend to be. Similarly for *trying* to relax, or *trying* to digest.

Trying is doubting, or not being sure of, the outcome of your efforts. It is not always unhappiness. E.g., "I am trying to carve this stone into a sculpture of an apple" can mean that insofar as I am able, I will, but the stone may crack and I may not have the knowledge or training necessary to achieve what I hope for.

Doing without trying is to decide to do it insofar as one is capable, or insofar as one's own good intentions and ability contribute to the outcome.

If I have decided that I truly want something or want to do something, then I can know that I will do it, insofar as the power is naturally within me and as long as I am wanting to.

For example: I want to read this book. My doing is: I now sit down and begin to read.

If my mind wanders and/or I keep forgetting what I am reading, the following is happening:

1. I am no longer wanting to read (I am not interested in the material enough), or
2. I am afraid that I won't be able to maintain interest or be able to concentrate or remember what I read, or
3. I believe that I should read and believe I will be unhappy, disappointed or some other way I don't want to feel, if I don't.

These apparently different phenomenal causes really all amount to the same thing, and call for the same solution.

Stop *trying* to read, and stop *trying* not to forget, and stop *trying* to prevent your mind from wandering!

Stop believing that what is natural needs help by your doubts and fears!

The solution in each case:

1. Decide anew whether you really would like to read (even though up till now you have lost interest since your first decision). Realize you might want to read and think, read and think, read, then think, and so on. You might not want to just only read. Realize that you might be interested in the material, or might not be especially interested, or not as interested as you had thought you were, but you still might want to read it, or might not want to read it now no matter how interested you are. You may want to come back another time. You can love changing your mind.

   Don't base these decisions on any self-doubts that you couldn't read if you wanted to, or on believing you should or should not read. If you do, your real problem is #2 or #3.

2. The fear of your mind sabotaging your desires is a perfect example of trying instead of knowing. If you really *are* wanting to read, and know how to read, nothing in you can prevent you unless you fear it will. You will read naturally because it is *natural*.

   You just haven't decided that you really want to read. The reason you haven't decided is because you believe that in this case, your decision isn't enough. You may even feel that you don't really "feel" like reading and are constantly "tempted" to give up.

   The reason you are not believing that your decision would be enough is probably "past" experience. You approach this book fearing that you might have the same "trouble" this time as you had in the past. Your problem in the past was that either you really *didn't* want to read, or that you tried too hard.

The solution is "Don't try. Want to, and just let it happen." If your mind wanders, don't worry; just re-decide whether you want to read more this time. You can't read by *trying* to read, but only by *wanting* to.

Know that if you really want to, then you will. You will have no "trouble."

"Really" want to means that you have decided that it *is* what you want, and that trying or forcing yourself is unnecessary (you naturally feel like it).

"Really" wanting to do something is believing that your wanting is natural and that you will naturally do it as long as you want to.

Not feeling like doing something you want to do is the result of believing that you may not do naturally what is only natural to do if you want to.

It is not fully deciding to do something because you believe your decision won't help or make you do what you want. But that is based on the belief that something (even, your decision) has to force you to do what you want. You do not realize that the decision that you really want to do something "frees" you enough to allow it to happen. It "frees" you to feel like it.

"Feeling like it" frequently is not a real feeling. In other words, it does not have a physical sensation. It is more like hope and determination.

"I feel like it" means that on some level I am already beginning to move toward what I am imagining.

One could "feel like it" about things or actions we want or don't want based on whether we are believing it is going to happen.

I will find myself "feeling like" something I don't even want if I believe that it is going to happen anyway.

Feeling unhappy is like this. If I believe it is going to happen anyway, whether I want it or not, I will "feel" unhappy.

Sex is like this. If I believe that I am going to be turned on to someone, whether I want sex with them or not, I will feel turned on.

The same is also true about "not feeling like it," if I believe I am not going to be especially happy or not turned on, etc.

"Not feeling like it" about something I want, will happen if I believe that I will not make it happen even though I want it.

Believing I will not make any consenting real moves, or decisive moves, toward what I want will produce "not feeling like it" feelings, which are like despair and repulsion, lethargy and the feeling that someone or something will have to make me do it.

Happiness and sex are like this.

If I believe that I will not make any moves naturally toward sex or happiness (no matter how much I want them), I will not feel like it. I will feel "blah" about them, and have a passive attitude (not to be confused with bodily repose). Affection and love are the same. If I feel or believe that I won't feel what I want to feel, even though I want to, then I won't feel it. The more I think I *should* feel it, the more I won't.

3. I "should" be reading is just another attempt to use "fear of repercussions" to motivate me to do what I want. Stop trying to motivate yourself.

Believing we won't do what we could *only* do by just simply wanting to and allowing the feelings to arise in us is the same as trying. Trying is not doing. Trying is not trusting nature. Trying is not allowing.

In fact, a person who is always trying will eventually believe that they must not be allowing themselves for some reason. They will even deduce that they must have something against what they're wanting:

Maybe I have some deep fear.

Maybe I believe it is evil, bad, wrong.

Maybe I believe that if I get what I want I will screw myself.

Maybe my wanting is not to be trusted.

Maybe something is really wrong in me. A basic contradiction working against me.

They are hinting at the real problem.

True, they are not trusting their wanting.

But not in the way they think.

It is not that they really believe their wanting will mislead them or is to be mistrusted.

It is that they do not trust that by simply wanting they will have the effects they want.

All their doubts and fears that there is something deep within them (impotence, fear, confusion, belief in evil which they don't really believe in) are deductions that are inevitable for someone who is sensing that there is no good reason why they should not be feeling what they want or are feeling what they don't want. They do not trust that by not wanting to feel certain ways they naturally won't (unhappiness, sleepless, turned on, turned off, etc.).

They do not trust that by wanting to feel certain ways, they naturally will.

Parenthetically, it is interesting to note that the terms "turned on" and "turned off" refer in the mechanical and technological world to the necessary primary functions to begin or end all other subsequent or previous activities. The switch that makes the difference.

No machine will begin to do its thing unless it is turned on.

No machine going in the wrong direction can continue to if it is turned off.

Trying to do what you *don't* need to try to do is the only cause of craziness.

It is the only cause of inappropriate and unwanted feelings.

Unwanted feelings are the only cause of unhappiness and confusion and self-defeat.

Unhappiness is the only cause of deducing that we believe that which we *don't* really believe, or like believing. This is the cause of feeling that there is something wrong with us.

Trying to be good is the cause of evil.

Happiness Is the Most Effective
Ground for Doing

June 25, 1975

I HAVE the awareness that I don't have everything I want, and that there are things that I have that I don't want. I have been happy, and felt good, and done what I wanted and that obviously doesn't work, because it hasn't worked yet for those things.

So: I've tried happiness, so now I'll try unhappiness, the only other thing to try. Ouch! Still . . . it might work . . . ouch!

Happiness didn't do me any good (get me what I want). Ouch!!!

I don't like feeling this way (unhappy). But if it gets me what I want then I'll be able to relax and be happy as a (useless) luxury. At least happiness enables me to enjoy what I have even though it doesn't work in getting me what I want.

The only problem with all of this is that every time I become aware that I want more, which is frequent, I'm unhappy. So, I'm unhappy a lot, because happiness doesn't work.

Maybe the truth is that neither happiness nor unhappiness does the work of getting me what I want. *I* do that work, however I do it.

But with happiness I feel better, and so when I find there's more work for me to do to get what I want I blame my happiness for not having worked, when actually if I'm going to get what I want *I* will have to do it, happy or not.

Maybe, also, I would like to feel good while I'm working for what I want rather than believing that the feeling good or bad, in itself, serves to work for what I want.

Feeling good frees me to not be concerned about how I feel, since how I feel is my first concern, my first want.

When I am happy (feeling good, feeling myself) I am free to give my whole attention, my whole mind, my whole heart, my whole self to doing and getting what I want. I then am free and am freed up

182

to devote myself to anything I want. In that way happiness is a very real cause of my doing and getting what I want.

Happiness frees my powers, happiness frees my ability, happiness frees me to be what I want to be, to do what I want to do, to get what I want to have.

When I decide that being happy didn't work, or hasn't worked yet, that must come from a desire to *do something* about the fact that I don't yet have everything I want, or the fact that there is more for me to devote myself to.

Only someone who does not have to attend to themselves first (in particular, does not have to attend to their feeling bad) can freely work, do, and be at their fullest abilities.

What are we truly capable of? Only by being happy will we find out, and see our capabilities manifested.

Summary: Believe in the power and freedom of happiness, no matter what more you are wanting done.

Whatever we want is okay to want. We'll do what we want most.

We want nothing more than we want happiness.

What I Can Do

August 12, 1974

Both happiness and unhappiness are descriptions of what one feels, which both mean (predict) nothing when these terms are used to imply that our feelings are caused by something other than what *we* are doing, that some external thing or internal thing has something to do with our happiness.

"Happiness" in this case means "that which I might feel in the future." I am talking about what I might feel in the future because I am saying that that feeling might be (or will be) something that I will call happy or unhappy.

To describe our feelings as "happy or unhappy" is a prediction that this present behavior or feeling or event will determine our future behavior.

True (perfect) happiness: I am doing what I am doing. I am not doing what I am not doing.

I may or may not speak of all that I am doing. I am still doing it. I may not recognize what I am doing. I still am doing it. I may not be aware of all I do. I still do it all. I may not think or acknowledge that all I am aware of is what I do.

All that I see and hear and experience is what I do, whether I deny it or not, whether I am aware of it or not.

I can do everything I *can* do, if I don't believe that I can't.

When You Don't Know What to Do

April 29, 1979

W HEN you don't know what to do . . .

Don't do "something," as if "something" had to be done and any "something" is better than nothing. Worsening a situation is not better than doing nothing.

Don't do "something" about it. First and foremost, do nothing. Then do anything you want, even if you don't know what it is "for."

Your behavior is not "for" anything but yourself, no matter who says otherwise.

When you don't know what to do (when you are bored, confused, facing an "urgent" problem, an emergency, a great opportunity or great danger) you are already free of any "problem." When and while you don't know, you don't know. It is the real truth of the moment. No fear or complaint ever changes that truth. There is obviously nothing you have to do yet, if ever. Do nothing or do anything. You are free of the obligation to do something.

Forget it until you know what you want.

Sometimes there is something you feel you should attend to, a chore, business, etc., but you don't "feel" like it; that is, you don't believe you'll do it, or you believe you won't. Just because you do not know that you'll do it, that doesn't mean you know that you won't do anything. That is your fear.

When you don't know that you will do what you would like to do, know that you *will*. Maybe you are presuming you won't because you have put off doing anything in the past (or put off things like it) or you believe you have a "problem" with such tasks, or feel like you need to take a break from chores but are afraid you will take too many breaks for too long and will never get to what you need to do in time.

This is a case of believing you know *what* to do but don't want to do it anyway.

When you know what you want to do, but do not know when you will do it, *don't do it now.*

Don't do it now as if it were "now or never," which you do not really believe, but only fear. You don't have to forget about it. Look forward to doing it later whenever you *want* to. Just remember it is not that you don't want to ever do it, but that you don't want to now. If you don't know when, then you honestly don't know when. You are free to look forward to it.

Doing as a Sign of Self

I F it is true that you do not or need not do anything in order to gain perfect happiness,

and all things you can do are good (in the sense that none can make you unhappy)

and none are better (in the sense that none or any can make you more happy)

but you have reasons for doing things

and you believe such reasons relate to happiness or unhappiness,

then any of the so-called reasons in those cases are really false—they are just beliefs.

Actually, it may be that all doing is in order to perfect our awareness that we are happy and that we will become more and more happy.

Perhaps all behavior (doing) is a sign to ourselves of where we are at. Some doing shows me that I am as I am.

Since there are no real (in the sense of "happiness-preserving or -maintaining") reasons for doing, perhaps doing is a sign of me to me.

SECTION V

Knowing

Knowing

To believe that there is something more you need to know before you can enjoy what you already know (and do not doubt, in itself) is not doubting what you know. It is ignoring it. It is simply not enjoying it (yet).

You will act as if you don't know it, of course. It is no mystery if you keep forgetting it! This can only happen if you believe there is something more important for you to know.

The process of ignoring may be the best thing to do if what else you want to know is more important to you than what you already know. Is it?

Believing and Knowing
January 7, 1974

THE fear of projecting and being deluded:

There are some things we *know* deep in our hearts but do not yet *believe*.

For example—we really know that we do not have to be unhappy but we don't always believe it.

We want evidence that we don't have to be unhappy, and believe we have evidence that we do have to be unhappy. We have no evidence of anything. We interpret. We either know or we don't. We either believe according to what we know or don't know, or we don't believe.

The fact that I am sick is no evidence that I have to be unhappy or afraid.

The fact that it seems that I have been scared and sad is no evidence that I have to be unhappy or afraid. We know that true unhappiness cannot exist; it is only a pretense, a fear which is a belief that unhappiness may come somehow in the future.

All so-called unhappy feelings that we experience are an act, an acting out our belief that we don't know, our belief that things might happen or work out or not work out in a way that will cause us to be unhappy in the future.

Knowing More

January 24, 1977

T HERE is no more I need to know and feel to enjoy and be happy with what I already find enjoyable and attractive.

Perhaps to know or feel more would be to make it more enjoyable or more attractive but I don't need to find it more attractive than I do. In fact, perhaps to know more about it would be to find out that what I believed I "knew" was not true and then it would be less enjoyable or attractive in the future. But I don't need to know if what I believe is true. I already believe it is. I don't need to know more in case I was wrong. If I start to believe I was wrong, then I do. Suspecting that I need to know more in case I'm wrong is already suspecting I'm wrong, is already finding it less enjoyable, is already believing that what I believed about it, I don't believe.

There is no more I need to know about things I do not find enjoyable and attractive. I do not need to find them more enjoyable and attractive. If I suspect that I could, I already am finding them more attractive. I don't need to know more in order to enjoy it as much as I already do.

I may need to know more if I am going to enjoy more or less what I already enjoy or do not enjoy, but I do not need to know more *now* in order to know now how much I value a given thing *now*. Believing I need to know more now in order to feel good now is a mistake. I am then ignoring what I presently really do believe, feel, and enjoy because I believe that since I *may* change my opinion, I ought to try to change it now. I wind up preoccupied and worried, not appreciating my ability to be happy now.

I know how to be happy now. I don't need to know more about what I like or don't like in order to be happy now. While it is true that I may be happier with something the more I know about it in the future, if I believe I need to do that now in order to be happy now, then that is a mistake. I am ignoring that I already am happy to some degree with this thing. I might be very pleased and already happy about what I already know about it, if I realize that I don't need to know more in order to admit what I already feel. I don't need to know more in order to realize what I already believe. To know more may mean to feel more or believe more, or it may not. To know more about someone or something may be only another aspect or version of what I already know and so it won't add or subtract to what I feel. But if I'm ignoring what I feel already, no matter how much more I learn or see about the thing or person, it won't matter. I'll still be alienated from my feelings.

For example, I may believe that you are a wonderful person, who could be very good for me to be friends with. If I think I need to "know for sure" and all I ever find out is more of what I already believe about you, then nothing has substantially changed. But one thing will change. Since I'm not appreciating and realizing what I already sense about you because I am preoccupied with needing to know more, I will be holding back, appearing reluctant, etc. and you will notice. I may notice what I'm doing. You may point it out. You may express the hope that I will view you as a wonderful person and expect me to act accordingly. I will protest that I think you are great and I don't know why I seem reluctant, or I may just feel bad that you would think that I don't appreciate you. Of course, I feel bad because I also believe it is true. I'm not appreciating as much as I can. This does not mean I'm not enjoying you now as much as I might in the future. The truth is I'm not enjoying you as much as I really *do* enjoy you now. I'm not realizing what I already believe and could feel now because of my "need" to know more before I affirm what I already believe.

It's like saying that I need to know that you're a good carpenter before I feel good about you're being a good artist. It's like saying I need to know that you're a good friend to Mary before I admit I believe you would be a good friend to me.

I know I love you; there can be no "I want to be sure." I already know what I felt. Nothing else can "prove it." All that is left is for me to express it. To believe I am not "sure" of myself is not saying anything real. It is just believing I "ought" to reconsider, when I really don't want to or need to reconsider.

COMMENTARIES

by Aryeh Nielsen on

"Wanting, Doing, and Knowing"

People Are Always Doing
What They Want

This commentary is a synopsis of ideas that Bruce Di Marsico expressed in many writings or talks, but did not express summarily in a single writing or talk.

WHAT is the full meaning of "People are always doing what they want?"

a) People are always doing what they want insofar as *they* are doing it. If someone has got strings tied to their wrists and is being moved like a marionette, then whoever holds the strings is doing the movement of the body, not the person whose body is being moved.

b) Sometimes, people are doing what they want *based on the mistaken belief that it is necessary to do what they want to do in order to feel the way they want to feel*. For example, someone may want to feel stupid when his boss yells at him because of his mistaken belief that this is only the only way he can motivate himself to not "mess up" at work, and that it is necessary to avoid "messing up" at work in order to feel the way he wants to feel.

   Note, in this context "feeling" always means "emotional feeling." Pain, insofar as it is a physical sensation, is called by some a physical feeling. Feeling bad or good about the physical sensation is the emotional feeling of pain.

c) Even when people are acting based on this mistaken belief, people are still aware of what they *really* want (sometimes called "in touch with their desires"). By "*really* want" is meant: what desires they are aware they would act on if they did not believe that it was necessary to do anything in order to feel the way they want to feel.

   For example, someone who believes it is necessary to feel anxious in order to motivate herself to drive safely, would in most cases admit that if she truly believed that she could drive just as safely with (non-fear-based) caution, she would merely be cautious, and not be cautious and also feeling bad. So what she really wants is to be cautious, but she believes she needs to be anxious. It could even be said that "She chooses to be anxious only because it keeps her in touch with her desire to be cautious."

PART V

Relationships

SECTION I

About Relationships

Relationships, Love, Sex, and Happiness
December 1975

RELATIONSHIPS do not and cannot exist as events that have the power to cause happiness or unhappiness. People simply do not need each other in order to be happy—they already have what they need.

Relationships can and will exist. Although they have happiness, they will ask each other to give it as a gift to each other. This is love and sex.

Love is wanting another to be happy.

Love is wanting to make another happy.

Love is making another happy.

Sex (desire) is wanting to experience the other's happiness.

Sex (desire) is wanting the other to want you to experience their happiness with you.

Sex (expression) is love-making and making happy, experiencing making happy, being made happy and experiencing the other experiencing you.

Sex (fulfillment) is the awareness of all the above.

The game of relationships is the Big Game: Give me what I don't need (to be made happy) without my asking. Let me be who I already am, for you.

SECTION II

*Happiness Does Not Depend
on Relationships*

The Only Kind of Happiness
Is Personal Happiness

February 1, 1991

THE only kind of happiness there is, is personal happiness.
Just as the taste in your own mouth is yours alone, so is happiness. There cannot be an objective happiness or a general happiness common to all people. The abstraction can no more exist than, say, health in the abstract. Only each person is able to enjoy his or her own health. It cannot be in another person and be your health.

Happiness, like health, means *my* happiness. Whereas another's health can be appreciated for the benefits it may afford you, if they choose, the benefit of happiness is personal happiness alone. Even if another were to happily do you a kindness, only in your own happiness could you enjoy it. In other words, your enjoyment is always your personal enjoyment.

My Wanting Is What I Intend
to Have or Do or Be

MY wanting is what I intend to have or do or be.
My having my wanting is how I plan to express myself.

My wanting is my awareness of what I am beginning to do, be, have.

Before I finish I may want something else, but now, I *want*.

I want my doing whatever I want to do to get me whatever I want to have.

What You Are Wanting Is Perfect for You to Want

If you believe that you are not feeling the way you want,

If you believe that you are not doing what you want,

Then know this truth:

What you are wanting is coming from your perfect happiness and is perfect for you to want.

You are not *wanting* to be Perfectly Happy. You Are.

You are Perfectly Wanting to do or to have something that your Perfect Happiness is moving you to do or want.

I Cannot Be Unhappy against My Will

I cannot be unhappy against my will. I can only be unhappy if I think I have a very clear reason to be.

I would never choose unhappiness over happiness unless I believed I had to and it was to my benefit.

I know that I have never chosen to become unhappy for no reason.

I know that I am as happy as I want to be right now.

SECTION III

Love

Happiness in Relationships
Monday Night Study Group, 1973

WHAT two people start complaining about in relationships is "you don't love me enough, and because you don't love me enough, you are going to leave me. And, if you keep that up, I'll be so miserable, I can't stay with you, I am going to have to leave *you*, because I am so afraid of your leaving *me*. I just can't stand you constantly being *this* kind of person because if you continue to be *this* kind of person, I am going to be unhappy enough to leave you, and that's what I am most afraid of. If you continue to keep coming home late, and being interested in other men or other women, then I am going to just have to leave you . . . because I want to be with you."

I have never known it to be different.

Take it from a bird's eye view. Here are two people who love each other, who are leaving each other, and what they were most afraid of during their whole relationship together was one or the other being unfaithful, or leaving them, or not loving them enough and therefore wanting to leave them. Somehow they're to the point where they are really glad to separate; yet if anytime during that relationship you ever tried to tell them that they didn't need to be unhappy with the other one not being there, that they never needed to be unhappy to not have the other one, that they needn't be unhappy if the other one didn't love them, they could never hear that and would claim it to be absolutely impossible. Yet, what they are saying by the end of the relationship is, "I can't be happy unless they're gone, it's impossible for me to be happy with them." And they are often glad to split up: "Thank God it's over." They were: "Thank God I don't have to learn to be happy without him; I don't have to learn to be happy without her. That's the thing I never want to learn." So now they *are* without him or her, and they go on through the same cycle in the next relationship and on and on and on.

We play a game that we have to move away from what makes us so unhappy. People do that with jobs. You want to make a move and get a better job, and you become very unhappy about where you are at. Mostly what you are unhappy about is that you are afraid of losing it. So you want another one.

Some fear that if they didn't think they needed something in order to be happy, that would mean that they wouldn't want it if they *were* happy. This comes from the idea that you need reasons to be happy. Many, in fact, have lived with others who never gave them anything unless they pretended to need it.

"Can I *want* what I don't *need*?" becomes the next frightening question. The answer is always assumed that, if I merely wanted it, that's not going to be enough motivation for me to get it. We've been believing that just wanting it doesn't motivate me to get it; that's not true. You haven't really been wanting it.

You have deduced that you wanted it because you were afraid of *not* having it, but that's not the same as wanting it. You think, well, if I don't need my wife, if I don't need my husband, if I don't need the person that I love, that will be same as not wanting them. Why? Because you think that wanting them isn't going to make it work. Why? Because you haven't really been wanting them. You've been more afraid of *not* having them than you have been in touch with wanting them. You are your own evidence against yourself. You are right: you wouldn't have them if you didn't need them—unless you started wanting them. Because you *haven't* been wanting them. What you *have* been doing is being afraid of *not* having them.

Being afraid of not having is not really the substitute we think it is for wanting. It is not the same as wanting. It's the other path on another road that goes another place. We often say, "well, but I *have* wanted it" and that's how we can come to the conclusion that wanting isn't enough, that wanting doesn't motivate us—but anybody who says that about something hasn't really wanted it. "Oh, but I have wanted it and I cried every time I haven't had it." That *might* mean you feared not having it, but that doesn't mean you wanted it.

And so each time you have had the feeling that you would want it and that wanting it wasn't going to work, and wanting it doesn't make it happen, it's because you haven't really been wanting it. How many of you have really wanted to be happy? How often have you instead been afraid of being unhappy? That's not the same as wanting to be happy. It's nowhere near the same. It smells very bad; it has nothing to do with wanting.

If you went shopping to *not* get an ugly dress, you probably would never leave the house. And then you might wonder "how come I am not going shopping, because I want a nice dress?" But every time you go out the door, you are going out of the door to *not* get an ugly dress, and you feel you might as well stay home. And how many people, when they go out on a date, *want* to meet another person? And how many on a date are not wanting to enjoy themselves, but instead are feeling "I don't want to be nervous tonight, I don't want to be bored," and so they stay home. You think that you are wanting to have a good time, and yet you find yourself not even leaving your apartment. But when you really *are* wanting something, there's no question. You don't go shopping because you *don't* want a can of beans; you go shopping because you *do* want hamburger or whatever you are going shopping for.

Questioner: *I believe there are certain life situations that would automatically make someone unhappy. For example, I have a patient whose husband has had a stroke and he is left physically impaired, and has had a personality change to being demanding and childish. He was a quiet man who now talks excessively and preaches to people.*

But what are *her* reasons for being unhappy? *You* might have good reasons to be unhappy in that situation, but are they good enough for *her* to be unhappy? Besides having a husband who has become an imbecile, does she also want to be unhappy? Isn't she certainly afraid that she can't take care of him or herself the way she wants to, things like that? Can you see that she started out wanting to take care of him or herself, and now that wanting has changed into fear, and now there is fearing instead of wanting?

And maybe questioning will lead to the fear of not wanting. You might ask, "Why do you believe you really want it?" There may be fear that they *didn't* want what they know they really want. There can be fears of *not* having fears. So, just question, and find out what comes up. Maybe there is a wanting underneath it all. Maybe there is no wanting anymore, just fear of the implications of not wanting. You'll find out. Questions are the best way to help someone get in touch with their wanting.

There is a kind of wanting that doesn't do any good, and there is a kind of wanting that does do some good. We've made the distinction: we called them wanting and needing. They seem to be two kinds of one thing. In a sense, though, needing is not really a form of wanting because it doesn't get you anywhere that you want to go. What it gets you is unhappy, which is not really what you want. And even if you get the thing you want, it doesn't get you what you wanted it for, which was to be happy.

People who are happy together are different because what they are wanting from the other person is exactly what the other person is wanting from themselves. If my biggest complaint in my heart is, "I am going through all of this hell because you are not wanting to be happy. I am wasting my time wishing you were happier," all I am saying, then, is that you don't want to exist as a human being and so basically I am accusing you of not being human. To ever be angry or unhappy with another human being is to basically accuse them of not being human, to say somehow that they don't have the same basic human energy need that you do, the same tending, the same desires, the same desire to be happier.

And so to hate anyone is to consider them not human. There are all kinds of corollaries; in the history of every murderer or any soldier, they cannot believe that they've killed a human being. In any case that I have ever known, everyone who has ever murdered anyone, they would never allow themselves to believe that what they killed was a human being. They always believe that they killed some kind of a perverted miscreant creature, some kind of creature that didn't want to be human and therefore deserved to die. It was okay to kill them.

Every war has a vocabulary that's meant to dehumanize the so-called enemy, whether it be "gook" or "kraut" or whatever. It is not wanting to believe that the enemy is human beings. Human beings simply cannot kill other human beings intentionally. They have no reasons to do so. So the only reason they have ever come up with is that they made those they kill not human in some way in order to be able to kill them.

When I am helping those who have hurt others physically, I help them with whatever form the guilt takes. They have to know what they did was out of unhappiness. They have to know that they lied to themselves to do it. It can be very easy to help them see that they didn't believe it was humans they killed, that they really aren't capable of killing human beings. You first dehumanize them.

The state can't even honestly admit that it kills human beings. First they have to call them criminals, which are something that is not a human being, or has to call them an enemy, and give a reason for killing the enemy by showing all kinds of inhuman things about them. "Look what they did here and look what they did there, they are inhuman!" They couldn't kill them any other way.

"Senseless" killings are hardly senseless; you invariably find there is great rationality behind it, overloaded with reasons. You have to think that you and I are not alike, that we don't basically both desire the same things, we are not both trying to be happy and that somehow I become a threat to you, an accusation against your happiness and your being.

Back to loving relationships. If you are counseling an individual, or if a couple came to you, or three or four or whatever constellation of people who have a relationship, you would be able to see that their problem, whatever it was, had to do with their beliefs about getting all kinds of proof that they were not loved. And that really bugs them—the presented problem is not what really bugs them.

For example, if a person is unhappy because her husband slapped her, she was never unhappy that she has been slapped, she is unhappy about what that means. It means he doesn't love her, that if he loved her, he wouldn't have done that. Anybody who has ever been slapped accidentally and really believes that it was an accident does not have an issue. In order to get angry at an accident, you would have to believe "if you loved me you would have been more careful." People do get angry at accidents. But first they have to convert that into "not really" an accident by saying "you wouldn't have had that accident if you were more careful and if you loved me." That's not the same as being happy with accidents, that's just *not* being *un*happy with them.

Your butcher and you may both be having a good day and you go to your butcher, and you are happy, and he is happy, and you meet this morning and you are gone. You loved each other. But there will be some people that we are happier with than others based on the flimsiest reasons, like we've known them for a while, or we are both interested in the same thing. There is a fear there, that is the reason we are avoiding being happier with other people, so we pick a few people to be happy with, and choose not to be happy with many others.

It seems like one of the signs of being a happier person is if you are more open to being happy with anybody. Even though you may not be making a move to love anybody, you could be very open to something going on, so that if somebody asks you to love them, they are only asking you to be who you are with them. Then you can say, "Sure," if asked, "Would you like to do this with me?" It wouldn't be decided anymore on the basis of whether you like them or not; it would be decided on the basis of whether you like to do what you are going to do together or not. If someone said to you, "would you like to go to the museum with me this weekend?" the response would be in terms of the museum, not in terms of, "I don't like that person. I wouldn't want to spend in the afternoon in the museum with them." There would be a kind of openness to "I would be glad to go with you any place that I would be glad to go by myself." You could be happy without them. Now, would you like to be happier with them?

You just know that you are going to be happy no matter what you do, whether you try or don't try, that you are going to be more happy every minute of every day. You won't be using desire to be happy, then, to make *decisions*. If you were just moving toward more happiness, no matter what you did, you can stay in bed and you would be happier, or if you got up out of bed you would be more happy.

On Loving

Monday Night Study Group, 1973

To use your past as evidence to make your decision will only be the same old decision: being at the place where you need reasons in order to be happy. Apparently to be happy with another is somehow a reason to allow yourself to be happy. You will perhaps be moody, grumpy or feeling bad or be depressed, but if somebody who you like comes into your room, it's all gone; you smile, feeling better.

You may find that it's easier to be happy under the "pretext" of loving another person. So that becomes the reason for you to be happy. In other words, I want to feel good with this person, I want to love them, and the awareness of doing that is able to obliterate all your preoccupations with your own unhappiness, so that you are truly not unhappy any longer and truly not afraid, just merely as a result of that decision. We apparently find it much easier to say, "I am really going to be happy with this person, I want to love them," than it is to say, for no reason at all, in an empty room, "I want to be happier." And apparently we have set up our unhappiness vis-à-vis other people. There is the question of whether unhappiness could even exist if there weren't other people, if somehow we didn't set it up in order to deal with relationships with others. So maybe that is the reason why therapy works, why we don't just do it ourselves, why we need another to help us so, why we use others to help us. Seems to me that after one session we could learn all the tricks of the trade to be able to apply it to ourselves from then on, and yet haven't because somehow there is that belief in the dependency. We can use that very same belief that shackles us to free ourselves, by deciding to love each other and just making that decision. You have found in your mind many times, when we have simply decided to love somebody, all your worries went, all your cares went, all your fears went away. Then you attributed the magic to them, but if you don't do that, you could really know where your happiness "came from," and really have it.

You use symbols of love, so perhaps there is someone in a distant city now: if you were to think of them, you could love them, you could feel good about them and be happy about them. Your expression of love, this is your way of letting yourself know that you *do* love. I don't think it is a necessary expression, but it is an expression, it is feedback to yourself, and it's the way of reminding yourself.

Now, if we are really happy, we become simple. We become our own symbol of happiness: "I just know because I know, because I know." But there may very well be signs left over from our own unhappiness that are just that: old signs.

A smile is just one expression, but there are other ways that we let ourselves know that we are happy and we love. The value in communicating our happiness to others is that so many of us walk around with one central belief: each of us believes to one degree or another that we are no good. Each of us believes that we are unlovable; we wanted to believe that, in order to make ourselves happier. And the more people there are around us to dispel that myth, and who *don't* support us in that belief that we really are no good, we really are worth avoiding, we really are not worth getting involved with, etcetera, the easier it would be to face that myth and to see that perhaps we are putting it on ourselves. Can you imagine a miserable person in a community of everybody who kept loving them no matter what he or she did, and no matter how he or she acted, and kept understanding, kept being patient, kept loving and kept being happy? If we do that for each other, we are enabling that to be done for us.

The advantage of a loving environment is that it becomes something to reflect upon, as feedback. We really would be doing ourselves a great favor if this were a very loving environment and if we loved each other very much. The big favor would be that when we individually don't feel happy, we still have a legacy that we have built up, all the happy people around us; and that's when it will really pay off. It pays to be happy just simply with yourself. And when we are unhappy we are somehow thinking that being unhappy pays off better and that's all. Just somehow we are believing that it's better to be unhappy, and I don't know how long we could keep that belief if everybody else wasn't supporting it so easily. Symbolic expression just put something out there that someday will come back to you.

Many of you may take this as a "should." It's not. It's practically advantageous, but has no ultimate bearing on your happiness.

I hear some say that for you to be involved with somebody else has to be to your advantage. "Why would I want to get to know more about so and so? He is a salesman or she is a housewife and they don't have anything in common with me as far as I know, I couldn't get anything out of a relationship with them." This is a myth. Perhaps one of the most beautiful or important things you can do is to be happy with somebody, with anybody. Why all the rules and measure of gains? You all have conditions and specifications about the kind of people you will allow yourself to love. They've gotten looked at in certain ways and you acted certain ways with them and have a certain past history and have certain hopes in future, etcetera.

And you've got all these rules about the people who you allow yourself to be happy with. Wouldn't it be easier to dispense with those rules? You all have the greatest thing in common; you all really want to be happier. Do we have to keep pretending that there is risk involved in loving others? It's only pretence, it's only a game and we don't have to play that game. What are you are going to lose? Why is that going to mean anything to you? Why is that going to make you unhappy? It's a big pretence. There is no risk.

Some of the ways we pretend: "I can't be happier here until I am a happier person. I can't be happier here in this room and that is just a reflection of where I am at." We don't have to believe that. The biggest pretending is pretending that you are not pretending. All the reasons, the rules, we don't have to keep.

I want to say something about a woman here tonight. She sat in group for almost a year without saying anything. She would cry occasionally, and every so often somebody would come up and try to stop her from crying, trying to "help" her, and she learned how to get rid of them. And this became a place where she was really allowed to just be. One of the biggest helps for her in her life was that there was a place where she was allowed to be, she didn't have to talk, she didn't have to bring her problems, and if she did, she didn't have to solve them, she didn't have to share them and she was allowed to be with people. It makes a fantastic difference to not take the responsibility for another person. People didn't take responsibility for her in the group, and so it became a really good experience for her.

Loving Has Nothing to
Do with Happiness

December 12, 1992

I WANT to deal with this myth that love is somehow an absolute; that it is to be universally admired, that it is a universal goal, and that it is in any way, shape, or form equivalent to happiness. It's not. It's not something to be sought as a god, as if it were happiness. Love is not happiness. Happiness is not love . . . any more than lack of love is unhappiness. That is just what the world has believed. That's the closest they've gotten.

Throughout history, the way to be happy was to be good. The way to be happy was to be good. The goal was to be good, good, good, good, good. Then, after the Christian era, it became: ". . . to be good is to be loving, to be good is to be loving. Good and love. To be loving is good." And then you can feel good about people.

I love whoever I choose to love, just like you do.

My point is, love is a mythological thing. Sometimes people call it an emotion. But the emotion of love is just feeling good. The feeling of being "loving" is like the feeling of being holy, or the feeling of being civilized, or the feeling of being noble, or the feeling of being an aristocrat. It is just feeling that you are being the way you should be, and you're really proud of it.

But love is like anything else. However you define it, you feel good if you get what you want. So if you're saying, "I want this person's love," and you get that person's love, then you feel good. If you feel that one of the ways of becoming a happy person is by being a loving person, then you can say, "I will be loving."

I know many people who try to justify every single thing they do as loving. No matter how obnoxious or stupid or ridiculous it is, they justify it as loving! They need to see themselves as loving, because that's the same as believing you are good. And then you have the right to be happy. If it wasn't loving, well then, maybe, I guess, I'd consider that I'm not happy. But I can justify everything I do as loving; if I give the drunk a drink, I'm loving, if I take the drink away from the drunk, I'm loving. You see, I got you either way. If I beat my children, I'm loving, if I don't beat my children, I'm loving. If I cheat on my wife, I'm seeking love, if I don't cheat on my wife, I'm giving her love. You screw it up every way you want and you justify everything.

The point is, "Being Loving" is just another one of those characterological goals that people set for themselves to consider themselves worthy human beings who deserve to be happy. Love is many, many things. It means many things in our language, but one of the most fundamental things, is "Being good to whom or for whom you choose." You love who you love—you are being good for them. I don't want to get into what "being good" means or what form that takes. But suffice to say, your loving somebody means you are desiring to be good to them. You want good things for them; you want to do good things to them. It starts in your mind as *your* belief that they are good things. This is one of the problems.

If you are trying to make love a universal principle, you are not going to be able to do it, because what is a good thing? To give the drunk a drink or not to?

Participant: *If I want to be loving, then I want for you what you want.*

Bruce: Why do you "want" to be loving? Don't you *really* love anybody? Why do you have to "want" to be? Don't you love your husband? Don't you love your children? What do you mean you "want" to be? Wanting to be loving is making loving some kind of goal to be. If you want to be loving, consider that just the same as wanting to be well-dressed, and fashionable. Figure out what it is and do it. But it's got nothing to do with happiness.

I love everyone. But I don't believe I'm *supposed* to love anybody. As far as I'm concerned, anybody can be anything they want to be, and they can be happy, and I'd be perfectly glad if everyone was happy, and as far as I know, I'm the only one I know who is even capable of wanting everyone to be happy. To really want the son-of-a-bitches to be happy, the nasty people to be happy, the murderers to be happy—I want that. It's okay with me. I'm glad for that. If you want to define love that way, "that love is wanting people to be happy," then I love everybody.

But I don't have to do that. I don't even consider that a goal. I don't consider it worth talking about.

I don't want to deify "loving." I don't want to canonize it. I don't want to, I don't want to, I don't want to. I don't want it to be second on the list; I want it to be like ninth, tenth, or eleventh! I want good television programs to be second!

If you are not loving, that has nothing to do with you having a right to be happy or not. You can still be the happiest person in the world, if you love anybody, if you don't love anybody, or if anybody loves you or doesn't love you. It's not a notch on your gun, if somebody loves you.

Someone took a lecture of mine, "To Love Is to Be Happy" (and I had very definite reasons for putting it that way), and then made it into theology, and I want to poke holes in that. If you do what you do, you did what you did, why does it have to be called loving or not loving?

If a person believes that what they've done could be seen as mean or nasty, they may very well try to justify it as love. But I wouldn't believe that anything I did was mean or nasty. But I wouldn't necessarily call it loving. The reason I don't have to be mean and nasty is that there is no such thing. See, mean and nasty is another person feeling bad about what I've done, and they are calling it mean and nasty.

If you are starving, and you come to my door, and you say, "Would you please give me some bread?" and I give you a stone, I'm not mean and nasty. But I'm not loving. I don't believe I'm being mean and nasty, but I don't believe I'm being generous, I don't believe I'm being loving. And I don't believe that because of what I did, this person had to be unhappy. Now, in fact, in the long run, if I was a Buddhist master, I could have a point of view that there is a great wisdom for them to see—I just enlightened them. You asked me for bread, and I gave you a stone—you don't see all the Truth in that?

Why do I have to judge every one of my actions . . . why *should* I judge every one of my actions as either fashionable or not fashionable, loving or not loving, cool or uncool, neurotic or non-neurotic . . . you name it, whatever has become the latest fad?

Say I have a child. He's two years old, and he is going to get an inoculation. And he's going to hate me for three days after that. He doesn't have a short-term memory like other two-year-olds. He is going to resent me, and when we get home he'll look for pins to stick me with. That's my child. And I'm going to give him an inoculation— I'm going to bring him to the doctor, and he's going to get a shot.

Am I loving him? Am I not loving him? Don't bother me with that nonsense! You can make this nice suggestion that you are "loving" your child because you are protecting him from disease, and you give him an inoculation, even though he doesn't appreciate it. And he'll know later when he's twenty years old that you were really loving him when you gave him this injection. But, on the other hand, right now, I'm going to be giving him an armful of pain, something that he's afraid of, something he's scared of, something that hurts, something he doesn't want, and something that in no way he would consider love.

I've got this dilemma. I'm doing something that I consider loving, but my child doesn't consider loving. So am I really loving or not loving? Shall I give the bum a drink, or shall I tell him I'm doing him a favor by not giving him a drink? "I'll take him to the restaurant and give him a cup of coffee, he'll really appreciate that, and if he doesn't, that's because he's sick."

Don't bother me with this! I'm doing what I want to do, because I feel like doing it. And my child's getting a shot, because I'm bigger. And I can help the child, and I can prevent the child from having a disease. And that's what I want to do. You might want to call that loving. I call that protecting. Then you might call protecting "loving." I've been "protected" . . . forget it! Haven't you? Don't give me "you did it for my own good!" Do you know how many things were done to me and to you because of that? You go into banks and they photograph you; you want to cash a check, and they fingerprint you; they are all doing it for your own protection. Yeah, right, that was Hitler's statement: "It's for your own good." No. Things don't have to be justified in terms of love and unlove. That's my point.

When you have to start calling everything love, then you have to start twisting your mind into describing everything you do as love. Nobody accuses themselves of not loving. Then you get all this self-righteousness. All the evangelists are very "loving" when they are condemning everybody. The most venomous, hateful people appear on television, preaching some gospel, which I don't recognize, and they are calling it loving. Why does it have to be twisted like that? Why can't it be that they are doing what they are doing?

The point is happiness is happiness, that's what counts. Love is no better a word, nor useful a word, than anything else you want. If love has a value to you, has a meaning to you, it's because it is something you want, however you define it. It's something you want for those who you love, it's something you want from others, but it's just a collection of a certain amount of things that you want. It's not divine. I hate that! God is "loving," that's why he blows up volcanoes, and smothers people, and drowns them. And then a hurricane goes through Homestead, and you get these little self-righteous people who say "God was with us." Well, what about your neighbor who just got smashed to pieces? God wasn't with them? "Our prayers were answered, God protected us." And he hated your friends?

Love, and "doing good" and getting what you want are really ways of saying the same thing . . . it's just another way of wanting what you want, getting what you want, getting what you consider good. You consider it good to get what you want.

Now, there are dilemmas. Once you start making love a thing to be sought in itself, you have the idea of "is this love or is this not love? Do I chain my wife to the bed so she won't eat anymore and get fatter and fatter and fatter?" So there is my idea of imposing my love on you, and you're not perceiving it as love at all.

The lecture, "To Love Is to Be Happy" was to show that you're not loving people by being unhappy with them, by sympathizing with them, by agreeing with them that they ought to be unhappy, by saving them from unhappiness—"Oh, you're afraid of spiders? I'll rescue you from the spiders!" That's not love. Love is to help someone not to be afraid of spiders, not to go around killing every spider you find. Love is to show someone they don't have to be unhappy, not to agree with them.

The comment I hear about love is that you sympathize with somebody who is unhappy; I was trying to make the lecture contradistinct to that. That to love is not to be unhappy along with them, to not agree with them, to not agree with their unhappiness, to not support their unhappiness, to not keep telling them they are right to be unhappy, and you're going to fight that which makes them unhappy. This was the point of the lecture; that kind of love turns upon itself.

And you wind up angry and unhappy at the people you love once you get into this idea that love is agreeing with people that they have to be unhappy. Now what happens when they are unhappy with you? And now you can't agree. The whole lecture was to show that we're not loving people by being unhappy.

Loving, and Wanting to Love
Monday Night Study Group, 1973

Wanting to Love

The alternate belief to "proving that I am not loved" goes something like this: "Although I am not loved more at this moment by so and so, because they are scared, I have not proved that they do not *want* to love me more." And that usually is very, very consoling and peace-giving for a person to realize.

Although I think I may have proven that they don't love me more, all I've proven really is that they're afraid. That doesn't prove that I'm unlovable. It only proves that because they're afraid, they can't love me more. It doesn't prove that they don't *want* to love me more, that, in fact, they're against loving me more. And I guess the question we could ask ourselves is, can we ever really find proof that another person wouldn't want to love us more? Who is there that wouldn't want to be happier? Who is there that wouldn't want to love anybody more? Who is there that wouldn't want to love us more?

You will find that there are different answers to that question. Sometimes you will find that people do not want to love other people more, for example, strangers, people they don't know. But in that relationship, who wouldn't want to love the other one more? Who wouldn't want to be happier? So we could see this for ourselves: they would want to love us more and they would love us more if they believed they could. It doesn't prove that there's anything wrong with us if the other is not able to overcome all their fears instantly. If the other people we love are not able to overcome all their fears instantly regarding us or other people, it doesn't prove that there's anything wrong with us.

They certainly would want to overcome those fears if they believed they could. But all the unhappiness that we have with them is based, somehow, on the belief that because I am who I am, they don't even want to overcome their fears of me, they don't even want to love me more, somehow because there's something wrong with me.

226

And that's where all the anger and the unhappiness and depression in relationships come from. And the confusion stems from this: in our emotions, and in our language we often believe that loving and wanting to love are identical, and we could say to somebody, "I love you." But we could really mean two things. We could mean, "I love you," or frequently, we could mean "I *want* to love you more." Which means: "I'm happy with you" or "I *want* to be happier with you." And both of those, we express in our language by saying to somebody, "I love you."

We could be angry at somebody and having a terrible argument with them, and say, "But I'm only doing this because I love you." That doesn't mean, "I'm happy with you right now." We can't possibly mean that. That kind of an answer means "I'm not happy now but I want to be happier with you."

We know that what we basically want, really, is for the person to want to love us. The fact that they do or do not love us, at any given moment, would never matter to you as long as you believe that someone *wanted* to love you and that what was preventing them was their own past, their own beliefs, their own fears, not *you*. On close inspection, it seems that what all people really want from others is for them to *want* to love. If we know that a person sincerely *wants* to love us, we cannot be unhappy because we cannot believe it is our fault.

We can only be unhappy when we believe that it is our fault, that there is something wrong with us. We cannot be unhappy when we don't believe it is our fault. People in a relationship cannot be unhappy with each other if they really saw that the other person was being unhappy and frightened and *wanting* to love them, but felt they were not able to.

If you've ever had that fear, it was the fear that somehow the other person didn't even *want* to love you. You didn't believe that they were trying with all their might. You didn't believe that they were doing everything they knew how to do and everything in their power to be happier. And you really believe they didn't even want to be happier with you.

"If you really wanted to be happier with me and if you really wanted to love me, you wouldn't do such and such a thing." That really is an impossible sentence filled with contradictions, because we can't accuse somebody of not wanting to love us more in any real way. We can't accuse them of not wanting to be happy, not wanting to be happier.

And if we can be in touch that our unhappiness with another person is based on the belief that they don't really want to be happier, we don't have to believe that, because it's impossible for another person not to want to be happier. So that huge belief, that cardinal belief, which is behind all the problems in relationships, which can be stated, "if you loved me more you would be such and such a way, or do or feel this or that," this can't be believed and felt if the person is able to see the inherent contradictions.

Okay, so what I really want you to see is how it's all based on that one belief. And that difficulties between people, no matter what shape, no matter what form, no matter what style, no matter what the roles, can still be boiled down to this very, very simple principle: "If you loved me more or if you really wanted to love me more, you would . . ."

And just by sometimes pointing it out, as we do for ourselves, how many times have our own problems with other people stopped, saying to ourselves, "They don't really mean to be that way. They didn't really mean to say that or they don't really want to be that way." How many times have they stopped when we saw that they were really very sorry and felt very bad.

Why did we enjoy their feeling bad about having been unhappy with us? Because it was their way of saying, "I don't really want to be this way either and I didn't really want to treat you that way." And when a person is very apologetic and falls all over you, why do you even allow that to let you feel good? Because somehow they're saying, "But don't you see, I really *do* want to be happier with you and I don't know what came over me. And I don't know what happened and I don't know why I'm this way and I don't want to be." And as long as they reassure you that they do *want* to love you, all is forgiven.

I've seen people that lived in what you would consider the most impossible situations with alcoholics and drug addicts, and could really love those people and be with them very much, when they realized that.

Feeling that You Are Not Loving Enough

I didn't speak too much about the second person who is unhappy about not being what they should. But basically all the dynamics are the same. That's their way of motivating themselves to be what they would like to be in a relationship, to do what they'd like to do.

"If you aren't what I want you to be, there must be something wrong with me that I can't give you whatever you need, to be the way I want you to be. There must be something wrong with me that I can't motivate you." And that person is very much in touch with it. And they feel, "I really don't love that person, I guess. But how come I feel so bad about it?" They are confusing loving and *wanting* to love. They're not in touch. But they do want to love and that's all that's needed. All you need to have a good relationship is to *want* to love. You don't need to love. Just want to be happy.

The person who is very frequently the withdrawn party or the abused party or the victimized party or the masochistic one, whichever you want to call it in a relationship, is very frequently feeling that they don't love the other person and they feel bad about that. "I try my best. I can't feel any better about her or I can't feel any better about him."

We can still let it be okay. We may find out that a person who is very unhappy with us all the time, in a sense, is just not there for us. It becomes easier and more possible for them to see that when they're being unhappy, that's okay. But that doesn't mean that we like it or we love it. We want to love them but we will never want to love their unhappiness.

Especially because we love them, we won't want them to be unhappy. So we don't have to be unhappy with another person's unhappiness. What if we're not really unhappy with their unhappiness? We won't be avoiding them but I don't suppose we'll be searching them out, either. It would be impossible for us to look forward to being with them, too. But that's all right. That's not a problem. Very natural resolutions come about in that respect. And the person who's very unhappy is just very unhappy and isn't really going to be any different regarding you anyway, and the unhappy person can really see that all they are doing is depriving you of a friend.

You won't keep getting in the way and telling them that their real problem is that they make you unhappy. Indeed, their real problem is they're making themselves unhappy. All they're doing is depriving themselves.

If someone was nothing for you because he was unhappy, then he would just be nothing for you. It'd be nothing for you to run away from, but nothing for you to be attracted to. And they would be being what they wanted and felt they needed to be.

If, for whatever reason, you wanted them to love you more, that's another thing and that's no problem really. If you wanted them to love you more, then you could easily help them. You could try to help them. And you could see that you didn't need them to love you more. They were an unhappy person. You would like them to be happier. You would want them to love you more. You would want them to be more happy with you but you would approach that thing a whole lot differently. And probably, in such a way that would make a real difference to the other person, because they wouldn't be able to use you as the thing to hang their unhappiness on.

Although they may be unhappy about everything else, they wouldn't necessarily want to bring that into your relationship. They probably would be quite willing to suspend their unhappiness when they're with you. And you may find that eventually, they'd only want to be with you when they were really happy. So they'd have that and they'd want to be with you and they'd be happy. And it would change things quite a bit.

SECTION IV

Intimacy

You Want to See My Love

WHEN I realize that I am not getting what I want from you, I also realize that you're not getting what you want from me (even if you aren't aware of it).

When I realize that you are unhappy, I also know that you want something from me. I am not unhappy nor am I glad for your unhappiness, but I am glad to give you what you are wanting from me.

You want to feel or see my love. That is what I want, too. I know that what you want is beautiful.

You want to know that happiness is real and can be yours.

I want you to know what you want to know.

Know mine.

If You Have the Attitude I Want

If you have the attitude that I want—

(that is, you are really happy and don't doubt it; you are happy with me, glad for me, pleased by me, happy about me.)

—then I have everything I want from the whole universe at that moment. Then I have the certainty, the sure guarantee, that I can have anything I may want with you.

But since there is no certainty that I will be wanting anything in particular with you in the future, I am certain that what I want now is: Your Happiness.

It is not that I really want the certainty that I can have other things with you, it is that I am wanting the certainty that you are happy—Truly Happy.

Commitment

A LOT of people believe they could never have a relationship on its own merits. They would need the person to promise to stick with them even if it doesn't pay off—that's what's meant by commitment: "you promise to stick with me no matter how miserable I make you." Commitment is "you'll stay with me even if you don't feel like it." Women are often aware of wanting that from men before they are married; men are often aware of wanting that from women after they are married.

The biggest destroyer of relationships is the fear of making the other person unhappy. Many people can't stand to believe they are making someone unhappy. Often, the so-called "fear of commitment" men have is the fear of making the woman unhappy, by disappointing her. "I don't want to make any commitments," meaning "I don't want to give you false hopes and then disappoint you, and then you'll be unhappy, and then I'll have to see myself as the cause of your unhappiness."

There Is No Doubt about It for Me

THERE is no doubt about it for me.

You don't believe that I love you as much as you want me to.

You are not as sure as you want to be.

You don't believe as much as you want.

You want me to express it more, in ways that you will be glad for.

The answer to your uncertainty, my natural response, is for me to want to make you sure, and to show you more in the way you want—in the way that will make you glad.

This is how I will do it:

I know that what *you* are wanting is exactly what *I* want. Your doubt and desire is beautiful; it is because you love me so much and want our gladness. I want you to have me exactly the way you want. I want you to have what you want from me.

Even though I am sure there is no doubt about my love, you are not sure that I have no doubt.

When you see how sure I think I am about my love for you, you could be confused and wonder why you are not glad, and wonder why you are not sure, and start to feel that maybe you are not loving me, when all you are really wanting is reassurance in the form you want. You want what you want, in the way you want it.

I don't want you to believe you don't love me, just because you don't think I love you as much as you want. I know you love me, and your desire and doubt is just a way for me to know what I want to do: to assure you.

When I see that you are doubting your love for me, when you get afraid of not having a certain feeling—it is for me to know something, it is my way of knowing what I want to do. I am glad for the opportunity.

Your doubts about yourself, your lack of joy are a question to me, a request. Your lack of feeling "glad" for me is a request without words. You are asking "Do you really love me as much as I hope you do?" I will answer you.

After all, you don't have to ask in words when you don't want to.

There are just some things we'd love to know without using words to ask. I think that is beautiful. I know when you are asking. I will be glad to answer in the best way I know.

You may think you know the best way for me to show and reassure you. Let us be open. I am going to be open to my knowing the best way to show you even "better" than what you think. If I am right, you will not have any complaints. If I am right you will be really glad for my way.

This is good to know when I see that I don't want to show you in the way it seems you want me to. I will let myself know that it is not that I don't want to show you; it is that I want an even better way to show you, and I *will* show you.

Maybe you are even wanting a wordless assurance.

If You Loved Me, You Would . . .

Monday Night Study Group, 1973

Why Lovers Split Up

I have never known two lovers to split up for any other reason except fearing unhappiness. I've never seen two people who have gotten divorced for any other reason. There may be other reasons but they're not the ones I've ever come across.

I think the confusion between loving and *wanting* to love is the basis for much of the difficulty in relationships. When two people are unhappy with each other, it generally manifests in two ways.

First, they are unhappy that they're not getting what they expect from the other, which is another way of saying that they're not getting what they believe they need, or they're not getting what they "should." What they believe they need could be functions and things from the other person, or good feelings from the other person, such as approval of love, happy with me, etcetera.

Second, they are unhappy about not being or not giving what they should to the other. That's the unhappiness about not being what one "should" be for the other, or what one expects oneself to be or what one is expected to be. And that also regards functions and things, or good feelings. In my experience, this is the person who will ultimately leave the relationship.

Even if the first feeling is predominant, that they're not getting what they want, and that has been predominant, there will be a point when that feeling converts to the second feeling, which is the feeling that they're not giving what they should and they're not being what they should. And it's when that feeling becomes strong that the person leaves the relationship. Both are feelings of powerlessness: in the first case the person believes and experiences that they have no power to motivate the other to give, and in the second case, they believe they have no power to motivate themselves to give.

If You Loved Me, You Would . . .

Each is using the other or expecting the other to affirm their worth. It usually starts off with this one cardinal belief upon which everything else hinges: "If you loved me, you would *X*." From that starts all the difficulties in relationships. We'll take a closer look at that sentence later—it's got a number of inherent contradictions and pitfalls, and in some ways it's really an impossible sentence—but, nonetheless, that's the experience of people who have problems in their relationships. "If you loved me, you would . . . Since you don't do this or feel that or be this way, *X*, it's because you don't love me enough. Why don't you love me enough? I do this and that and that. And I do all of those things. Why don't you love me enough? Why isn't who I am, what I do, why isn't that enough for you to love me more? Why can't I get you to love me more?" And it's a question, but the answer is often implied. "What's wrong with you that I can't get you to love me more? What's wrong with me?" becomes the immediate corollary. "I'm unhappy that you have made me feel that there's something wrong with me by your actions, by your behavior, by what you do. You've made me feel that there's something wrong with me."

"You've made me feel that there's something wrong with me. I'm unhappy that you have made me feel that there is something so wrong with me that I can't get the only and the simplest thing that I want, which is for you to be happier with me and to love me more. That's all I want." Of course, the feeling was not caused by the other, but follows from the premise "if you loved me more, you would *X*." This could be totally unspoken between a person and another person.

For example, I could just observe you sitting there with your legs crossed, and writing. And I could just say to myself, totally within me, "If you loved me more, you wouldn't be doing that." That's all. It doesn't take any more than that to start the whole thing. Then I could follow with, "Since you are doing that, you don't love me more. That's because you don't love me enough. Why don't you love me enough? What's wrong with you? What's wrong with me?" And now I'm unhappy that you are making me feel that I can't motivate you, that there's something wrong with me.

Then there is the second frame of reference: "If *I* loved you more I would have *X*, if I loved you more I'd feel such and such, or if I loved you more I'd do this or that. What's the matter with me that

I don't love you more? Why don't I love you enough?" The same reason would be to continue using myself as the one I'm expecting something from. Now the whole dilemma is based on the belief that my wanting you to be happier should make it so.

So it's all based on the belief that my wanting you to be happier should make it so, the myth that I should be able to motivate you to overcome every fear and hang-up you ever had. And you'll find that this is usually what the parties are saying in a relationship that they're unhappy with.

Proof That You Don't Love Me

I had a patient that reasoned like this: "My mother is afraid of mice. If she loved me, she would not be afraid of me if I dangled a mouse at her." That may seem patently absurd to you but that is what you'll find some variation of in any relationship that you find is in trouble. So he dangled a mouse at her, she got frightened, then she got angry. And he was satisfied that he had proved that she didn't love him at all. And he was very satisfied. He was sure he now had proof that she didn't love him at all or, at least, not as much as he needed.

In this model, although it's extreme, I think you'll see you can fit anything into it. "So-and-so is afraid of such-and-such. So-and-so is threatened by such-and-such—my husband, my wife, my children, parents, whatever. If they really loved me they would not be afraid of such-and-such, if I did it." When others fail our test for love—this test being, "if you loved me more you would . . . ," we believe that we have seen evidence that we're unlovable or evidence that we're not worthy of being loved, or evidence that we're not good, or evidence that we're really unable to motivate others. It's all basically the same evidence.

When others fail our tests for love, all that happened is that we have discovered the basic reality of human relations dynamics, which is this: people love only to the extent that they are happy. That's all we ever find out when we test love.

Love means "happy with." If we are or do what others are afraid of, to that extent, they cannot love us. That is, if we are or do what others are afraid of, to that extent, they cannot be happy with us. People can only love what they are *happy with*. Now we could say that if they are usually happy with us, then I think we could say they are usually loving us and vice versa. If they are usually unhappy with us, then they are usually not loving us. Because they're really one and the same thing.

Not Allowing Others to Be Unhappy

If we are, or do, what others are afraid of, to that extent, they cannot, absolutely cannot, love us. They're mutually exclusive terms. One cannot be afraid of and love at the same time. I do want to point out something which we'll get into later. That doesn't mean they can't *want* to love us, which is usually the confusion. But they certainly cannot love us at that time.

So, for example, a person may say, "If I discover that people will not be happy with me and cannot be happy with me if I scare them, that bothers me because I believe I need them to be happy with me." The only problem I've ever seen in relationships is that people will not allow others to be unhappy. We have all kinds of ways of not allowing others to be unhappy; they're as varied as attacking them or leaving them alone and everything in between.

If we want another to be happier, for whatever reason, that's one thing. If we want another person to be happier with us, for whatever reason, that's one thing. But if we *need* them to, we are resorting to trying to motivate ourselves with unhappiness, in order to motivate the other to be happier.

Once we need someone to be happier with us, we'll try to motivate them in one of two ways. One, by giving what they "need or want"—for example, being really being nice and giving—or two, by denying them, and depriving them of what they need or want, hoping to motivate them by unhappiness. So we're either hoping to motivate them by happiness or hoping to motivate them by unhappiness. But there's a built-in pitfall in either of these, a seed of destruction in either of these approaches when it comes from our own need.

Anything that we may do to get someone to love us from our own need is doomed to failure. When we're trying to motivate the other person by giving them everything and removing fears, we come to feel that we are catering and placating, and that, eventually, we're going to feel that we have to continue this behavior or we'll not get what we need. We're going to feel that we have to keep giving to them, that we must. It's going to become a feeling of a "should." We eventually resent them for having their fear. We resent them for having their need that we keep catering to. And we wind up only realizing that we were confirming our original fear in the first place, which is, "you'll only love me as long as I do this or that. You'll only love me as long as I'm, and only if I'm, generous, kind, patient, always looking the other way, never criticizing, always bringing home the money, never yelling at the children, whatever that is. That's the only reason you love me." And we wind up not feeling loved at all, because the other person is only happy conditionally and we encouraged that and we played with that, and we never really dealt with it.

The other approach by which we try to motivate the other is by making them more unhappy, in trying to prove that if they need something from us, they will never get from us what they're unhappy about or while they're unhappy. We try to prove to them that if they need us or need something from us, that they're going to be making us unhappy, which, of course, was their fear in the first place. So we punish them.

And this is very much like training a person to not need anything from us with the hope that if we succeed, they can't be unhappy with us because we could never fail them then. So if I could train a person by making them feel very bad anytime they've ever needed something from me, every time I've ever disappointed them, and somehow punish them for that, my hope would be that I would train them not to need anything from me. And so if they don't need anything from me, I can't fail them and they can't be unhappy with me.

Both of these approaches begin with an absolute terror of anybody being unhappy with us. That is the thing that is just not allowed, which is what I began with in the first place: we just cannot allow people to be unhappy with us. And we resort to any extreme to prevent it. We'll either sell out and sacrifice everything and deprive ourselves and constantly give, give and build up feelings of resentment, or we'll do just the opposite and try to show them that we'll give nothing and we'll just give them more misery, more unhappiness and anger until they learn to stop being unhappy with us.

Both of these approaches only continue to increase unhappiness. They never solve anything. If these approaches were truly adhered to and stuck to rigidly, to an absolute degree, it could lead to death within hours or minutes—each person believing that they would kill each other, and they do. Most times, though, people would rather give up their relationship. They'll kill the relationship instead of killing the other person.

The new belief that can make the crucial difference: that in a relationship, no matter how you try to test love, you are never proving, really, that you are unlovable or that you're unloved. All you prove is that you know how to tap another person's fears. In a sense, it was proved that one wasn't loved more or enough at that point. But a person wouldn't be unhappy if they had another corollary belief to go along with that. So when a person says, you know, "This proves that I'm not loved, this proves that they don't love me," you can point out that it doesn't prove that they don't love them. It only proves that in that moment, in that place, and in those circumstances, they can't be loved because the person is afraid of them.

Time and Feelings
January 15, 1977

NOTHING we desire to do is ever, in itself, an unlikeable chore. We have always believed that we could want to do something we don't "feel" like doing. Life, we were told is full of "unpleasant" tasks that are nonetheless necessary in order to achieve what we really want. For example: one "works" at a job in order to earn money. The money is desirable for what we can do with it and what it gets us; that is, the real things we want. The garage mechanic "works" on cars and "relaxes" in his carpentry workshop. The carpenter works in his woodshop and relaxes by "tinkering" with his car. Some actors drag themselves to work for an 8 a.m. rehearsal (or refuse rehearsal time) and other actors (usually amateurs) volunteer for any job that is even remotely related to acting (sets, ushering, etc.) for no pay and longer hours.

Many people can't wait to work in their new professions. They begin with great enthusiasm and later the zest not only wanes but is replaced by outright hatred for their own professional endeavors. A rookie policeman is willing to take any assignment. After a while, he is a failure if he is found "pounding a beat," etc. The new doctor or nurse is willing and eager to do anything asked and even more— not so, for most after a while. Every vocation has similar examples.

There is an American phrase that is taken as an axiomatic principle of human existence. The phrase is believed true about all human relations with other people, places, things, concepts, events, etc. It is some version or another of, "When the honeymoon is over . . . ! Things become routine. We get into a rut. We all eventually take things for granted. Familiarity breeds contempt," etc.

The opposite is believed about certain things also. Some things, we are taught, get better as time passes. We learn to appreciate better something as we get "used to it," like exercise, in-laws, teachers, certain "serious" music, fashions that grow on us, new smelly cheeses, etc. "You'll like the boss as you get to know him (or her) better."

A favorite belief of people in authority (parents, teachers, doctors, judges, etc.), and which is even sometimes verbalized, is, "You'll thank us for this later!" or "Someday you'll appreciate what this means for you" (this education, this six-month sentence to the work farm, this diet, this straitjacket or whatever). The subtle equivalents are often some variation of "This is harder on me than on you!" or "I don't enjoy this any more than you!"

At first sight it might seem that they are agreeing that the situation they are imposing is distasteful, but they don't mean distasteful for you. What they really mean is this: "I've got good reasons for not liking this but I want you to realize that you don't have to dislike it. I hope you'll appreciate that I really believe this is good for you (something for you to be glad for) and the fact that you are too ignorant to realize it makes it painful for me to impose it on you. Of course, you understand, that this is the very reason I must impose it. You are too ignorant to volunteer for it." It all amounts to trying to get across that you might be able to dislike it less if you understood it more.

We do believe that time affects enjoyment; that more, or further, or deeper experience affects our gladness. Sometimes it adds, sometimes subtracts. All agree that it is not the thing in itself, but greater experience of it, more exposure, etc., that causes the change.

Why must this be so? I ask this especially in regards to this complaint: "Why must I love you less in the future, or why can't I love you more now as I might in the future? Why must the honeymoon be over? I love this so much!" or the opposite: "Why must I have absence to make the heart grow fonder?"

Sometimes we are on the other end of these "facts." We are the ones who are less appreciated the more we do. It is sometimes the ones we love and want to love us who need more time to come to love us and understand us, etc. We should all know that it is precisely because of the belief in these axioms as "facts" that they become actual experiences.

Imagine, if you will, two people attracted to each other who want to have a very enjoyable relationship. He believes that in time all strong emotions taper off unless increased efforts are made. (Belief A: "The honeymoon dies if not renewed.")

She believes that a relationship is more worthwhile in the long run if they don't rush into it. "A good thing is worth waiting for." It is good if it will withstand the test of time and deprivation (Belief B: "The honeymoon dies if not forestalled and stretched out. Absence [of strong emotions] makes the heart grow fonder.")

He will be hot, she will be cold!

He will pursue, she will retreat.

She will resist, he will insist.

Their relationship is doomed to frustrations, arguments, hurt feelings, misunderstandings—not because of the inevitable "facts of life" but because of the inevitable consequences of the beliefs in just what those facts are. They have the two basic varieties of that one belief that nobody likes and everybody tries to overcompensate for. *Any* compensation for a non-existent thing is over-compensation.

How does one properly arm oneself against an imagined future dilemma? Well, it doesn't matter how, because however we do it, we are not going to enjoy it. It is our preoccupation with the fantasy that is the cause of ignoring the present reality. These two people could be enjoying themselves now, *this* now, and every now they will have together.

Their one common belief is that continued experience changes appreciation.

The corollary experience is that the more important or desirable the event, the more important to assess and predict and prevent (or assist) that change. The greater the experiences hoped for, the more to dread undesirable changes in appreciation, such as a cooling of the relationship, or hope for desired changes in appreciation, such as a greater eagerness to engage the relationship. The greater the hope, the more drastic the possible change. Each tries to express their hope by their style of appreciation, cool or eager.

She hopes for a fantastic future to grow from the present attraction if they are not too eager now. He fears that a fantastic present attraction may shrink in the future if they both are not eager enough now. She assumes he could not be able to appreciate her as much now as he could in the future. He believes he could never be more turned on, he's so eager now.

I'm not sure we have to explain why they start with the opposite roles. Even if they both had the same beliefs, the resulting life styles would still be unsatisfactory. If both are eager, both are trying too hard, both are expecting it to die; a one-night stand is the order of the day. In the extreme, they both believe that their initial experience is their tops. If it is not fantastic now, forget it, don't bother. These types are called fickle, promiscuous, etc. If it is great, they will continue until they see the first signs of it dying. In the extreme, they then call it quits. It's only "a matter of time" before they feel impotent.

If both are cooling it, both nonchalant, both businesslike, both slow to move closer, if they ever develop anything more than a polite "civilized" relationship, it would be a miracle. In the extreme, this is a no-night-stand. They don't even notice each other. If introduced, they can begin. Circumstances will dictate the relationship. They will get together if they have nothing better to do. In years to come they might form a polite marriage. Both will experience bitter self-recriminations and fantasize what it might have been like with someone else. They may argue, not so politely, about each other's failure to keep bargains and agreements about the pets, the garbage, etc. They are waiting for the other to appreciate the other more, and are often guilty for being cold. They will settle for being proud of how long they have stuck together. They will sagely observe how those passion-filled romances of the others "burn out" while their cool light glows dim but steady.

The "hot" shots wisely observe how the cold ones live dull, uneventful, routine lives. They shudder with chills at the thought of being trapped in a solid (but ice-solid) relationship. Each set believes the others must secretly hate their life styles.

Each combination of these relationships is unsatisfactory to the parties involved. Granted that extremes are not the usual; the usual has its extremes in different settings. In any one relationship we might find one combination regarding sex, one about new friends or movies and one about their children.

For example, he's more eager and she's more reluctant about sex. Both love lavish parties for business associates yet have polite and somewhat boring evenings for old friends and family. Both eagerly await a new movie and are usually disappointed with the ending or bored halfway through. Both are so careful not to spoil their children, they are distant, proper and stern, maybe even cold.

These are consequences of *beliefs* about experience, not just the consequences of experience. Therefore, the truth can now be told: love something as much as you want now—that can't ruin it for later. You may or may not love it the same way in the future but it won't be because you loved it too much or too little now.

If you don't love something now as much as you think you might in the future, so what? If you do, it won't be because your appreciation "grew"! What will happen then? Simple. You will always appreciate and love anything you want to. You will love it differently, not better or worse. I love you today by writing to you. Tomorrow I might love to meet you. It is still I who loves and you whom I love. We are the same us—we don't grow—love doesn't grow or die.

I am not saying the feelings don't change. They may, but they are all enjoyable.

More experience of you will not make me feel better or worse about you. More experiences are more experiences to enjoy or not. If I do not enjoy the experience you give me today, it does not mean that I will enjoy it more or less if you repeat it. Understanding it better does not in itself mean more or less enjoyment. There will be the truth of the moment, whatever it is. More may be desired or more may not be desired. Time does not make the desirable more or less enjoyable in the getting or losing. Time does not make the undesirable more or less enjoyable in the getting or avoiding. Experience changes no one's feelings. Repetition does not create love or hate. Time creates nothing—it allows creation. Time does nothing, it is the name for what we recreate or newly create.

There is no "work." There is only privilege turned into burden by a belief. There is no growing love for the one thing. There is the joy of new love for new things that the one thing creates or reveals. There is no dying of love for any one thing. There is either new love for new things or there is no love for the new things the old thing creates or reveals.

There is no hate for new revelations just because they are new. They are either desirable as now seen or not. It doesn't matter that the revelation is an old one. It is new to us. It is also sometimes news to us that some knowledge is old.

The newness or oldness in itself affects nothing in our appreciation.

There is no such thing as not liking what we want. There is only the belief that these are the facts of life.

Belief—"Some things that we want are no fun!"

Truth—"The above belief is merely a belief." This truth (belief) is unquestionable and unsurpassable unless the above belief is true (even for those who don't believe it).

All unhappiness is the fear that you "know" to (that is, want to) do other than what you are doing and wanting.

This is what was meant by sin and evil. It is impossible to want to do something you "know" not to do. You do not ever know better than to want what you want. Doubts are questions, not knowing.

On Solitude and Close Relationships

NEITHER closeness nor solitude has much value if they are not satisfying to us in the way *we* want them to be. It is better to not have closeness with most people if it isn't the kind of closeness we enjoy.

We may sometimes be suspicious of our desire for solitude. It is of utmost importance that we don't be suspicious about our desire for the solitary life. A fruitful and satisfying relationship ability can only flow from a person at peace with themselves first—a person who accepts their desire for solitude. It is only from the same kind of approving of whatever we want (in or out of a relationship) that the honest approval (and lack of defensiveness) of all our desires within a possible relationship can be achieved. If we are not unhappy (or worried) about our own desires we can really let someone know who we are, and what we want.

We sometimes feel it is hard to want something we believe is impossible. If we really believed something was impossible, by definition we wouldn't want it. It really isn't hard to want something we think is not probable, if we don't believe it is wrong to want it. Sometimes we think it is "wrong" to want something because we haven't got the slightest idea of how to go about getting it. In that sense it may seem impossible, but what we really mean is, we just don't know how we can justify wanting it since we can't imagine how we will get it. Yet, we want what we want.

We can know about ourselves that we do not have to be unhappy if we don't get what we want. Our job is to want it, not to guarantee it.

Our partners will come from the people who see us as generous. We are rich in many of the things our new friends will want. These may even be things we don't much value—things that we just do naturally—throwaways.

We want to be loved, yes, but only for what we want to be loved for. If we are loved for reasons that we don't think are good enough we won't be satisfied. If we decide that what we want to be loved for is something called "sexual attractiveness" then that may have the closest meaning to "loved for ourselves"; for our own sexuality is something that has a deep, personal meaning to us, and it is a kind of synopsis of how we see our deepest, most secret, and yet most public self. How we see ourselves sexually is how we see ourselves, period.

Our happiness and our "sexuality" are, in a way, one and the same. Sexuality is a phenomenon of unspoken joy of the heart for the earth; manifested in our eyes, our movements, our ambition and our tone of voice. It is seen in our confidence, in our desires, without apology. We can want what we want without apology, put ourselves behind our desires—wholeheartedly—without apology. They are ours, and that's just the way we want it—without apology.

Nothing is emotionally "difficult." Nothing is hard in this life, except unhappiness and fear. Everything else is what *we* want to do, or *not* what *we* want to do.

What I Do, Alone, Is My Doing Alone

August 25, 1975

WHAT I do, alone, is my doing alone. What you do, alone, is your doing alone. What we do together is everything.

When I love you, it is my love, my very own. When you love me, it is your love, your very own. When we love together, it is God's love.

Our loves were first manifested individually, when our united love was first known by us; even though it was not yet existing or real, we knew we wanted to create it. We foresaw the possible and were captivated by it. We called this "seeing God, knowing Perfect Happiness."

SECTION V

General Relationships

I Can Want You to Want Something

August 1976

I CAN want you to want something. I can want you to be a certain way.

My wanting is not relevant to your wanting. You can only also want it, or not.

If you believe you "don't want to want it" or would "hate to want it," you are thinking that "wanting it" would really be a situation where you would be doing it and not loving it. What you really mean by "don't want to want" or "hate to want" is believing you *need* to not want it to avoid unhappiness.

You don't want to need anything or need to be any way in particular. Need means you believe you would be unhappy if it was taken from you. Do you believe that?

Unhappiness is depriving yourself of what you can do for you, and depriving yourself of how you'd love to be, for no good reason other than you believe you'll be unhappy if you don't deprive yourself.

In this case, you are depriving yourself by believing you don't want to want something because you don't want to need to have it. That is the same as already believing you need it. You are, in effect, deprived of it now and unhappy now because you don't have what you want.

You cannot know happiness if you are against anything that you believe right now you could want some day. If you are against something you believe you could want some day, you are *needing* to not want something; and even though you may or may not want it now or ever, you are afraid you will "want" it—but really, you are afraid you will *need* it.

To be afraid you will need something, to try to avoid needing (which you sometimes call "wanting"), is to believe that you need something to be and feel the way you want, which is happy.

You are afraid that you may need what I want from you.

I want something from you, but not if you don't want it for yourself. I want *you* to want it. I don't want it from you if you don't want it for yourself. I am not wanting to get it from you if you don't want to give it to me.

You see that I want *you* to want it. And the reflection brings up the question of whether you want it for yourself.

Asking and Giving

November 30, 1973

I F I don't know or see any reason why my wanting to get something from you will prevent me from having more from you, I will try to get that thing.

I can want something or anything but not necessarily try to get it if I think that it causes me not to get something I want *more* from you, or to get something I am not seeking, For example, if I want $100 from you, and don't foresee that your giving me that $100 prevents me from getting another $200, then I will try to get it. If I foresee that you will resent my wanting it and will not give it, I will not try to get it.

If you feel guilty about not wanting to give what you want because you are afraid not to, I can bail you out of feeling guilty by saying "I don't want it. Thank you for the thought." I do not have to be afraid that I am lying and denying what I want. I want it, but I more want it freely. I am not saying I never wanted it and never will want it again under any circumstances; just that right now, under these circumstances that you are creating, although the object or action would be nice, or is attractive, I really would rather not have it because I would not want to pay the price of your resentment and guilt, which leads to your avoiding me and not giving me other things that I want.

If I give you a kind of permission not to feel that I need it and show you that I don't need it, that would be true. There is really no denying that I wouldn't want it and that it isn't good for me. If, for now, you want to believe that because I don't seem to want it, I *really* don't want it, that is your interpretation. You need to believe that it is okay for you not to want it and as a justification you can use my permission as an excuse not to feel bad about not giving me what I want, or what you want, or what you think I want, or what you think you want.

It is not my fault if your happiness depends on my permissions. I don't want that.

When Two People Have the Same Experience

Two people experience the same awareness, instinct, feeling, or belief (almost simultaneously).

It feels like knowing what the other person is believing, etc.

Sometimes they think they know that I am unhappy.

Sometimes I think I know that they are unhappy.

Sometimes we both feel we are both unhappy.

Sometimes it seems to them that they are just unhappy themselves, but it turns out that I was feeling similarly.

When someone and I experience the same belief, does it come from me, them, both, elsewhere, or does it matter?

Are we experiencing the same wanting, the same dream, ideal, etcetera?

Are we acting on our wanting independently?

Fearing the Attitudes of Others
June 29, 1979

WE do not fear real things or real events. What we fear are illusions or an illusion. Since it is merely an illusion, there is nothing to fear or hate.

To hate unhappiness is not to feel hatred as if there was something
to hate. The true relationship to unhappiness is to have nothing to
do with it (no respect for it, no interest in it, no use for it, no value
for it), because it is nothing but an unhappy person's view and reaction to an illusion.

Unhappiness makes statements, has views, does actions that are
related to illusions. Unhappiness fears what cannot exist. What we
do not want (dis-want) or fear from people is their unhappiness,
their unhappy delusions about the world, about us, about themselves,
about the reality of reality?

But their unhappiness is not contagious, because it is not a reality.
It is a narrow, distorted view of reality. The attitudes and opinions of
others are nothing to fear when they differ from our beliefs, opinions
and attitudes.

When we love another person's attitudes, it is because it is another
form of our own. "We love it" means we recognize our own view,
which we don't merely love or approve of: we live it, we are it.

When we fear or hate other attitudes, it is because we believe it is
a distorted form of our own beliefs, or no form of our own beliefs.
In short, we fear or hate because we don't want to agree with it. We
dislike a belief not merely because we do not agree with it but we do
not want to agree (as if we could be made to).

What is the sense of disagreeing with another attitude? What
is really happening is that your own beliefs recognize that certain
attitudes are foreign or contrary to yours. They are not yours. That
is all. That is everything. There is nothing to agree with. There is
nothing to disagree with. Why? Because you believe that the other

belief is a distortion of reality or based on a distortion or illusion. Because you believe it is nothing.

When a person brings news that you will or will not believe, your emotional reaction is not to the news but to the views.

For example, news about killing. You may find all these views, and concomitant emotional reactions:

1. People are being killed by people,
2. People are being horribly killed by horrible people,
3. Horrible people are being horribly killed as they deserve by courageous people,
4. Horrible people are being humanely exterminated by honest but misguided people,
5. Misguided people are being efficiently dispensed of by right-minded people for their own good,
6. Stupid people are being massacred by savage people,
7. Innocent people are being humanely dispensed of by honest but misguided people,
8. Innocent people are being efficiently exterminated by selfish desperate people,
9. Something not really human was annihilated.
10. Something not really human was annihilated for its own good.
11. Something not really human was annihilated for your good.
12. Something not really human was annihilated for another person's good, and
13. I will tell you what you should believe.

Enjoying Differences
March 24, 1977

IT is not necessary to understand why a person is different than you or others (or vice versa). It is not even necessary to know *how* they are different or to what extent they are different or *if* they are different.

The differences that are relevant will all be experienced the same way: namely, the other will not give or offer what you want or will not respond the way you want. The differences will be experienced simply as not getting what you expected or desired from another. They may not theoretically be different from you in any other way.

Other differences may be experienced as your being given or offered what is desirable to you before you were aware of the desire. The differences are all distilled, as you are given more or less than you desired. You are given "other" than what you want or expect. You will either enjoy the experience or you will not. You may be different in that way.

If another is different from you, then so are you from them.

The experience of yourself as different may be desirable or undesirable as you focus on the difference.

You may like that you are not like them or not like (dislike) that they are not like you.

You may like that they are not like you, without disliking that you are not like them.

You may like that they are like you want to be, and experience it as liking yourself for the desire to change. This can be experienced as "I like being that way too. In some way I have been like that. I shall expand the ways to be that way." Or, you can dislike yourself for not having been that way and wish you could and feel bad that you will not.

When it is experienced as "That is the way I have been wanting to be, but have only just realized (believed) how desirable it is, and possible," that is a happy experience. "I never knew how nice it could be for me or I would have wanted it before," is, of course, the only true reason why we now want to be different.

On Being Special

Monday Night Study Group, 1973

For some of you, there is something uncomfortable with the idea of being special, or of being into something special.

Maybe people have made idols out of things such as The Option Method, and they have worshipped their institutions and they have worshipped their movements. And all of those movements that they worship, they worship them *in order* to have some peace or some happiness in themselves. To be aware that you have something valuable to yourself, and to acknowledge that, is just to say what you know is so.

On the other hand, some of you fear being common. You've got certain fears that, for instance, to form a group, to be close to something, to love, to really get in touch, all is bad somehow because it makes you like the rest. To avoid things that others use, to not use certain things because others are using them badly or wrongly, to shy away from everything just because it seems idolatrous and religious and institutionalized is to sell yourself short. When you are depriving yourself, you are simply depriving yourself.

How can you help someone else to be happier if you can't make the assumption that it might be possible? What makes you special is your hope that people can be happier. You have a hope that others do not dare to have—not all others, but most others. Many others do not even dare to hope, that maybe to be really happy in all things is really possible. I want to point out to you that that is special—to help you stay in touch with it, so that you can use each other more, so that you can love each other more. Sometimes that isn't a truth that we allow ourselves to know, that it's special. How many of us can really say that we really, really know the value of wanting to be happy, and being happy, all the time? Of wanting to be happy and being happy, and how do you use it? How many of us really help ourselves as often as we might to be happier? It's neither modest nor immodest somehow to be aware of your specialness. It would only be a problem if your specialness functioned somehow to delude you into thinking that you are better than others.

When there is a certain arrogance about others, or a certain lack of understanding for other people, and a putting down of others, you cannot help. If you help others to see what they are not seeing, that is a very special role, and to excel at that enables you to get touch with something. You could see yourself as a servant of others, and that for some reason you have been put in charge of the warehouse and they are coming to you. That doesn't make you the owner of the warehouse or anything better than anybody else; but if you have gotten things that others want, you can dispense them, but you cannot dispense them unless you are aware that you are standing at the gate of the warehouse that contains what others want.

COMMENTARIES

by Aryeh Nielsen on

"Relationships"

Freedom in Relation to Others' Wanting

This commentary represents the editor's synthesis of ideas Bruce Di Marsico expressed only in fragments.

Example: Dressing Like Your Parents Want You To

Your parents may desire that you dress a certain way. They want *you* to want to dress that way. They do not value coercion, but rather that you realize how beautiful their taste is.

How does that feel?

The stereotypical child accepts all of their parents' taste on principle. They *need* to want what their parents want them to want, which is to dress like them.

The stereotypical adolescent rejects all of their parents' taste on principle. They *need* to *not* want what their parents want them to want, which is to dress like them.

A happy person might want to dress in the same way their parents want them to dress. They might not.

They might want to dress in the same way their parents want them to dress because they have similar tastes as their parents. They might want to dress in the same way their parents want them to dress because they want to show their parents they care about their parents' taste.

They might not want to dress in the same way their parents want them to dress because they do not have similar tastes as their parents. They might not want to dress in the same way their parents want them to dress because they want to show their parents they are indifferent to their taste.

This is knowing your freedom in relation to others' wanting you to want something. Unhappiness is *needing* to either want what someone else wants you to want, or *needing* to *not* want something because someone else wants you to want it.

PART VI

Believing Yourself

SECTION I

About Believing Yourself

Believing We Need Help to Be Happy

UNHAPPINESS is believing, in practice, that we need (help) to be happy or we need something (i.e., help) to avoid the need feelings or the condition of need.

Unhappiness is the fear of not believing that we need things, in case we are wrong and really *do* need help to not be unhappy. It is believing we may really have needs that need to be satisfied, even though we don't like being that way (i.e., needy).

SECTION II

Self-Creation

People Choose Their Beliefs, Every Belief
1990

People choose what they have hope in. People choose what they have no hope in.

People decide what they want, and they decide what they don't want.

People choose to believe that they can't do something, or can do something.

Pretending and Lying

People choose to lie or tell the truth.

People choose to make believe and say they know what they do not know,

or they choose to admit that they do not know. People choose to make believe and say they don't know that they do know,

or they choose to admit that they do know.

Freedom

People choose what they feel and think about anything. People are free everywhere, and yet choose to believe that they are constrained in their opinions. beliefs, attitudes, decisions, and *options.*

Why Do People Believe Thus?

They choose to believe that they do not choose. In some way they must believe that they would be responsible for something bad if they had to realize that they freely choose. People fear being free because if they were free they would be "too" free and would do evil or something bad.

Consequences

People choose what to forget, and what to remember. This is not wrong, nothing is. There just are consequences. These consequences are not good or bad. Those are also choices of judgment. This is also not wrong, to judge. There are just consequences for that.

Happiness and Unhappiness

The consequences of judging are not good or bad. The consequences are happiness or unhappiness.

People choose what to do, and choose what not to do.

This is not wrong, etcetera.

People choose what to feel emotionally, and choose what not to feel emotionally. This is not wrong, etcetera.

People choose their postures, etcetera.

People choose their mannerisms, etcetera.

People choose their speech, language, inflections, etcetera.

People choose what they learn, etcetera.

People choose their tastes, opinions, attitudes, etcetera.

People choose their superstitions and religions, etcetera.

People choose what they believe is proof of anything, etcetera.

People choose what they believe is relevant and pertinent.

People choose what they think about their lives, their dreams, their memories, their thoughts, affections.

People choose whatever they think about anything.

Fear of Unhappiness

Fearing Unhappiness

The only thing feared is unhappiness. That is all you can fear. Fear means anticipating unhappiness. Fear, as we are using the word, is an emotion: not the desire to avoid, or the decision to avoid, alone, but that along with the belief that if you do not, you will become unhappy.

The Only Thing Feared Is Unhappiness

Unhappiness is believing that something makes you (is making you, or will make you, or has made you) feel or otherwise be (act, think, have emotions, desires, etc.) a way you were not allowed to (or not supposed to) be.

Unhappiness, as we have already seen, means to feel bad. To feel unallowed or undeserving of happiness is the same as feeling you are bad. The reason feeling bad feels bad is because of what we believe about "bad."

Bad, whether it is about us, or about what happens to us, means that we should feel bad. Bad means deserving of punishment. Punishment is anything that can make us, or is supposed to make us, feel unhappy, or that we are bad.

For punishment (*poenis* in Latin means pain) to work as punishment, it must convince us that we don't deserve to feel good or be happy. It must be convincing that we deserve to be in pain or unhappy. We must feel bad. If not, then it is not punishment.

People get unhappy when they don't *get* what they want, because, in a sense, they feel they are being punished; even if they don't know why.

Unhappiness
  is believing
      that something (even you)
proves you are (makes you feel or be)
    a way
        you should not be,
        (which is bad for you, which means it makes you bad)
and deserving of feeling bad.

"Bad for you" means you will have to *feel* that because of what was "bad for you," you cannot feel the way you would like to feel. It also has the meaning that you cannot be the way you are supposed to be.

SECTION III

Being Allowed

All People Are Allowed to Be Happy at All Times

January 26, 1991

ALL people are allowed to be happy at all times, forever.

This is happiness; to know you are always allowed to be happy no matter who you are, what you do and no matter what happens to you.

All people have the right to be happy.
Those who know it are happy forever.

Happiness is being allowed to be happy.
To be born is to be allowed to be happy.

Happiness is not fearing you will have no right to be happy.
Happiness is not believing you should be unhappy.
Happiness is not believing you have to be unhappy.

It is evident:
God permits you to be happy no matter what or when.
Nature permits you to be happy no matter what or when.
The only permission you need is yours to be happy all the time.
You don't have to deny your happiness ever. It is not wrong to be happy always. It is merely believed to be wrong.

Allowed to Be

You, and Everyone Else, Are Absolutely Innocent,
and Completely Forgiven for Everything.

Let's make it simple.

Whatever you have been, considering what you believed, and how you perceived things, you were being the way you were supposed to be. You couldn't have been different.

If that helps you to understand your life, it is because it is true.

If that feels relieving, or like forgiveness, that is because it is true.

True forgiveness is knowing that there is nothing to forgive. There is no evil, and there was never anything that wasn't supposed to be, or was not allowed.

Let's keep it simple.

You have always been what you were supposed to be, and you are now just what you are supposed to be.

You have always been allowed to be exactly what you were, and are now allowed to be exactly what you are.

Whatever you are going to be is what you will be supposed to be.

The above is true and nothing can prove it isn't. Whatever befalls you cannot prove the impossible. You are, no matter what happens, exactly what you should be. Just because you don't get what you want doesn't mean you were not the way you should have been. Nature doesn't punish you for not being what you should have been. God, or Nature, or the Universe of reality cannot have such insane concepts. To make a joke: Nature does not speak in human language, so therefore cannot make the play on words that unhappiness demands. "You are not what you would have been if you were not the way you were."

The correct meaning of *should be, needs to be,* and similar concepts means that whatever is, is caused by what necessarily causes it.

Saying that you are "allowed" to be the way you are might not seem so good. Sometimes being allowed seems to mean merely allowed, and that is not good enough for us. We worry that being allowed is like being tolerated in our wrongness, as in "just for today, everyone is allowed to behave badly."

Because you may think that way, I will clarify.

You are not being allowed to be bad, because it is impossible to "be" bad. It is possible to try to believe, and you are allowed to try to believe, that you are bad, and you are allowed to spoil your appreciation of all that you are. That is possible.

Remember, to believe that you are bad is to believe that you are not allowed to be what you are, or have been, or will be. You are allowed to believe that, but you are also allowed to know that it isn't true.

You are the allower of yourself. That is the way it is supposed to be. That is the way it has to be. As we said, if "supposed to" or "ought to" or "should"' has any real meaning, it means "must of necessity." Well, you *are* the allower of all you do, and that is the way it is. You allow. You must do the permitting. That is the way it really is, and the only way it can be.

You can't be bad, and you are the one who has to allow yourself to know that. If you don't, that doesn't make you bad, but you will feel that you are.

Let's try again to make it simple.

When you are unhappy you are believing you are a way—or you feel, or you think, etc. a way—that you shouldn't, or even a way that you don't want.

You can't think or feel a way you don't want. You can believe that you can. That believing feels like a feeling that you wouldn't want. Who would want to feel that they feel a way they don't want? That's unhappiness. You want to feel bad when you believe that you have to feel a way you don't want. Even though that never happens, believing it does feel bad.

You cannot be a way that isn't you. Period. No matter what anybody says.

Simply:

You always did what you wanted.
You are now doing what you want.
You always will do only what you want.

SECTION IV

Your Feelings

You Don't Want to Feel Bad

You are allowed to do anything, be anything, feel anything, think anything, but no matter what it is, it will always be you and what you wanted to be. You don't want to feel bad about it. In fact, you don't want to ever feel bad. You just have not always believed this about yourself. You, indeed, don't want to feel bad.

Can this truth about yourself help you to never be unhappy?

Sure! Just know this:

You don't want to feel bad.

You have believed you did. You have believed that it was "good" to feel bad. That's all.

You thought you wanted to feel bad. You thought that was really what you wanted. Here's why. It was so much of what you believed was naturally you; you believed you had to be that way: the way you wanted. The things you "had" to feel bad about were things you *believed* you had to feel bad about because that was being true to who you believed you were. You believed that was "good."

What you never realized was that:

You don't like to feel bad means you don't really want to feel bad.

You don't want to believe you're bad.

You don't want to believe you are the way you shouldn't be.

You thought it was right and good to feel bad, and you always want what is right and good. You thought you were being what you shouldn't have been, or something was happening that shouldn't have been happening, so you wanted to feel bad.

Feeling bad is believing that you (or something) are being a way you (or it) shouldn't be for you.

You, everyone, and everything are exactly what should be for you. You were wrong when you felt otherwise. That's all. If you want it different, then want it different. It is not what it should not be. It's just a way you don't want. You need not feel different about it. You are allowed to not want anything; anything at all. Just because something is, doesn't mean it has to be wanted by you. Let those who want it do so. You don't.

Wouldn't it be true to say:

You now don't want to feel bad?

You don't want to believe you have to feel bad if it isn't true, do you?

Since it is impossible for you or anyone or anything to be bad, it follows that it would be impossible to feel bad.

Could it be you are believing it is possible to feel bad just like you used to believe it was possible to be bad? Are you believing that feeling bad is another way of being bad?

Could it be that if you have a feeling you call "bad" it is because you are believing you could want to feel bad, or could need to feel bad? Do you believe you deserve to?

You only need to know something. The truth is that you don't any longer want to feel bad about anything. You don't believe feeling bad shows the truth of anything. Besides the fact that you don't want to feel bad, no feelings are "bad," or shouldn't be.

You have been believing (feeling) that you should feel a certain way (unhappy), and now may realize that you believed you wanted that feeling, and now you don't want it anymore. It's not "bad" to feel bad in either case.

Feeling bad about feeling bad, or feeling that feeling bad is bad, is no more than doing what you did to feel bad in the first place. You are believing that something that has a perfect truth (a reason or cause) in being should not be, and is bad for your happiness. When we believe that something is bad for our happiness, we *must of necessity* feel bad about it.

Feeling bad is not bad for future happiness. Feeling bad cannot cause any further feeling bad. Fear of it does. It could be over immediately.

If you know, or believe, or decide that you don't value and don't want to feel bad, then *you can't* any longer. It is over. Whatsoever you then feel, it is not bad. Now what do you feel? *That* is the truth.

A Simple Option Method

Is what you are feeling okay?

Even if you don't feel very happy, is what you are feeling something you want to be, or deserve to be, unhappy about?

Decide! Know yourself! What is *the* truth? Realize that you only want to *be* happy, and at least not unhappy, about the way you feel or don't feel.

Now, is it you? The truth!

For whatever cause you feel what you feel, it is not bad, is it? It's okay with you, isn't it?

We Are Here for Happiness

Our only issue here is happiness.

Our only questions here are about unhappiness.

Our only answers here are about happiness.

Whenever you ask yourself the question, "Why are you unhappy?" and answer it, "I am not" and ask yourself the question, "What can you become unhappy about?" and answer it "I can't be unhappy," then unhappiness is no longer the question.

Then you will know what other questions there are.

Do you believe you are not very good at being happy? Do you believe it takes practice?

Are you allowed to be happier than you are now? Do you believe you will be?

PART VII

Forms of Unhappiness

SECTION I

About Forms of Unhappiness

Unhappy Motivation
Monday Night Study Group, 1973

U NHAPPINESS can make the goal impossible, especially if the goal is happiness . . . and since the goal is happiness, unhappiness makes it absolutely impossible.

But unhappiness also makes all those things impossible that call for ease of body, that call for relaxedness, that call for lack of tension, that call for clear thinking.

Many do not let themselves want, but believe they must first ascertain if they're able to achieve what they want. There is no problem in wanting to estimate your probability of success; happy people might want to do that too. But when we're unhappy, why do we want to estimate our probability of success? The person who predicts that they'll be unhappy if they do not achieve what they want, they'll be in a position of saying to themselves, "Well, if I can't get what I want, I don't dare want," and so can't now decide whether they really want it or not until they know whether they can get it.

Many things can't be gotten unless you want them, such as personality states, and if we insist that we be guaranteed getting them, we are doomed before we even start.

So the problem is not in wanting to estimate the probabilities of success. I want to repeat that. Both happy and unhappy people do that. But the unhappy person wants to estimate for a reason, which is something like, "If I don't get it I'll be unhappy, and if I'm going to be unhappy I better not even want it." Wanting leads to unhappiness, with this belief.

If we hedge it on the condition of getting what we want, we wouldn't even efficiently estimate whether we can get it or not because now we're thinking through fear and out of fear, and out of, "If I don't get it I'll be unhappy. Oh boy, I better make sure I can get it before I can even let myself want it." And that becomes a big game because you wouldn't even want to estimate unless you've already decided that you wanted it somehow on some level.

If we don't freely want, we will not even begin anything. After a while we'll get to see ourselves as people who do not want to get, and that only leaves us with a sense of deprivation, a sense of stupidity, and a sense of paralysis. The antidote is obvious: if we are willing to want before we even know whether we will get it or not—in other words by not fearing not getting, but not needing to get—then we can increase our wanting, increase the probability of having it, increase the chances of success, increase our estimation abilities, increase our happiness. If we can want without even knowing whether we're going to get, we'll be happier. Unhappiness is only to help us to do that.

So if we make our happiness contingent on getting, we wouldn't even allow ourselves to want, we couldn't even begin wanting. And if you can't want, you can't get.

Let's say, for instance, you're screwing a screw into a hole, which depends on a certain competence and skill of your own. If your fear is that if you don't do it you'll be unhappy, that has to destroy wanting, it has to increase the fear of not doing it. If screwing it depends on any kind of calmness in the hand, any kind of relaxedness at all, that won't be possible. If you increase your fear of not succeeding even more in any way, you won't even begin to pick up the screwdriver. You can so destroy wanting that you don't want to screw in the screw! You start off by wanting and wind up not wanting, not being able to move, which now leads you to see yourself as somebody who doesn't do what they want to do, which is a very hopeless feeling. It leads to tremendous depression.

"I can't even want what I want," becomes our feeling. "I'm afraid that I really don't want what I do want and I see myself not doing what I want to do." And I guess all of us could write a list of things that we say we want to do and don't do. And if we look very closely we'll see that this is the phenomenon that is taking place behind it, because we've already set it up that if we don't do it we'll be unhappy, and that's why we won't do it, why we can't even begin to do it.

Fear of Being Stupid

If, after wanting to learn, you began feeling, "I'll be unhappy if I don't learn," forget it. That's the end of it. You will not learn. To whatever degree you need to learn, to that degree you will never learn.

The more you believe you *need* to learn, the less you learn. The most "stupid people" that you'll ever meet are the ones that really think thinking is tremendously important. We might make the mistaken guess of saying, "the reason they think thinking clearly is so important is because they're stupid." No, it's the other way around. They are stupid because they think thinking clearly is so important. And by "so important" I mean something to be unhappy about if we don't achieve it.

If it's really okay not to think clearly, we can let ourselves still know that we want to think clearly, and thinking is one of those processes that just by wanting it makes it so. If you do anything more or less than want it, it becomes impossible. If you began with the belief that it's possible for me not to think . . . that's it. That's not wanting it, because if it's possible for me not to think, then I can begin to be afraid of doing that. You can't really then be in touch with wanting to do it because you're really into the fear of not doing it.

Now, how can you extinguish the fear of not thinking? By thinking or not thinking, which is it? And you're faced with one of those two ways. The only way you can extinguish the fear of not thinking is by not thinking further. We can overcome that whole phenomenon of fearing being unable to think by knowing that even if, perchance, for some reason you couldn't think, it wasn't for lack of *wanting* to think. If the reason you couldn't think was because there was something chemical going on or electrical going on, you'd never be upset about it. People who really have brain dysfunction are not upset that they have brain dysfunction. You can only be upset about not being able to think clearly when you think you are the cause of it or you know you are.

So if a person had the confidence that, "I may not think of some things, I may not understand what I'm about to hear, I may not comprehend it at all but that won't be for my lack of wanting to," they can really be okay, because the only reason that the fear is there is to increase their wanting. The only reason that the fear is there is to affirm to themselves that they really do want to learn. So they would be fine if they could stick with, "I really do want to understand, and there's no reason that I won't learn insofar as it's within my power as long as I keep wanting to." If it's not within their power, all the worrying and fearing in the world is not going to change anything.

More Examples of Unhappy Motivation

Consider anger, depression, jealousy—most of the personality traits we have that we make judgments on. If we fear our own personality traits, whatever they may be, we intensify them. The angriest person you've ever met is the person who hates anger most. Again, we may make the mistake of assuming, "Oh, the reason they hate anger so much is because they're so angry all the time." No, it's the other way around. The reason they're so angry all the time is because they hate anger so much, because they need to not be angry. And they just absolutely hate themselves for being angry. Who is angrier except people who hate themselves, and hate their anger?

And yet such a person believes that it might be possible for themselves, and that it's possible for everybody else, to not to be so angry, and will ask "How come I'm so angry?" If he gets angry enough at himself and hates himself enough, maybe he won't be angry; but that's the cause of anger: self-hate. The most angry person is most angry because they hate anger the most. They're most judgmental about anger. We very frequently get into that, trying to root out what we call so-called personality defects. We've got this tremendous system that points to certain kinds of behavior as being defects or wrong or bad. And they really don't do anything to anybody, but somehow we've gotten to believe that they're wrong because we hope to use that to stop ourselves. Instead of wanting, we're using fear as the motivation.

We get all the symptoms from fear, expressions of our having lived with fear: headaches, stomachaches, anger, bad temper, bad smell, whatever. When we go to root them out, we use the same technique again: fear of them, anger at them, hatred of them, dislike or disapproval of those things, judgments upon them. So for instance, as stupidity is from fear, when we try to root out stupidity with more fear, we only wind up being more stupid. When anger is from fear, we try to root out the anger with more anger; we end up more angry with more fear. It's as if we were using an immunization technique that doesn't work. It's like in order to cure cancer you get more of it, in order to cure tuberculosis you get more of it. "I'll show myself. That'll stop me."

And so all of these things that have to do with your own person-alities, no one of you will be more destined to fail than whichever one of you is the most into a self-improvement project. And any of you who have any idea of improving yourselves has got to be the one most destined to fail, because that word "improvement," in this context, is loaded with disapproval, loaded with the concept of fear.

That's why diets don't work. People on diets can't get into wanting, they're always into fearing and the cause of their eating is fear, and so they always want to console themselves. So they make themselves feel bad about going off the diet, then they go on a binge to console themselves. Now they feel so bad that they failed on the diet that day. Say they were on a diet, they're losing weight; now one day they felt bad and their symptom of feeling bad is to eat, that's the way they express their fear and console themselves. So a dieter will have an extra piece of cake or a piece of pie or a sundae or whatever. Now she went and did that: "Oh, no!" She did that out of unhappiness, and now she becomes unhappy that she did that, because she's off her diet. She becomes so depressed: "Forget the diet!" The diet now only becomes an occasion for failure; the diet now only becomes another thing by which she can fail and feel bad about. "I'll go on it again next week, starting next Monday," and so she goes on a binge again.

Now the person who can succeed on a diet is when they go off a diet knowing, "I did that because I felt bad; I did that because I was unhappy," and stands up, brushes themselves off, and goes right back to their diet. They'll succeed. But a person who tries to counteract their so-called failing on a diet with more fear won't succeed. And so the average fat person that you've met will tell you that they've lost thousands of pounds in their life. It's an on-again-off-again type of thing, because their motive and their way of using it has been the very same thing that's always caused their gaining weight: fear, disapproval.

Wanting without Knowing the Outcome

So we can increase our wanting if we'll just be willing to want before we even know what the outcome is going to be. Let's want it first, then estimate it, then see if it's possible, then see if we want to go through all the trouble that it may take. Let's see if we then want the intermediate steps. But first, let us get in touch with wanting, and in doing that we can clear all the middle ground, and we can properly evaluate it for ourselves, and we can really be in touch with what we might want more. And then our life can be, "I want this, but I want that more." And there's no sense of deprivation, there's no sense of failure. There's no sense of never having been what you wanted.

Say I want to learn the piano by this time next year. What will I need to do to get to that? Now you could begin with, "Well, I don't know. Let's just try now and learn the piano." Fine, in a short while you'll begin to see that you're not making too much progress unless you give it a little more time. And the question immediately comes up, "Do I want to spend more time practicing the piano or do I want to spend more time doing other things that I like?" That sets up this kind of a process of choosing, "What do I want more?" That is going to be determined by another ultimate goal. And so, you're not going to be able to make that decision unless you get in touch with an ultimate goal and compare them. And in each way the ultimate goal that's the more "important one" is the one that'll win regardless of the intermediate steps that might be involved.

I want to learn the piano by next year and in order to do that I find that I'll have to practice more. But by practicing more I'm going to work less hours, I'll have to take some time off work or find a job that takes less time or cut down on my social life or something like that. Let's say it means I'm just going to have to work fewer hours.

And then I start making the decision, "What do I want to work for and what do I want to learn the piano for?" Whatever's behind each of them have now come into conflict, have now become a question. And I haven't thought about it really, why I wanted to work and why I wanted to play the piano. But now that's it's going to be a tradeoff, whatever it is that I want to play the piano for is now in conflict with whatever it is I want to work for. And I just compare the two of them and the one that's more important to me, or the one that I want more, determines my choice. And I want to play the piano more because it'll make me more popular at parties and give me greater love. And I want to work more because it'll give me more money and enable me to throw nicer parties.

Okay, now you still haven't done it. So you go to the next step: what makes a nicer party, playing the piano or having more money? And whichever it is that you're finding is more important is going to be the choice for you.

The Names of Unhappiness

September 21, 1975

WHEN the world becomes perfect,
When you become perfect,
When you go to heaven,
When God comes to earth,

Everyone will know something they never knew,
You will believe something you never believed:

You will realize and
God will let you become aware that

Nothing can make anyone unhappy.
Nothing can make you unhappy.
Nothing and no one has the power to
Make you feel bad (i.e., make you make yourself unhappy),
Judge bad (i.e., make you see things as unhappy),
Want bad (i.e., make you want something that can cause
     unhappiness),
Be bad (i.e., make you be a cause of another' s unhappiness).

Unhappiness has only been a belief in a power that does not
     exist.
There is no power in the universe to make you
Want what you don't want,
Believe what you don't choose to believe,
Know other than what you choose to know.

There is the power of happiness, truth, God
To enlighten, expose, manifest
What you really do know,

What you really do believe,
What you really do want,
What power you really have,
What you really do.

The truth is,
No one can make you believe that you can cause unhappiness.

The truth is,
It only looks that way to people (and you)
If they believe they have the power to make unhappiness.

Unhappiness goes by many names:

Theology: The Devil, Divine Justice, Hell,
Professional Psychology: Neurosis, Psychosis, Aberrations,
    Deviance
Medicine: Psychosomatic Illness, Disease
Folk Psychology: Feel bad, doing what one doesn't want,
    believing what one doesn't want to believe, acting in a
    way one doesn't really want, believing in the ability to
    cause others to experience the above.

You can't make anyone believe that they have to be unhappy.

You could give them the opportunity to expose their belief that
they could make you believe that *you* have to be unhappy.

You cannot make unhappiness be. Others may believe that you
are mistaken about this. They believe this is a delusion of yours.

You can't make unhappiness *be*, and any contradiction or manifestation of other than this is merely and simply an erroneous, superstitious belief.

SECTION II

Flavors of Unhappiness

Fear Itself Is Often Worse
than What Is Feared

WHAT happens with anybody who has a fear? They frequently rush headlong into that fear to undo it. The fear of death is much worse than death itself. No problems are ever really solved by fear—not personal problems, not emotional problems. It's very much like the child with the bad report card. They'll come home and confess, rather than live with all the fear of what will happen if you eventually find out. Compulsive "addicts" (gamblers, "alcoholics," "kleptomaniacs," etc.), compulsively play out their addiction just so he can get rid of the fear they are going to do their "addiction." Because one of the things that happens after you do your addiction is that you don't feel like doing it again. A compulsive addict is not desiring to do their addiction, but is desiring to be *rid* of the desire to gamble, drink, steal, etc., and the best way to be rid of the desire to do it is to do it.

Or take a kid who steals. He steals compulsively, telling me his reason for stealing was that he feels so bad when he realizes that he's stolen something. He believes that if he can feel bad enough, he'll stop stealing.

When he steals, he removes his desire to steal. But the desire to steal, in the first place, came from feeling horrible, and the feeling of guilt that comes after is almost a relief: "I feel terribly guilty but I'm glad that I feel guilty about it and that I don't want it anymore." Until they desire to steal again in response to feeling so bad.

For instance, take compulsive drinkers. Drinking was a way of feeling good that applied very much to their problem, which might have *not* been feeling good. Not feeling loved, not feeling deserving of any pleasure. Very frequently they don't have a single moment of peace or happiness in their whole day, except when they drink. The fear becomes that that's going to be all the pleasure they're going to have. The drinking becomes an escape from feeling bad. That, in itself, is something to be feared.

It's coming from unhappiness. Every compulsive drinker, if no one ever told them that it was dirty, if no one every told them that it was wrong, would make it wrong. Guilt only exists in our society because it exists in us, as individuals. And it doesn't come from the society. That is just simply a myth. We create guilt every time that we notice any behavior that comes from unhappiness.

So anything that we've ever done or ever do that comes from unhappiness that we do because we're unhappy, we feel guilty about. And so now, the person saw that this was a relief, something they did from their unhappiness that felt good. They didn't want to feel good about feeling good this way. What they really wanted to be was a happier person. Every drinker I've ever talked to said that what they really wanted was to deal with what was making them unhappy, and if they drank, they would have no need to deal with what made them unhappy. "If I could always make myself feel good this way, why should I deal with what made me unhappy?" That was the fear. What helped them was if they could see that they could drink and also not forget that they were unhappy. And as soon as they didn't forget that they had problems, they immediately stopped feeling guilty about drinking, and drinking frequently diminished quite considerably. And when they did drink, they would enjoy it much more.

Fear

June 27, 1977

UNHAPPINESS is the fear:
I may be against what I love (my happiness). Some or all that I want is what I suspect only a person who is destined to destroy their own happiness would want. I need what I want in order to stop feeling that I wanted it because I was bad; or if I get it, it proves I was "right," not crazy or self-defeating to want it.

I suspect that in this case what I want would only be wanted by me if I was out to destroy myself, my happiness, what I truly love, my dreams, other real desires, etc.

Corollary: I believe that what is happening to me or has happened or may be about to happen to me (some undesirable event) would only happen to me if I have been motivated by some inner self-destructive desire or force.

Or:

What happens to me proves whether I am motivated towards (really desiring) my unhappiness or not.

I need what I want to stop feeling (believing I am) bad for wanting it.

This belief is what can make a person hate what they love, fear what they want, seem self-destructive to themselves, angry, depressed, distrustful of feeling good and all the behavior that comes from this. They are against themselves *now*.

To hate or fear what another wants is a protest to make sure *we* don't ever want that thing which we believe would destroy *us*.

Guilt

GUILT is feeling bad about feeling good when you thought you were supposed to feel bad. We don't want feeling bad to lead to anything that feels good. We don't want bad feelings in us to lead to something productive or lead to something good. We don't want to reward our bad feelings. Drinking can become a reward for bad feelings and an escape from them, and we don't want that so we feel guilty about resorting to that. A person who's guilty will be very depriving of themselves in many ways. The whole idea of feeling guilty is to not enjoy yourself and to feel guilty about every enjoyment, anything that may come from unhappiness.

People, very frequently, will then fear that they won't deal with their bad feelings, and they won't deal with what originally made them feel bad, and that they won't make themselves feel better, except by a particular method, and that method becomes an addiction. The more I believe that alcohol is the only way that I'm going to feel good, the more I'm going to hate the fact that I drink. The more I hate the fact that I drink, the more I'm going to fear it. The more I fear it, the more I'm going to desire it, the more I'm going to drink. Nobody hates booze more than an alcoholic. They *want* to feel bad about feeling good.

And the addiction becomes secret behavior. The big cesspool becomes sex. That's the thing everybody does behind a door with three locks. Nothing kills sex worse than somebody knocking on the door. Have you ever noticed that people who supposedly think that sex is beautiful, sex is wonderful, sex is all kinds of great things, but when somebody knocks on the door while they're having sex— they're not so sure!

Example: Guilty about Coming On to Pretty Women

There's a man. Every morning he's standing at the train station and watching the pretty girls go by. Sometimes he'll make a derogatory remark and sometimes he won't. But he feels like he's got to do this and he feels terrible about himself. He believes that somebody who has everything on the ball, like him, shouldn't have to do this. And yet he's doing it.

"I shouldn't have to do this. There should be another way for me to feel good. I disapprove of the way that I'm taking to feel good." Feeling bad about feeling good about feeling bad.

Look, for some reason he's doing this in order to feel good. What's so horrible about that? He's hoping that the worse he feels about it, the better he is, he'll stop. Why does he want to stop? Because he's recognizing that somehow he's doing that to feel good instead of what he really could be doing to feel good, which is—to just feel good! Well, the problem is that he insists on feeling bad about something in the first place. And rather than give up feeling bad about that, he resorts to some other things to make himself feel good.

It makes him feel good to be derogatory toward pretty women. He doesn't like that he needs that. But he is believing that he needs something in order to be happy, for instance, that pretty women are only out to get him. And he feels he can't stop believing that because if he did, what protection would he have?

On Anxiety

March 6, 1991

A NXIETY is an unhappiness not unlike any other.

A sense of bad luck or doom is a ramification of anxiety belief.

Free-floating anxiety is the need to avoid "something" but not knowing what or how.

Anxiety or worry is the kind of fear that one has by believing there is something we need to do or we can't be happy.

The belief that there is something left undone, needing to be attended to, or needing to be fixed is worry; the worry that we will be bad for ourselves if we don't. The "surety" that we will feel bad if we don't do this thing is the cause of the worry. The doubt that we may not do it, which is caused by the feeling that we don't like it or may forget it, intensifies the feeling of anxiety.

The belief that we don't even know what it is, but have to do it anyway, often describes this free-floating anxiety. It is the fear that even if we were to attend to something, that would not be enough. Something has been left undone or something else will still need to be done.

This fear is usually accompanied by the feeling of impending doom or bad luck. It is actually the same fear. The fear that something bad will always be just around the corner is a kind of depression which is being manifested by this anxious belief that we won't or can't do what we have to do to be happy.

Our guilt for not having done what we should have done is the prompter of this fear. If we have already been teaching ourselves that we should feel bad for past negligence and incompetence, we are now ready to promise ourselves that punishment for any future neglect is our expected lot. We are ready to regret something. The anticipation of that regret is called worry or anxiety.

The important question is, of course, "Why do we believe that there is something we must do to be happy?" Why do we believe that we will have to be unhappy if we fail to do some good thing?

Despair

July 31, 1975

THE fear of being crazy is the fear of being unhappy for no reason. Along with it come the feelings of hopelessness and craziness and the fear that no one will notice you need help until it is too late, the fear that you will never ask for help and no help would help anyway.

Unhappiness is the only feeling that must have a *reason* for being, even though it is not real. Even though the only real reason unhappiness exists is in order to not be unhappy, which we would not be if not for having a "reason" to be.

The fear of being unhappy for no reason at all is the reason for despair.

That belief is the belief that you are unhappy about.

We despair in order to prevent the unhappiness we get as a result of trying to prevent unhappiness that never would be, if we were not trying to prevent it.

The Basis for Shame

January 19, 1992

IF you don't demand that people be prettier and more attractive than they are, then you can't be ashamed of yourself. If you don't demand that people be more beautiful, and more virtuous, and more skillful than they are, and be more attracted to you than they are, you can't ever be ashamed—because the only basis for shame is someone telling you that you aren't good enough for them.

Fear of Self-Deception

Often, people are afraid to believe they are special. They believe they are supposed to be afraid of feeling very, very lucky, of feeling very wise, of feeling very enlightened. And they believe that people who think that they know it all are deluded. It's a fear of self-deception.

What was the problem with the man with the diamonds?* Not that he started to believe that they couldn't be diamonds, but that he threw them away. He was thinking, *maybe* they are not diamonds. So why throw them away? Why, "it can't be true?" Instead of throwing things away, people can just hold on to them, find out, explore, enjoy, test.

And so, when people feel special, feel wise, feel enlightened, they could just enjoy, find out, and explore if these are so, instead of rejecting these feelings on the presumption that they could never be that lucky.

---

* Here, Bruce refers to a story of a man who finds many diamonds and, concluding that to find so many diamonds must mean they must not be real, throws the diamonds away.

Fear and Unhappiness
(Sadness and Anger)

THE two forms of unhappiness are myriad forms of sadness and anger. Anxiety (or worry) is fear, another kind of feeling which really is the anticipation of unhappiness (feeling bad). All fear is the fear of feeling bad (unhappy). This is expecting being a way that we will then feel is wrong. It could be expecting to behave in a way we believe will prove we are against ourselves. We could fear being directly self-defeating, like an hysteric. It could be expecting to be treated in a way we believe will prove we are against ourselves. We fear bad luck like a paranoiac. It could be expecting an undesirable event, which is a combination of both the above. It could be the experience or the anticipation of a mysteriously caused, or random, accidental bad luck which, we don't know how, but somehow it does prove we shouldn't have been the way we are.

Paranoia and Hysteria

Paranoia: I might not be able to stop when I want to, because I am feeling like doing it now. I will do things I don't want to because I feel like it. My enthusiasm screws me—I must cool down.

Hysteria: I might not be able to start when I want to, because I don't feel like doing it now. I will not feel like stopping doing things even though I want to. My coolness screws me—I must be more enthusiastic.

> The antidote to paranoia:
> My wanting is good
> My enthusiasm is natural (good)

> The antidote to hysteria:
> My not wanting is good
> My lack of enthusiasm is good (natural)

Both believe that they don't know how to feel other than they are feeling except by feeling bad about how they are feeling—paranoiacs putting down their enthusiasm, and hysterics their coolness—and so paranoiacs play down their enthusiasm, and hysterics force themselves to act more enthusiastic.

These experiences come from trying to do what you can naturally do without trying, just by trusting that what you want is natural.

Why Aren't You Perfectly Happy Already?

For some, there is the feeling that, no matter how far you get, no matter how happy you are, no matter how much you learn, that something somehow is missing, something is wrong. There's some kind of a final hurdle to jump that you're not jumping, some kind of a final door to open that you're not opening—something that would really finally free you to be as happy as you want to be.

All of you and each of you have told me, at one time or another, that you were faced with the dilemma of really wanting to be happier, knowing that you choose your own happiness and yet not being able to account for the fact that you're not happier. You are knowing everything that you'd ever need to know about being unhappy and are still unhappy. Being unhappy and not wanting to be leads many of you to the feeling that there's just something basically wrong with you, which you sometimes express with the feeling, "Well, I guess time will take care of it."

I see in all of you that you really don't believe that time would take care of it. How much time? What more experiences do you need to have that you haven't had? What more time do you need that you haven't already had? What is that one thing lacking? That basic flaw in you? We talked once before about "what's wrong with me." And then you found out that what was wrong with you was that you thought something was wrong with you. And what did you do with that?

Why wasn't that "it"? Why wasn't that the final door, the final key, the final hurdle? Why is it that once you've worked through a belief and you no longer believe that you have anything to be unhappy about, that you'd still be unhappy? And indeed, many of you become unhappy about things that even you know you have no reason to be unhappy about, yet you know the only way to be unhappy is to believe you have a reason to be.

How is it that you could be unhappy, knowing that you don't have a reason to be? You all know that you don't have to be unhappy. That is not even a matter of belief anymore for you. You've experienced it. You know it. You all know that you can only be unhappy when you have reasons to be. And you all know that you don't really have any reasons for being unhappy.

Depression Is Being Scared of Yourself

You know that ultimately you really don't have to be unhappy. We can use a word to describe this phenomenon, this feeling that you all experienced. The word I'll use is a word that's been common. It's been used: Depression. You're all depressed. You've been depressed for a long time. Depression is being unhappy about being unhappy. Depression is being disappointed in yourself for being unhappy, while at the same time you're believing that you really have nothing to be unhappy about.

"I'm unhappy and I have nothing to be unhappy about. Boy, am I unhappy. Boy, am I in trouble. Wow, have I got it bad. I can even be unhappy when I know that I really don't even have a reason to be unhappy. And I know, ultimately, if I were to work it out, I would see that I don't have a reason to be unhappy." Depression is being scared of yourself, when you find that you're feeling bad, and yet realizing that you really have no reason for feeling bad.

Depression is being afraid that you are unhappy when you're not unhappy. You're not unhappy about anything, but when you're afraid that you might be unhappy about something, *then* you're unhappy. It's being afraid of being unhappy, even when you're happy. So that if you're happy, and you try to maintain that happiness by being afraid that you won't be happy or that you're not happy, you're depressed. Depression is being afraid that even though you have no real reason to be unhappy, you still are.

Depression is believing that you are afraid of being happy. Some of you have said what you think the problem is, is that you're afraid of being happy somehow. That's depression. Depression is believing that even though you have no reason to be unhappy, you still will be. Depression is believing and deducing that you must be afraid of something that you know you're not afraid of and have no reason to fear.

You look at yourself and you say, "Gee, I'm feeling a certain way. I'm doing something and I must be afraid. And I have no reason to be afraid." That's depression. You came to the conclusion that you're afraid when you're *not* afraid. And you become afraid of being afraid when you know you're not. And you're faced with a kind of terror that says, "I think I'm happy and I'm really not. I feel good, but I'm really unhappy."

Depression is being afraid that there must be something very wrong with you if you're unhappy, that when you experience yourself as being afraid and knowing that you have no reason to be, you believe that there must be a reason that you can't know, a reason that you'll never find out, a reason, perhaps that isn't really a reason, a cause that you'll never know. A cause that you'll never be able to deal with because "I'm afraid and I know I have no reason to be. I'm unhappy and I know that I have no reason to be." If you believe that, you're depressed.

Depression is being afraid that there is some power inside of you that can make you unhappy even after you have searched and searched and found that you don't have a reason to be unhappy and you really don't believe that there is anything to be unhappy about.

Depression is the only unhappiness. Depression is the only craziness. Depression is the only cause of psychosomatic illness. Depression is the only cause of anger. Depression is the only cause of mania. And depression is really the only cause of not loving others. Depression is believing that you cannot be what, indeed, you would be if you weren't depressed. Depression is fearing or believing that you couldn't be that very thing that you would be, in fact, if you weren't fearing that you couldn't be it.

For example, depression is believing that you cannot enjoy what you would enjoy if you weren't afraid that you couldn't enjoy it. Depression is believing that you cannot learn what you very well would learn if you weren't afraid that you couldn't learn. Depression is believing that you cannot be happy when you would otherwise be happy if you weren't afraid that you couldn't be. I could be as happy as anything until I become afraid that I *couldn't* be as happy as anything.

Depression is deducing and fearing that you must be unhappy when you are not feeling or acting in a way you believe you would if you were happy. That's depression. It's depression if you come to the conclusion, "Gee, I must be unhappy because I'm not physically feeling a certain way or I'm not acting a certain way," that you believe that you would really be acting, would really be feeling, if you were happy. Depression is not letting it be okay to be unhappy, because you fear that if it was okay, you'd be unhappy even if you didn't have a reason; that somehow, if you let it be okay to be unhappy, you'd go ahead and be unhappy even if you never had a reason to be.

And so you use the fear of being unhappy. And that's depression. And that leads to all of these other things that we talked about. Depression is putting someone down for being unhappy. Depression is criticizing somebody for being unhappy. That's depression. Depression is disliking someone who is unhappy. Not being depressed or being happy is knowing that you cannot be unhappy unless you have a very clear reason for being so.

Knowing That You Would Never Choose to Be Unhappy

You cannot be unhappy against your will. You cannot be unhappy accidentally. You cannot be happy for some kind of a vague *je ne sais quoi* ("I know not what"). You cannot be unhappy unless you have a very, very clear, clear reason to be. A reason that you accept. A reason that you believe. A reason that you want. Not being depressed, or being happy, is knowing that you would never choose unhappiness over happiness, unless you believed you had to and believed it was to your benefit.

Depression is believing that you're feeling something that's not to your benefit. Not being depressed, or being happy, is knowing, really knowing that you never, ever have chosen, you never ever have ever become unhappy for no reason. It's knowing that every time you ever became unhappy in the past, it was because you believed it would make you happier. There was never a time in the past that you were unhappy for no reason. You always were unhappy because you believed it would make you happier. Not being depressed, or being happy, is knowing that even depression and all its fears and all its beliefs were something you have been doing in order to be happier.

So depression is believing that if you're afraid enough of feeling bad, you'll be happier. If you're unhappy enough about being unhappy, you'll be happier. Depression is believing that you are and can be unhappy for no reason, even when you don't want to be. Depression is your way of trying to be happier with your awareness that you're not *yet* happier.

If you believe that unhappiness happens for no reason, that you're not happier for no reason and you can get unhappy for no reason, even when you don't want to, "Now I know I want to be happier. and I'm not!" becomes my statement. That means, I can't be what I want to be. Even when I want it. And I get unhappy about that just so that I won't feel so bad. Because by being unhappy about that, I'm not accepting that I want to be happier, and I'm not.

So in a very real way depression is your way of accounting for the so-called fact of not being happier even when you know you want to be. Not being depressed is knowing that you are happier. Depression is what prevents that final step. Depression is what prevents you from making that final conversion from being a victim. It's why some of you seem to yourselves as not to be getting where you want to be.

How do you account for not being happier? For not being as happy as you want to be? By believing somehow that you're not as happy as you want to be. And yet, you know, at the same time, that you're as happy as you want to be, right now. But that you want to be happier. You're as unhappy as you feel you need to be. But you want to be happier. So without depression, if you were unhappy, all you would need to do at that point would be to look at your belief. You see, all you'd have to do is simply untangle it.

Question your belief. If you weren't depressed, you'd move, right away. Depression is what prevents you, even though you go through all of your beliefs and you come back to the fact, "I have no reason for being unhappy about this." Yet still nagging in the back of your mind is the fear of "But wait till tomorrow. I'll be unhappy about it again, even though I have no reason to be." That's a constant thing that you all walk around with, manifested in so many things that you do and say. It shows on your faces. It shows in your behavior. It shows in what you talk about and how you talk about it.

You don't have to be depressed. It's just something that you're doing. It's not something you need to do.

What Is Depression?

* Depression is the feeling that something is missing, something is wrong.
* Depression is the dilemma of really wanting to be happy, yet not being able to account for being unhappy.
* Being unhappy and not wanting to be.
* "There is something basically wrong with me."
* "Will time take care of it? No, not really."
* "What more do I need? What is lacking; what basic flaw?"
* "I am a living contradiction to everything I know."
* "How can it be that I can be unhappy, knowing that there is no reason to be?"
* Being unhappy about being unhappy.
* Disappointed in oneself for being unhappy.
* "I can be unhappy when I don't have a reason to be unhappy."
* Being afraid of yourself.
* Being afraid that you are unhappy when you are not unhappy.
* Being afraid of being unhappy.
* Believing that you are afraid of being unhappy.
* "I must be afraid of something that I know I have no reason to be afraid of."
* "I think I am happy, but I'm really not."
* "Something is very wrong with me if I am not happy or unhappy, therefore there must be a reason that I will never know."
* "There must be a power in me that can make unhappy regardless of all I do know."
* "I cannot be what I would be if I were not depressed."
* " I fear that I wouldn't be what I *would* be if I were not fearing it in the first place."
* "I deduce and fear that I must be unhappy if I am not feeling or acting as I believe I would be if I *were* happy."
* Depression is the only unhappiness.

Being Appreciated

January 19, 1992

Referring to a case in which a woman says she is talented, beautiful, and feels hurt that no one appreciates her.

W HAT is the belief that would have to be necessary for this woman to be unhappy that nobody appreciates her—even if she was right? If it is true that she is worthless, how could she feel bad about that without having a certain belief? She is believing that if she is not appreciated, that is something to be unhappy about. She is unhappy about not being appreciated, therefore she is believing not being appreciated is something to be unhappy about.

Being stupid is one reason to not be appreciated. It doesn't matter if they are right about her being stupid or not. Her real reason for unhappiness is the belief that she should be appreciated. Even if they were right, why is that something to be unhappy about? "Because now I don't have what it takes to be appreciated."

On the one hand she says, "I have what it takes to be appreciated, but I'm not being appreciated," and then she imagines "Maybe I don't have what it takes to be appreciated, maybe I'm really stupid and ugly." But in either case, "Woe is me, I can't get appreciated." And she believes she ought to be appreciated.

If she didn't have the belief that she ought to be appreciated, could she be unhappy about those things? She couldn't be unhappy. It is that simple. No matter how beautiful you are or ugly you are, no matter how talented you are or how untalented you are, if you believe you ought to be appreciated, you are going to be unhappy.

She thinks she's talented and beautiful, and can't understand why no one appreciates her. Then she starts to wonder, "Maybe I'm not talented and beautiful, and don't have what it takes to be appreciated." She'll question it both ways, and either way, "There's something wrong here," and the only reason she believes there's something wrong is that she believes she ought to be appreciated.

Why should a beautiful person be appreciated? Why should a wonderful, kind person be loved? That belief will make a person unhappy. So maybe she's afraid it's true that she's *not* very talented. That only still refers to her belief. How come she would be unhappy if it was true that she was not talented? Why is it mystifying to her that she thinks she is talented and yet nobody appreciates her? Because she wouldn't get appreciated, but she should.

The belief is the same thing as the unhappy feeling. The belief is the cause of the feeling. If you take away the belief, the unhappiness is not there.

"I feel bad about not being appreciated" means "I believe I ought to be appreciated, and there is either something wrong with them, or something wrong with me, if I'm not." And you can go on for five thousand years trying to figure out what's wrong, instead of going right back to "Why do you believe you ought to be appreciated?"

Safety and Boredom
May 4, 1979

No children want safety from anything but boredom, and neither do adults. All our concepts of safety are meant to save us from incapacitations that threaten the mobility of health or wealth so that we can move around better to explore more and longer.

The punishment of prison is that it offers great safety. This incarceration is the old childhood punishment of "staying." Any prisoner would be glad for any kind of "rehabilitation" program that offers relief from monotony.

The fear of boredom causes wars, crusades, etc. From the boring desert come fierce warriors dying to sack, pillage, rape, burn, do anything. From the boring cities on hot boring nights rises a smoldering fire of hope for relief. A riot suffices. The lights went out. My God! What an opportunity! Heaven (or greater powers, like the electric company) has decreed a time for change. Joy fills the streets and a jolly good time was havocked by all.

Poverty is boring. Safety is boring. Sickness is boring. Ignorance is boring. Peace is boring.

In times of peace there is the need for great (even extraordinary) goals and prosperity and/or success within that society, or there will be an explosion of warlike energy toward the universe beyond.

The attention span of a child, an adult, or a nation is another description of the universal desire to experience change from static situations.

If nature abhors a vacuum, it is because it detests boredom.

Nothing is more boring to the human mind than a subject completely understood.

Repetition is boring when one believes nothing much more will be gained (or changed).

A bore is someone who repeats themselves when they are already understood too well.

A bore is someone who tells you more than you want to know about something.

"Beating a dead horse" is the epitomized expression of over-doing, over-killing, over-telling, over-satisfying.

Over-satisfaction cannot exist; boredom replaces satisfaction that is pushed.

SECTION III

Mistaken for Unhappiness

Unhappiness Is Not a Physical Feeling
December 1987

WHEN someone has an emotion, I want you to see someone who's choosing how they feel, and then see that in yourself. If it's easier sometimes for you to see it in others, don't deprive yourself of that. It's a perfectly good way of learning.

You'll notice that especially when people say, "I just can't help it, but I feel disgusted at this" or "I just can't help it, but I feel . . . ," you can at least know what you know, and that becomes a perfectly good time to remind yourself. It doesn't mean you're not willing to see it in yourself, but sometimes it's very obvious and very clear and very easy to see it in others. Then, at other times, it's much easier to see it in yourself and to use yourself as the example. It doesn't really matter which one as long as you do both.

See through when someone says "This makes me unhappy," "That makes me unhappy." See through "Knowing about this makes me unhappy, experiencing this makes me unhappy."

Distinguish the behavior from the feeling. Crying isn't a feeling. Screaming and yelling in anger is not the feeling. The physical feeling is almost not relevant to it. For instance, you wouldn't call that feeling "anger" if it was there without the belief that something bad happened.

The belief causes the emotion, and that makes it seem like that emotion *is* the belief. So, in other words, if you have the feeling of anger, which is a feeling that you have in your chest or someone else has it in their throat or someone else has it in their stomach, why we all call that anger is because we're all believing this has got to stop.

This belief that this has got to stop, that is really the emotion. That's what really creates the illusion that these feelings are the ones of anger. Although it's true that the body responds to those beliefs, how and why it responds isn't a concern, really, because that's going to be different for each person.

When a person says they're feeling bad, the physical sensation isn't in itself the feeling bad. If a person is experiencing shakiness which they are worried about, they could say, "God, I'm nervous," and feel very worried about that. Now, the shakiness might in fact be physiological to start and there'd be no emotion there as such. But their belief about it *now* is the emotion called worry.

Besides the fact that you have judged your physiological responses, how do you know you feel bad? *Why* you feel bad is beliefs about the future. *How* you feel bad is stimulus-organism-response. Now we're talking about "how do you *know* you feel bad? How does anyone know they feel bad?" We only have their word for it.

In itself, to not want something, or to want something different, doesn't mean you have to be unhappy. If you're glad that you want something different, is that unhappiness? Just the act of wanting something different has nothing to do with anything in terms of emotions. That's just a decision of your desire. But if you're uncomfortable with your own desires, that can become an unhappy experience. If you don't feel that you have the right to want something different, then you could feel bad about wanting it different. If you feel that the thing you're wanting different shouldn't be that way, if you have the belief that it shouldn't be that way, then that's unhappiness—but not just wanting it different.

Unhappiness is not really a feeling. We've learned to talk about it by talking about the feeling, but the actual unhappiness is not a feeling, but an attitude. It's a judgment *about* that feeling, a judgment before that feeling, but it isn't the feeling.

Let's say you had a tumor on the brain and you went to a doctor and you got some treatment, and he says to you, "When this tumor starts to shrink, you'll get headaches." Every time, you'd be looking for the headache and be glad to have it. So how do you know an emotion is a bad emotion? It's not the tears that are unhappiness, or the screaming and yelling of anger. When you decide that something shouldn't be, that's the unhappiness.

If your heart is beating faster, some would call that fear and unhappiness. To me, that sounds like a person trying to run away from something and escape. That's the flight mechanism. If you were believing "I want to run away," you might organize your body in such a way that you would start to prepare for that. Is that a bad feeling?

Or would you have to be feeling bad in the first place before you'd call it a bad feeling? Your heart beating fast in and of itself is not a bad feeling, but coupled with believing that something *shouldn't* be, or you *should* be getting away from it, or it *can't* happen, that is unhappiness.

Wanting to get away from something wouldn't be an unhappy feeling. Your question is, "I thought there were beliefs, then there were feelings, and the beliefs cause the unhappiness." But the part that is the unhappiness is not the feelings, it's the belief. If I gave you a pill that mimicked certain physiological feelings of unhappiness, that wouldn't mean you were unhappy, even though it made you feel the same way that you would have felt when you were unhappy.

Getting unhappy about physical symptoms, or judging them as unhappy, often exaggerates the symptoms. Nervousness turns to frantic panic. Sadness turns to debilitating depression.

On the other hand, if you change the physiological feeling, you haven't changed the unhappiness. In other words, if you give a frightened person a tranquilizer, you haven't changed their belief. You've covered up the belief, in a sense, by not allowing it to have its normal expression. But they are still unhappy, they still have the same belief, they still believe that something is bad.

If your expression of unhappiness is tension, and now you no longer believe you have to do that, you may feel residual tension, just as if you've been exercising and you stop exercising. The physical tension may be lessening. Things are moving in ways that they didn't move before. And you can either know that you are now not unhappy, or be unhappy that your body has not fully moved to the state you expect it to be in.

To be meaningful as unhappiness, unhappiness has to be something you yourself would agree is unhappiness. When you see somebody shaking, it isn't long before somebody says to them, "You're nervous," and they learn the name for that. Without the name, the chances *may* be that there's a similar belief involved, but we don't know. It may be true that we express that we're unhappy somatically, but even if we couldn't, we'd still be unhappy; if you have a schizophrenic who's flailing and throwing himself against the wall and you put a helmet and a straightjacket on him, you don't believe you've really done anything for his emotions, yet the expression is not there any longer. Or if you internally straightjacket them with drugs, we agree, too, that that hasn't really changed their belief. If they still think their mother is evil, they're still going to believe their mother is evil. Though, altogether, they may actually not feel as bad because they may no longer be feeling bad about the symptom.

A person that's unhappy about having certain physiological feelings, if you cure those feelings, the person is not going to be unhappy about that. If a person's unhappy about being poor, and you give them money, they won't be unhappy about being poor. You've done them a great favor, but you haven't really dealt with the issue of why and how they got unhappy. That's changing the event, and that's what people have thought they needed to do: get the power to change the event in order to stop feeling unhappy, and have constant power and constantly increasing power to do so. The thing is, that doesn't stop people from then being unhappy about the next thing they think they ought to be unhappy about.

Pain and Unhappiness

QUESTIONER: *I have a question around symptoms. You talked about "you give yourself the knot in the stomach." But say a person has a physical problem. They have an illness. And then with that illness comes symptoms that one might call pain.*

Okay. So the big trick is to not be unhappy about the pain, or the illness for that matter.

Questioner: *But I think for many of us the pain and the unhappiness are so tightly linked together that the pain and the unhappiness all happen at the same time.*

There are many of us who know the difference between our pains and knowing we're not unhappy about them. But the person who has an arthritic joint and feels tremendous pain, the question of whether they're unhappy about that or not is still a valid question. Because what pain says is that you don't want it. The very fact that you're experiencing it, I already know you don't want it. But people don't know that about themselves. And they're afraid, sometimes, that pain says they do want it. And what they feel bad about is that they could have pain for that reason. For instance, how could a person who doesn't want pain have pain? How could they be so shameful as to have the pain?

So there are lots of connotations to pain that have nothing to do with the pain itself. I've worked in this business long enough to know that the greatest problem with pain is embarrassment. The real problem with pain is that you believe it's going to make you act like a schnook or a schmuck. Something like that. That pain is going to make you ugly, unattractive. And especially when you yell and scream in pain. Nobody's going to want to feed you, clothe you, keep you warm and make sure you get a good place to sleep that night.

You're afraid if the pain continues, you're going to be unfit for human consumption. And that's what I have found that people are afraid of when they're in pain: not the pain, but what they're afraid it'll make them be, do or seem. And those are fears and beliefs. And so we look at those beliefs and we can help them. And when they're no longer afraid of their pain, for one thing, it feels differently. If it doesn't, in fact, go away, insofar as some pains are caused by the tension and the fear of having a pain and prolonged because of that, the pains could actually subside. Not to say that fear made them have pain. I don't subscribe to the idea that unhappiness causes pain. But lack of unhappiness might well lessen pain.

And happiness might well allow the body to do whatever it best can do to take care of it so you don't feel it as pain. Even if it gave you just enough brains to go to the doctor to get rid of the pain. But people who over-psychologize are always in trouble, whether it's with pain or a stutter or a tear in their eye or fast movement or anything like that. Because they're always psychoanalyzing themselves. And they're always looking for fault in themselves.

There's a very good reason why people do that, I should add. And it's very good in its intentions. You hope that if you're at fault, you can fix it. So you're looking to find yourself to be the nut. You hope that you're the crazy person who's constantly screwing yourself like this, and it's not God, who you strongly suspect, or the whole world, which you've already learned is paranoia. And you don't want to do that.

So some people are very quick to look, "What's wrong with them, what's wrong with me, what's wrong with . . . ? If I don't get what I want there's something wrong with me. If people don't like me, there's something wrong with me. If somebody doesn't read my mind in the right way, there's something wrong with me. If I don't get the right change there's something wrong with me. What did I do that they cheated me? What did I do that they lie to me? What did I do that they love me? Why am I followed by all these little ragamuffins and beggars?" Whatever your dramatic melody may be. The point is, people often want to see themselves as a cause of their pains and a cause of their problems.

But pain and unhappiness aren't the same thing. The fact that people may connect them is matter for question. I agree. You say they automatically connect them. Well, I say that just proves good learning. They just learn to do that and they just always do it. But it is certainly possible to have pain without unhappiness. But the way you would start is not being unhappy about the pain. Because you're unhappy about the pain because of what it means. Remember that?

If somebody's unhappy about their pain, they're unhappy about what it means. Not the pain as such, because the pain makes them do things, right? It makes them act like a baby. So now we've got a whole bunch of people who feel bad; feeling like a baby. Because when you are in a lot of pain you feel like a baby. Don't you? Have you ever been honest enough to admit it? I've been in enough pain to admit it. When you're in a lot of pain you feel just like a baby. You don't know what to do to help yourself. If you're very sick you feel like a baby.

And all of a sudden, you know you're over twenty-one and you wonder, "Is it okay to feel like a baby?" You just assume there must be something wrong with you that you feel like such a baby. You must be frightened. You're feeling like a frightened baby.

No you're not. You're feeling like a baby. You're feeling like a helpless infant in all the ways that you actually are helpless, at that moment. That's not a frightened state. When a child is helpless, a child is just simply helpless. A child isn't necessarily frightened. You think it's bad to feel like a baby.

And that's one of the things that we could question in looking at pain. Or we could question that you're a burden on others when you show them how much pain you're in. They all feel that they have to do something about it and they haven't got the slightest idea what to do about it. You're dying of cancer and everybody else is pulling out their hair. And you don't know how to stop them. What can you say? What can you do? Are you supposed to say something? Are you supposed to do something? How guilty do you feel for not knowing what to say and do?

Nothing Causes Unhappiness

So those are things that are involved. And there you are suffering in pain, and not knowing what to do, and feeling like you're stupid. And now comes the question. Here's your test: are you allowed to be happy when you're stupid? I like to tell my clients right up front, at some point, somewhere around the 1,000th session, that they're never going to be happy until it's really okay to be stupid. Nobody can be. It's got to be okay to not know. And I don't care what that is, but it's got to be okay to not know it. Until it's okay to be stupid, you'll never be happy.

Because all forms of unhappiness are these regrets that you've made yourself ignorant, and you've made your brain not work right for you, and you've made yourself not be on your own behalf. When I've told you all the definitions of unhappiness, and said "unhappiness is this and unhappiness is that," unhappiness is certainly the fear that you don't act on your own behalf, that you don't always do for your own good and for your own happiness. But that's only just simply a myth. That's just a problem.

Because you believe there are things you can do for your happiness. And you're afraid you don't do them. And you're afraid you passed up some of those things you need to do for your happiness. But there aren't "those things." There isn't anything you need to do to become happy. There's nothing you're supposed to do. And in The Option Method that's what you get to see. There is nothing you're supposed to do to stop being unhappy. And there's nothing you're supposed to do to be happy. Nothing.

And I literally mean it. And I can prove it. And that's what The Option Method shows you. And as you can see, if we use this paradigm and use the questions I'm asking, a person would be able to see that there's nothing they need to do to be not unhappy. There are no steps they need to take. There's no pain or process they need to go through. Nothing. Nothing. The bottom line of The Option Method is that some people have learned that nothing causes unhappiness.

As controversial or as strange or weird as that may sound, there are some people who know that nothing causes unhappiness. N-O-T-H-I-N-G. Nothing. That's what causes unhappiness. Now people want to know the weight of that nothing, and the size and shape of that nothing, and how long of a life does it have, and especially how expensive will it be. But nothing causes unhappiness. And so nothing needs to be done to be rid of it. It was only believed in. We find out that all the unhappiness that people have, they believed in. Nothing was causing it.

And there's quite a big difference between something being believed in and something existing. Believing that something exists gives it a kind of fictional existence. But it doesn't give it a real existence. It just gives it a phenomenological existence, which is not the same. See, exorcisms can work then. Flea powder could work. The weight of something that doesn't exist can't be heavier than something else that doesn't exist. You know, there are simple fundamentals in life that people don't understand.

You'll all agree with me that five years ago is the past and doesn't exist. But you probably all believe that 10 years ago is twice as long ago. I'm not trying to teach you philosophy; it's just a little joke to show you how the mind works. Something 10 years old is not something twice as old as something five years old; we just say that for convenience in order to run insurance businesses and things like that. We have purposes for making these comparisons.

But they're not real. Something that doesn't exist can't be compared to something else that doesn't exist. Someone asked me, "Is happiness and unhappiness not equal?" and I asked them, "Which is heavier, three or green?" If you say they're of equal weight, we're not talking about the same thing.

So when we're mixing all of these quantitative measurements and judgments, we say, "Is happiness equal to unhappiness? Is something equal to nothing?" Something that's nothing is nothing. So it isn't a something. You can't measure it against a something. Unhappiness, if it's nothing, can't be weighed or compared against happiness, which is something. It is the way you really feel. Happiness is the feeling of freedom. Freedom is real. Freedom is "That's the way you go, baby. You know, just go." That's freedom. And that's what I love. And that's what you love.

Unhappiness is "Where should I go? Can I go now? What'd you say? How much does it cost? Who's looking? Should I? Shouldn't I? Can I? Can't I?" That's unhappiness. And you're not talking to anybody about anything. You're relating to nothing. If you say, "Well, I'm following a law"—there is no law for unhappiness! All of the laws having to do with unhappiness are made up. There is no law in nature for unhappiness. Is there? And those are the kind of challenges that unhappy people present to us.

And that's what The Option Method is exquisitely designed to deal with, just those kinds of challenges. We just know that emotions are what we're talking about. And you have emotions you don't like. I'm not here to fix your good emotions. And people say, "You know, I'm in love with somebody. Can you help me stop? I'm really turned on to certain kinds of things and I need help to stop." That includes gay people. That's a very common complaint among gay people. They say that they don't like that they're attracted to what they're attracted to.

But, of course, they are. They love what they're attracted to. If they were really honest, what they don't like is the rest of us, who say that they're wrong. Of course they love what they're attracted to. They're just sick and tired of hearing how bad they are for it. Okay. They may believe they're bad but they don't believe they're not attracted to what they are attracted to. And they don't believe they don't love it. They just merely believe they're bad. Well, we can do that about anything. No big special class of people there. You rank with stepmothers, other ethnic groups and slave owners and rich people—all the kinds of people that people hate.

Pain

November 5, 1977

Pain is wanting to be *not aware* of a sensation, but believing that we *should* be aware of it.

An analogy: if you were in a hotel, wanting to have a conversation with a friend, and finding it difficult to hear her because of a loud TV in another room, you might first investigate to see if the TV could be turned off. If the TV was in the lobby, you might ask the receptionist to turn the TV down. If the TV was in someone's personal room, you might bang on the wall. If you didn't want to (or couldn't) take any action to have the TV turned down, you might then proceed with your conversation to the best of your abilities, unproblematically, with the TV blaring. Now, alternatively, you could instead ruminate on how the TV "shouldn't" be so loud, and be unhappy about the noise of the TV.

In this analogy, the TV is a bodily sensation that is present to your awareness that you don't like. If you find the bodily sensation informative (for example, you realization that your hand hurts because it is touching a hot stove), you will naturally act upon this information (and so remove your hand from the stove). If you find that this bodily sensation (for example, the throbbing of your hand after it has been removed from the stove) has no relevance to what you want, then you might first see if you can "turn it off" or "turn it down," by taking a painkiller, for example. If you find that this bodily sensation cannot be "turned off," then you could simply proceed doing what you want, unproblematically, in the context of this bodily sensation. Alternatively, you could instead ruminate on how the bodily sensation "shouldn't" be, and so be unhappy about your awareness of the bodily sensation.

RELATIVE to pain, to feel bad is to believe that *lack of awareness* is desirable. The need to change such a feeling is based on the decision, belief, or judgment that it is a bad awareness.

All feeling bad is about what might be our feelings in the future about our desires now—in this case, the fear of not feeling good about things we do not feel good about, but are afraid we will regret

339

not having felt good about. It is the disapproval of the present state of feeling.

To feel bad about pain is to believe that lack of awareness of a bodily sensation is in itself a goal to strive for. Pain is believing that being aware of a bodily sensation is undesirable. Pain is *trying* to not be aware of something (as opposed to *merely* not being aware of something).

Pain is fearing what will happen if we ignore what we choose to ignore and do whatever we want. Pain is simply being aware of something that is not relevant to our goals now.

If there is something we want to do, we will do it if we are not busy with pain or avoiding it. Pain is not the awareness of something that is happening. It is *trying* to remove the awareness of the event instead of either a) changing the bodily sensation simply because it is not desired or b) forgetting the bodily sensation until you want to change it or do something about it.

a) Changing the bodily sensation simply because it is not desired: in other words, eliminating the obstacle which "causes" the pain—but *not* because it causes pain, but only because you don't want the bodily sensation, in itself, to get in your way. Pain will not get in your way until you feel it as pain and need to direct your energies to relieving the pain or trying to relieve it, or feeling it, and not doing what you would want instead if you had no pain. Awareness of wanting to change something doesn't get in your way until you get involved with the awareness instead of the desire. Then it is pain.

b) Forgetting the bodily sensation until you want to change it or do something about it. For all you know, the event that caused the bodily sensation is over. If the cause has passed, or if you don't know if it has, or what it was, then pain is trying to get rid of an awareness of something that you are no longer aware of wanting to do something about.

Pain is the feeling of trying to ignore an awareness because we object to the so-called effects of the awareness and what the awareness of those effects will do to us. It is believing that your bodily functions and sensations are ruining your life, your happiness and your fun.

Psychological Hypochondriacs
November 11, 1995

You've heard of hypochondriacs. Well, there are psychological versions of hypochondriacs. It doesn't mean that there's anything wrong with them. They just use feeling bad to explain every mistake they make, every error they make: every time they mess up and every time they don't succeed, they say they were sick. I'm not meaning it as a put-down. There is a range of people who excuse their mistakes by saying they're having a problem. And that they set it up so that they have the problem ahead of time to explain the mistake they're going to have later, in case they have one.

It has nothing to do with unhappiness. It's just that some people will see through you and some people won't. And you might be unhappy if people don't believe you when you say that you're unhappy. That might make you more unhappy than anything. Does it bother you if somebody doesn't believe you're unhappy?

They are not really unhappy about anything but they have to set it up that they're having some kind of problem to excuse any failures or errors or mistakes, which they would really feel bad about when they happened.

If you're afraid that you're going to make yourself be a jittery mess or a frightened person or you're going to have all these symptoms (which is really just feeling your physical body), you can have unhappiness to account for why you make mistakes—you can always have that as a way to forgive yourself. But the problem is you have to blame yourself first.

Physical Symptoms
November 11, 1995

Does the fact that you anticipate a certain kind of physical feeling mean you're worried and unhappy, if you don't see that feeling as a bad feeling? Especially if we really stuck with physical feelings as physical feelings, such as excitement, or sleepiness.

I can imagine certain phone calls, if I got from some people, I would just instantly fall asleep. What I'm really imagining is that I won't deal with that phone call. Can you see the way it'll translate in my body? I just don't want to deal with that phone call. So I won't deal with it. Now I don't have to fall asleep. Some people would say, when they think of getting that phone call they'd get depressed instead of simply admitting they don't want to deal with that phone call.

All feelings just basically run the gamut of two kinds. The quiet feelings that go toward peace and sleepiness that can be called either "being at peace" or "being depressed." And the other feelings that go toward exhilaration and joy or frenetic wild anxiety and nervousness. So there are the active feelings of something stimulating, which can be either called good or bad. And there's the peaceful, quiet, down feelings that can be called either good or bad.

So if you're compassionate towards yourself and you're in a good mood, and you're not out to rake yourself over the coals, you will say you're just being at peace while everybody else says you're depressed. And that you'll move your ass when you goddamn feel like it. The reason people can't get out of bed because they are depressed is because they won't give themselves *permission* to do that. If they really allowed themselves to be at peace and knew that they were allowed to stay in bed as long as they wanted, they would soon find out how quickly they get bored. If they didn't keep thinking they have to do something about their constantly oversleeping, they would see what they would like to do that day. Then there are all those "hyper" feelings, which are judged as frantic or anxious, and frightened, or excited and joyful. And when you can't justify your joy, you're going to have to call it somehow "anxious."

COMMENTARIES

by Aryeh Nielsen on

"Forms of Unhappiness"

Joy, Peace, Mania, Depression

This commentary is a synopsis of ideas that Bruce Di Marsico expressed in many writings or talks, but did not express summarily in a single writing or talk.

BRUCE Di Marsico outlined four fundamental attitudes, two Happy and two Unhappy, that provide a broad view of the possibilities of engagement in the world. Often, when he uses the words describing these attitudes and their concomitant motivations, he is using these words in a precise manner, as outlined here.

The four fundamental bodily attitudes:
* Joy: The *active* bodily attitude of Happiness
* Peace: The *inactive* bodily attitude of Happiness
* Mania: The *active* bodily attitude of Unhappiness
* Depression: The *inactive* bodily attitude of Unhappiness

Peace and Depression are characterized by a lack of motivation (in the case of Peace, a completely benign lack of motivation—everything is felt to be sufficient as it is).

The two fundamental motivations of Mania are:
* Paranoia: Unhappily moving away from
* Hysteria: Unhappily moving towards

The two fundamental motivations of Joy are:
* Avoiding: Happily moving away from
* Wanting: Happily moving toward

In refuting arguments against happiness, four questions can be asked:

1. Could there ever be a situation in which Mania was more practically effective than Joy?
2. Could there ever be a situation in which Depression was more practically effective than Peace?

3. Could there ever be a situation in which Paranoia was more practically effective than Avoiding?
4. Could there ever be a situation in which Hysteria was more practically effective than Wanting?

PART VIII

Arguments against Happiness

Arguments against Happiness
November 11, 1995 Lecture

Now I know many, many, many miserable people who don't want to be happy. That's very threatening. I often tell my students, "It's like this: if I had a person who came in and they were afraid of spiders, I don't think I'd say to them, 'Okay, listen, when I'm done with you, you will be so not afraid of spiders you'll be able to eat them.'" I don't think that's very promising or much of an offer for help. Okay. Even though I might think that's a great idea, you see, that's not the point. There are some people who give meaning to happiness and insofar as they give it that meaning, they certainly wouldn't want to be happy. Some of the meanings they give to happiness are really another form of unhappiness, that's all—somehow being something against their will. But that's unhappiness under another name.

So unhappiness really goes under two names which I discovered. It goes under the name *unhappiness* and all its kindred spirits, from anger to hatred to annoyance to fear to rage to depression. From the slightest negative bad feelings to the most intense negative bad feelings. That's all unhappiness. And then a whole gamut of some things that we would call *happiness* also fit under what some people consider unhappy.

So The Option Method has this as its start: someone, a human being who makes up their own mind, who says, "I want to be at least less unhappy than I am now." They will certainly not ask for perfect happiness. That's stupid. But they've heard at least that people maybe have problems and something in themselves they could change and be happier or less unhappy. They've heard of phobias and fears and they've heard of manias and things like that. So they've heard of therapies and ways of help to be happier or ways of help that they have interpreted as ways to be less unhappy or happier.

So, that's all you need—thinking human beings. We can't use dead ones and we can't use people who are incapable of logical thought. They're perfectly fine, right? They're not making any judgments to question. Insofar as they are, okay, then maybe we can help them.

Being Too Happy

SINCE people believe that unhappiness will always be necessary at times, they do not experience their desire to be happy as an actual desire to be happy.

It will be felt as a desire to avoid greater unhappiness as much as possible and to endure slight unhappiness in pursuit of greater happiness.

When there is no question of ever being unhappy, there is no desire for happiness as such, just for anything else that might be desired.

There is no desire to be happy except theoretically when a person fears or believes they will not be.

Unhappiness is believing you may choose to have any feeling, behavior, etc. you believe you do not have to choose and don't yet want to choose (if ever).

It is not trusting that your own decisions count with you. It is believing that if you change your mind, you really didn't mean to or intend to or choose to.

"Too happy" means the same as too unhappy. It means feeling more or less or differently than you desire. It is fear.

There is of course no such thing as too much feeling the way we want. Too happy means too excited or too lethargic or too unaware, as in "too ignoring of my opinions." Too unhappy may also mean the same but with conscious dissatisfaction of the feelings. Too happy means feeling the same as unhappy feelings, but somehow without awareness that you are unhappy.

The fear of being too happy or feeling too good is simply the fear of not feeling the way you really believe best, or would choose, and not realizing you aren't feeling the way you want. It is fear of regret when you come to your "senses." It is the fear that automatic and natural choices of feelings, and not censuring or questioning them, allows the possibility that we do not choose them by our "best" methods.

It is the belief that if we fear and believe that automatic choices of feeling are not best for us, then that might cause us to choose "better" feelings and awareness.

Fear gives "caution" which leads to better choices of feelings.

The feelings are called bad, now. We feel lousy and scared of ourselves and believe that we can now better select what to think, do, choose and believe about things.

Being unhappy is fearing being too happy or too unhappy. Being unhappy is trying to attain the proper degree of fear of our natural, automatic, instantaneous choices. Being unhappy is trying to attain the proper degree of distrust, an honest appraisal of our "self-deceiving" impulse or "healthy" respect that our automatic ("natural") choices may have a need for correction. Being unhappy is believing "hesitation and self-doubt is God and man's way" is proper.

Unhappiness is believing (doubting, hesitating to believe) that we don't automatically choose to feel the way we most want and like best for us.

If you think twice about what you believed or felt or decided, if you feel like checking them out (so-called reality testing), that is another automatic natural choice.

Fear is believing you have to, must, believe either the way you felt, or the way you would like to feel on reconsideration, or both.

Fear is believing that reconsideration of how you feel is a problem and detrimental.

Fear is believing that there can be too much or too little reconsideration of anything. There can only be as much as you consider best for you—no more or less.

It is believing you should or should not consider any longer. It is fear of delay or impulse.

You are always evaluating what is the "best" (most desirable for you) approach to any event or imagined events. Desires are part of the consideration, and "new" or "renewed" desires are the effect.

E.g., Considering what I believe is true, feel that I know, believe that I would like, what may happen, etc., what do I "feel" now (want to do, think is the best point of view, prediction, etc.)?

What is best, since I only do what I think or feel is best?

To think one thing best and to desire another (feel "for" it) is to be considering.

We may keep reconsidering for years or may choose one or the other. Resolution of consideration is thinking and feeling the same way. You feel what you think (believe) is best to feel about things. That is a way of experiencing thoughts, beliefs, desires, knowledge, etc.

If the feeling is "bad," it is merely because you believe you should be more or less questioning and considering than you are. You believe it is possible to go faster or slower than you think is best.

If you believe you should stop or start before you feel best, you are believing in an impossible thing. You are asking the impossible of yourself and will feel sick.

Too Good to Be True?

THE unhappiness of feeling "It's too good to be true" as a reason for rejecting the good means I should be able to be very happy even if the truth I believe is true were not true.

I shouldn't have needed (knowing, doing, having, a person, etc.) this to happen to me to be this happy. I should have been this happy before (or this happy without, or this happy on my own).

If what you're saying is true and makes all the difference in my life, I should have known it before.

Since "unhappiness doesn't happen" must be true (as you say), I should have known it before this. It is too crucial, the only knowledge, too essential to have been deprived of; therefore it can't be easy to know. I can't really trust it.

This can't be so easy to believe, as I do, or I would have. This is so easy to believe. I'm able to. It's perfect. I'm afraid of being able to succeed at believing it. I'm believing this and I shouldn't.

It should be more dramatic, fanfares. Not so easy and ordinary and unawesome. It's so big and important; it should be impressive and scary.

I should have to be persuaded more and convinced more. It should be harder to be believed, since it is so important.

The truth is:

The most important truth should be and would be the easiest and most natural to accept. The greatest truth would be quite ordinary. The awesomeness would come from being glad and seeing the implications slowly as they unfold forever in the future.

It wouldn't take time or effort to believe what is simply the truth or what is necessarily true. It only takes time in appreciating it. It takes time for the benefits to unfold. The fruits and particular applications will be numerous and take time in the future.

Decisions, Decisions, Decisions

"Even if I knew what I wanted—I wouldn't do it."

"I'll probably regret my choice—I should have known better."

This is using fear of not knowing what you want in order to decide what you want (now).

Unhappiness Is "But"

THE only reason anyone can get unhappy is because they are believing that it is necessary to make them do what they want (including knowing what they want, or what they want to do—health, awareness, etc.).

After getting unhappy, it is not obvious to them why they did it—even though it may be apparent to others. It often feels to them that they are not getting what they want, but the real fear is that they were (and still are) afraid that they are not doing what they want (or may not do what they want) about what is happening. "I want to do what I want, but . . ."

Getting unhappy, feeling bad, etc., is the same as the awareness (the self-message, the personal belief, the reminder, the most effective-efficient means of implementation, the undeniable director, the guarantor) that it is necessary to believe "it is possible not to do what we want" in order to assure that we do what we want. "I want this, but . . ."

Although we may not do what we now want (we may change before we complete our goal, i.e., change our mind, etc.), it is not necessary that we believe it as a way of prodding or implementing or guaranteeing that we will do what we now want. "I may still want it, but . . ."

Some fear that they may not be doing what they "really" want now (although they like and want it now)—insofar as they may not be considering what they will want in the future, which they now also want to prepare for; e.g., "What I am aware of now is, or seems, fine for now, but how do I know that my present awareness is all that it could be for the future? I may find out in the future that I was not now aware of what I would have wanted to be aware of and could have been aware of (should have been aware of) for the good of my future desires. Also I find that now I realize that I should have been more aware in the past. If I was, I would have been better prepared for now, I would now already have had more of what I want."

"This is what I want, but . . ."

The beliefs seem to be:

"I may not do it *and* will still want to,"

which becomes: "I may not do it *but* will still want to."

"I may want to *and* not be aware of it and not do it,"

which becomes: "I may want to *but* not be aware of it and not do it."

"I may want it (really, in my heart) *and* not do it,"

which becomes: "I may want it (really, in my heart) *but* not do it."

"I may not want to *and* really want to,"

which becomes: "I may not want to *but* really want to."

"I want to *and* don't feel like it,"

which becomes: "I want to *but* don't feel like it."

"I feel like it *and* don't want to,"

which becomes: "I feel like it *but* don't want to."

Etc.

These beliefs are believed necessary as a means of doing what we want. "*But* I may not do what I want unless I believe I may not do what I want."

"But I may do what I don't want, unless I believe I may do what I don't want."

It probably amounts to a physiological expedience and experience of being aware that "I may not do what I want"—a double or multiplied awareness. But, But!!! But I may not do what I want, unless I expect to not do what I want.

I must believe it is probable in order to certainly prevent it.

I want to believe I won't do it so that I can believe I will.

This is necessary.

I need to tell myself the opposite of what I hope (want) in order to assure it.

If I believe I cannot do what I can do, then I will do what I can more surely.

If I doubt, I will be sure.

I am better motivated in reaction to undesirable ideas than by attractiveness.

I am better repulsed than attracted.

I move most easily by repulsion.

Fear is joy? (Joy is fearful.) God is Unhappy.

You will give me more by hating who I am than by loving who I am becoming.

The avoidance of feeling bad is a surer movement than the attraction of joy.

Force me into gladness. "Scare me out of my fear.

"Since I am sure that I always want to feel good, and do what I want, I want to guarantee it by moving toward it (wanting it) by avoiding its opposite. What opposite? No matter that there is no opposite, there is now. I want the opposite of the opposite of what I want. I am afraid of (want to avoid) the opposite of what I want, am afraid it is more of what I want than just wanting what I want.

"Wanting what I want is too simple. I am not simply wanting it. I am avoiding that too. I am doing double good at once.

"I do not (simply) want what I want, I need. Need means I 'twice it': I don't want its opposite as well, and for 'good' measure."

Nature vs. Belief

September 20, 1975

In this writing, Bruce Di Marsico addresses the attitude: "I should have known better. I'm such an idiot, I'm such a loser, I'm so stupid, I'm so lame."

The core belief behind "I should have known better" is a person's belief that their not having known something earlier in time than they actually did is a sign that there is something inherently wrong with them. For example, if such a person made an investment that failed, they would feel that they have proof that something is wrong with them that they did not know that the investment would fail *before* they made the investment.

The core belief behind "I'm such an idiot, I'm such a loser, I'm so stupid, I'm so lame" is a person's belief that they have evidence that there is something structurally wrong with them, something that has always been there and will always be there, as opposed to mere evidence that they *didn't* know something—and now they *do*.

Précis of "Nature vs. Belief"

Many people become unhappy again and again because they don't believe that unhappiness is a matter of belief. They get unhappy about their behavior because they believe it reflects their basic natural self. They don't realize that what they dislike is what they believe is natural, not what is natural.

Much of their behavior, which they believe betrays their stupidity, is a perfectly natural lack of skill which they naturally want to improve—except they believe they should have known what they naturally could not have known.

Why do they believe these skills are so necessary for their lives? Because they believe they need to be certain ways other than they naturally are in order to be happy. They believe that they can't be happy by starting where they are. These people believe they need certain personality qualities in order to be happy, usually relational commodities such as sex-ability, charm, gracefulness, intelligence, etc.

Self-identified "stupid" people believe they need these relational commodities in order to be in a good bargaining position to get from others the things they need to be happy, such as money, approval, etc. They believe that feeling bad is the best way to change themselves. They believe that they need to be or should be "happy" in order to be happy. They believe happiness is success, and success is better than happiness, and that success at being happy will make them happier. They are wrong. Simply mistaken.

Nature vs. Belief

Many people become unhappy again and again because they don't believe that unhappiness is a matter of belief.

There are people who consider themselves stupid. Others usually agree with them that they truly are stupid. They learn over and over again and yet never seem to learn. They are often "lovable" people (insofar as they are often engaged in "doing" nice things for others). They love to receive attention and affection, to a point. After that point they feel that they have been exposed as unresponsive. In short, they fear looking stupid and reluctant.

These people do not consider themselves as unhappy. They attribute their unwanted behavior to their "stupidity" or "coldness" or some other quality which they consider "natural." In short, they believe that their unwanted feelings and behavior are natural rather than from beliefs.

These people believe that their behavior (internal or external) comes from their "true selves," instead of their beliefs about themselves. They get unhappy about their behavior because they believe it reflects their basic natural self. They do not accept that this behavior is unhappiness.

They believe they are unhappy about their natural behavior (which they don't want). They find themselves hating what they believe they naturally are. They don't realize that what they dislike is what they *believe* is natural, not what *is* natural. The very fact that they dislike their behavior is an indication that they are unhappy.

Much of their behavior, which they believe betrays their stupidity or "wrong" feeling, is often perfectly natural behavior which a person will also perfectly naturally not want to repeat. It is a perfectly natural lack of skill which a person will naturally want to improve—except they believe they should have already known what they naturally could not have known.

They believe they must account for "lacks" in themselves, whether those lacks are lack of skill or lack of imagination or lack of feeling or lack of caution or lack of prudence, etc. They account for these lacks as natural enough; but by the concept "natural" they mean "unfortunately natural," as if "natural curse" was the meaning of natural. They see natural lack as evil defect. Even if they come to see these lacks as a result of their unhappiness, they then believe that their unhappiness is a natural evil or defect or a result of one.

But natural lack or natural unhappiness in this sense is a transient thing, which will naturally fill when exposed. In fact, the "evil" of ignorance is only noticed when the person is beginning to learn and is no longer ignorant. Youth becomes maturity, lack of skill becomes skill, ignorance becomes knowledge, and with time comes experience.

When a person makes a "mistake" out of ignorance, the time of ignorance is naturally over and the time of "knowing better" has begun. We were ignorant "up till now" and "from now on" we know better.

Stupid people only see the "knowing better" now as a reason for being unhappy about the being ignorant "up till now." This they can usually justify because the so-called ignorance has been corrected previously and perhaps frequently in the past, yet they still make the same mistakes. Still, the reason these "mistakes" are now culpable and "stupid" mistakes are because they see them as natural proof that they are naturally intractable.

They do not see ignorance as merely natural, as a natural consequence of simply not yet having learned or a natural consequence of not being able to learn because of fear; but even worse: they see ignorance as natural evidence that they *do* not learn. Their proof is that, although they want to learn, they can't. Their proof that they want to learn is that they feel bad for not learning or not having learned. This is not proof of anything except that feeling bad about being ignorant prevents natural learning.

The belief that they ought to feel bad in order to learn is simply the belief that what they just learned, they didn't learn—the belief that learning should take place before they learn. They believe they should not have to learn the way people naturally learn—by simply being aware of some new desirable knowledge. They do not believe that the knowledge they now realize they want is desirable now. Their complaint is something like, "Now it is too late, I already made the mistake. What good is knowing and learning now? I am already screwed. See, I am a loser and stupid and don't learn."

They are so disappointed in not having already known because they believe there is something wrong or bad with natural ignorance. They only believe this because it embarrasses them. Embarrassment is only another way of saying that they showed to the world their evil defects and imperfection.

What is it that makes these defects so important, so crucial? Why do they believe these skills or feelings are so necessary for their lives? Simply because they believe they need to be certain ways other than they naturally are in order to be happy.

They believe that they can't be happy by starting where they are. They believe that something is missing—a feeling, a necessary feeling; a skill, a necessary ability to learn that they do not now have.

They simply believe that they do not have what it naturally takes to be happy.

Just like people who believe they need things from others to be happy (money, sex, love, approval), these people believe they need certain personality qualities in order to be happy.

These qualities always amount to what another would love to have from them also. Such qualities as affection, sex-ability, conversation ability, charm, gracefulness, intelligence, etc. are what many other people believe they need from them in order to be happy with them. These are relational commodities that are valued by most people and make interaction worthwhile and rewarding.

The rewards of interaction might be seen in one sense as arbitrary: copulation, dialogue, working together, etc. They almost seem to be endeavors created just for the sake of having something to do with someone. Actually they are truly valued naturally because they are the natural expression of free happy people manifesting their joy over another person's happiness which is also naturally manifesting itself.

In short, the "values" of relationship are not the *causes* of a happy relationship, but the *fruits*. Happy relationships are not the causes of individual happiness but its natural fruit.

Stupid people believe they need certain desirable "good" qualities in order to be in a good bargaining position to get from others the things (money, approval, etc.) they need to be happy. They dream of the lover who will be the key to unlock their passions or wisdom— then they will be able to see themselves as successful human beings. Then, they believe, they will be very happy.

The truth is, of course, that no one, not even a true god, could unlock what isn't there or free something that is already there freely.

Naturally you will be successful if first you are happy. Being happy is the true successfulness stupid people are striving for. They only want these qualities in order to be happy about who they are. They can do that now. Only their belief that they should be unhappy until they succeed is the cause of their unhappiness and "stupidity."

When they finally realize that no one may be able to "make" them into what they want to be, they believe they need supernatural help. They turn to drugs, stars, saviors, Christs, cosmic love—you name it. They despair of nature and its god who has not yet helped them but who someday may get "good" and change them or the world around them to suit their stupid ideas. Their stupid idea, of course, is that something, some necessary thing, is missing for their happiness.

They just simply believe that unhappiness is natural to them and don't believe that that is a belief. They, of course, believe it is an indisputable fact, which they, of course, can easily prove.

They wind up with a universe with no meaning, no natural goodness or happiness. They have a god who doesn't love them enough or who isn't god enough to straighten them out.

They do not believe that they choose to get unhappy with what they want to change, which would change naturally were it not for their anger.

They get unhappy about their behavior. They believe that is the best way to change. That is why they do it. Not because they are stupid or evil. They believe that feeling bad is the best way to change themselves. They are wrong. Simply mistaken. They then believe that the best way to learn what they just learned is to get unhappy about not having known it before.

They believe that changing themselves is more important than anything. They act like it is more important than happiness. But they only value changing themselves in order to be happy, and changing isn't necessary for happiness. Happiness is natural when you do not believe that anything is necessary, including "learning" to be happy.

These people find themselves striving for happiness so that they will be good and therefore happy. They see happiness as a "smart" way to be so they still strive for right, smartness, goodness, etc. in order to be happy.

Happiness is what happiness is for. They still believe that they need to be or should be "happy" in order to be happy. They believe happiness is success and success is better than happiness. Success at being happy will make them happier. In a way they could be right. But these people want to be right rather than happy.

They are idolaters—they believe that pleasing the idols of social values is where true happiness lies. They worship success, money, sexual prowess, intelligence and the successful interaction of these abilities. They believe that one can buy the other. Being a good lover can make them free to be good workers and one or the other can be traded to good advantage.

This point of view or way of life is indicating someone who does not desire happiness, but instead fears unhappiness.

Happiness and Safety

February 20, 1974

In the essay "Happiness and Safety," Bruce Di Marsico addresses the argument against happiness: "Perfect happiness would make me a willing victim of others, or would cause me to not take care of myself."

In summary, his rebuttal is that perfect happiness is the absence of whatever doesn't belong there. And if, for us, what we would want in our happiness is to be assertive, safe, and taking care of ourselves, then to define our happiness as not including these qualities is merely to call unhappiness "happiness," and then argue against unhappiness.

A distinction used in this essay is between *reason* and *cause*. Reason meaning, "the purpose for"; cause meaning "the generative force." For example, if I dropped a water balloon on someone, the reason (purpose for) their getting wet was to entertain me. The cause (generative force) of their getting wet was gravity, the velocity of my throw, the force of impact, etc. Gravity, since it is not a living entity, has no purposes—gravity does not make things fall for a reason, as a matter of intentionality, in order to accomplish something; rather, gravity *causes* things to fall.

Wanting is the cause of doing. Ultimately, there is no reason for your wanting. A simple example that Bruce Di Marsico used is: "What is the reason that you like the color of the shirt you are wearing today?" The only answer most people can give is that "they like the color." But liking the color is the cause of them selecting which shirt to buy; there is no purpose (reason) people have for liking one color more than another.

Ultimately, there can be the realization that there is no situation significantly different in cause and reason than liking the color of your shirt: you did whatever you did because you tended toward doing it, liked doing it, or doing it was to your taste (three equivalent statements)—and there is no ultimate reason for why what you did was to your taste.

Précis of "Happiness and Safety"

Unhappy people are just not able or willing to imagine perfect happiness as happy. Perfect happiness is the total absence of whatever does not belong there. Anyone who refuses to believe that they really want perfect happiness must find themselves balancing between "too happy that makes you unsafe" and "too safe that makes you miserable." Trying to balance yourself is manic-depressive. Trying to balance others and your environment is paranoiac-hysteria. What did the fear of perfect happiness consist of anyway, except that either everyone else was out to take advantage of you, or that without unhappiness to goad people, they would not work for what they wanted, or wouldn't even want anything?

What people mean by unhappiness is not feeling the way they want. The dilemma of this whole crazy belief system is that I can get a lot of what I want by not having the feelings from myself that I want. The belief is that I am some kind of absurd animal who must give up my good feelings in order to be good enough to myself to get what I want. The fact is, unhappy people are the most destructive of themselves, and never achieve what they want.

If I could distill the whole problem of human existence into words, it would sound like this belief: "Perfect happiness is not good for me." That belief can be made self-proving by manipulating the meanings and loading the words so that the terms are mutually exclusive. When pressed into seeing the contradiction, those who believe happiness is not safe rejoin with "happiness is unhealthy-making because we would not desire safety." They gloat at their intelligence in being able to come up with the perfect "reason" for fearing perfect happiness: it will kill them. They practically promise, "Make me perfectly happy, and I'll kill myself by not caring." There is a total disbelief that the life instinct they attribute to amoeba and grass and jackasses is present in them. We are scared of perfect happiness because we desire it more than life. This is precisely because we always play one against the other in order to motivate ourselves. Just because we may believe that perfect happiness is more desirable than safety, that doesn't in any sense imply that safety is not also desired more than anything else that could come second to happiness.

Life can never "mean" more than happiness. Anyone who believed that they could never be happy again would kill themselves.

The cause of wanting is before reason. I come up with reasons after I notice that I am wanting. Ultimately, wanting without reason becomes mere doing. It is only because we believe we have to have reasons to justify everything we want that we fear that perfect happiness is a place devoid of wanting. We have cause and reason so mixed up that we even say that gravity is the "reason" that things fall.

You find that when fear is gone, you don't believe in anything, since you don't have to justify what you want. You eat because you find you want to. You go and do and be what you want.

Happiness and Safety

The Option Method Trainer is not what is usually meant by a therapist, counselor or any kind of advisor. He or she wants to help the individual client to become happier. He wants to help by an exploration of the beliefs that make a person feel unhappy so that ultimately the individual clients will experience and know the freedom not to believe what are unnecessary beliefs, since they want to be happy.

The premise, as in all Option Method endeavors, is that all persons want to be as happy as possible. This, by definition and by nature, means not being any less happy than a person believes necessary for their being "most" happy.

The Idea of "Too Happy Is Bad for Me"

Since people believe that a certain amount of fear (unhappiness) is necessary for being happy (fearless), we will use a method that enables the most efficient exploration of that central belief.

To be as happy as possible is to be as happy as one believes possible without endangering (or making less possible) future happiness.

This presupposes a future, and a future belief which will have been determinable by a present experience of believing.

Since all present happiness is experienced only insofar as one's present beliefs allow, all so-called future happiness would be experienced as a present-time experience not determined by our past any more than any "now" experience is.

This myth of endangering future happiness also presupposes that if any endangerment is possible, it will be caused by being "too happy" previous to that "future" time.

No one seems to know what "too happy" feels like. They seem to believe that its effect would be to make one stupid, lackadaisical, carelessly carefree, un-ambitious, off-guard, reckless, unaware of danger, gullible; in short, an idiotic asshole. They also believe that being like this will then allow or encourage the surrounding world to take advantage of them, "walk" all over them, try hard to cheat them, "abuse" their openness by heaping them with insults and disregard, to neglect their desires since they are so easy to please and impossible to displease, and eventually to kill them. This all assumes that being "too happy" brings out the "worst" in others.

This may indeed be the way the world treats an idiotic asshole who does not care for himself. It is built into the description of the too-happy idiot that he possesses the most disastrous belief of all: that the world will love me and not hurt me.

"Gullibility" implies believing others will protect you. Why believe that? The same for "carefree," "lackadaisical," "restless," etc. The attitude of the idiot we fear being is that "nothing will hurt me and it doesn't matter if it does."

So it seems that "too happy" means not only believing that nothing will make me unhappy but nothing will even try, and if it does, I won't try to do anything about it since my happiness is assured anyway.

Somewhat concisely expressed, "being too happy now brings unhappiness later" means: "I will want things but I'll be too happy to want them enough to do anything to get them and I'll wind up wanting them enough to get them when it is too late to do anything."

More concisely put, "being too happy now brings unhappiness then" means that in the future: "I'll want things enough to get unhappy (regret) if I don't get them but not enough to do my best to get them. I will blame my happiness for that."

That attitude and behavior is no different now except that we blame our happiness under different names. We believe that if we are cheated, lied to, insulted, neglected, stupid, blind, etc., we say that we were too soft, too careless, not firm enough, etc. If someone we love disregards us, we believe there is something wrong with us—we were too accepting, too easy to please, but also not attractive and loving enough. On the one hand we become aware that if we are more happy, we would be less of a scaredy-cat and more confident and more loving, but on the other hand, we would be too patient and more tolerant of others. Our goal is then to gain the confidence and equanimity of a happy person but the uncompromising assertiveness of what we think unhappiness is. So we are believing two things: happiness brings love, peace of mind and loss of ambition, and unhappiness brings ambition of mind and loss of peace and love.

Therefore we strive for the goal of not too much peace nor too much agitation. A balance between misery and joy. A wife is angry because her husband doesn't love her more. She knows he is not inclined to love an angry woman but she also believes that if she is more loving, she will be encouraging and giving permission to his disregard and therefore get more disregard.

What if the premise to this whole dilemma is mistaken?

Being Happy and Being Assertive Are Not Incompatible

The premise behind the concept of being "too happy" is that one will become more permitting and accepting of what one does not want by being happy with whatever one does want.

Why can't the wife love her husband more, be more affectionate, be more encouraging of his love without also believing that she must enjoy his disregard of her? Why can't she be honestly where she's at? She wants more love and less disregard. That cannot change, whether she is unhappy or happy. If she becomes "too unhappy," she supposedly will not care about getting more love (she will be "fed up"). If she gets "too happy," she supposedly will not care about getting less disregard (she will be "complacent").

Neither of these sound like happy alternatives. Could it be that what we keep calling happiness is just mania? Another kind of un-happiness—euphoric depression? What if "too happy" is just another posture of fear, the fear of rocking the boat, upsetting the applecart, or basically, the fear of making another come to grips with your happiness?

Why couldn't a happy person fearlessly be assertive and ambitious and at peace and be loving all at the same time?

Why do we have to believe that a happy person can never say "no"? Why do we have to be angry in order to stand firm or work hard for what we want?

The happy person who is the idiotic asshole is not a happy person. He is very scared. Since he doesn't want to be angry or unhappy, he believes he has no way of mobilizing a "no" to come out of him since he also believes that it takes unhappiness to be assertive. With no way of saying "no" he must become subservient, blissful and peacefully unaware of anything he wants that might entail saying no.

He does not believe that there is a difference between the arrogant "no" of a fearful, angry person and the unswerving "no" of a peaceful confident person who just knows to act in his own best interest. He is afraid that if he stands firm, it must mean that he is unhappy and he is not wanting to be happy.

The truth is that this "too happy" person has the same mythic beliefs of the so-called "balanced" person. The way it is set up by popular acclaim, happiness "means" unhappiness one way or another. "Too happy" means another kind of unhappiness. Why must we conform to the popular belief that being very happy means being stupid and careless? Could not a confident person simply naturally be careful and joyful? The only way we keep ourselves from finding out is through the fear of being too happy.

Why do people want the ambitiousness if not to get what they want? And why do they want to get what they want? They will say "to be happier."

That contradiction is the very mistake. They find themselves wanting what they want in order to be happier. Everything they want they want in order to alleviate unhappiness or to increase happiness. Why do they have to connect them? Why can't they want what they want and also be happy? Why can't happiness be independent of all wanting? Not a help or a hindrance, just separate? Why must they always make the happiness and the decrease or increase of it at stake every time they begin on a course toward getting what they want?

It is like a person who, wanting to go for a walk, takes off his head and throws it down the road. Then he says "I must take this walk in order to regain my head."

Why can't he take the walk because he just simply knows he wants to? Why does he have to create an artificial reward or punishment system?

The "too happy" person not only will become unhappy but is unhappy if he believes that being happy and wanting have anything in common.

All unhappiness comes from the belief that I need it as punishment for not doing or getting what I want, and using that belief as a motivation to get me to get what I want.

Again: I believe that I can be unhappy in order to motivate me to be and do what I don't believe I would be or do if I didn't believe I would become unhappy.

My patients, one after another: "If I was perfectly happy, how would I motivate myself to get or do what I want?" or "Why would I want anything since I would not need it to be happy?"

Why indeed? These are fantastically beautiful questions and the relevance of these questions captures the profundity of the universe.

Happy Wanting

To answer these questions, you cannot be the one who asks these questions. You have to be the one who says, "I want perfect happiness more than I want anything." Then you could see that perfect happiness would not be a condition of depriving yourself of what you want, but getting what you want most.

The answers to the questions are deceptively simply. First: If you are perfectly happy, you would not motivate yourself to get or do what you want by unhappiness or the fear of not getting or doing. However you would motivate yourself, it would not be that way. Indeed, must you think in terms of motivation? If you were happy, you would not have to motivate yourself to do or get. You would simply do and get whatever was in your power and ability to do or get.

Second: If you were perfectly happy, you would not want anything because you needed it to be happy. Whatever you would be wanting, it would not be for that reason. If you were wanting, then you would be wanting. You would do what you wanted. What else could you do? The only reason you ever had for not doing what you wanted was fear, and that would be gone.

If you were perfectly happy, the cause of your wanting would not be the need for happiness. Whatever the cause of your wanting, it would not be fear or need of happiness. The cause of whatever wanting would be the same as the cause of your wanting that you experience now that is not connected to your need to be happy. Like your wanting to breathe. You can make up a reason for wanting to breathe, but the fact simply is that it is in you to know to breathe. You really don't even experience wanting it unless it is questioned. You can say you "want" to breathe to live and "want" to live to be happier, but what is the cause of your wanting to be happy?

The cause of wanting is you, your nature, yourself, your life. Ultimately you might even ask what is the cause of you, your nature, etc. Some say Nature, the Universe, a God, etc. Whatever causes the tree to "want" to grow and the man to be happy will be the cause of your "wanting" when perfectly happy.

At worst, since you will have no happiness-connected "reason" to want and it was possible not to want one thing more than another, because of that you could create a system of reasons. You could want some things for life and health, others for financial reasons, others for social reasons, etc. But there would be no need to disguise the reasons or pretend that you had to have health, wealth, love, etc., in order to be happier.

If you fear that a perfectly happy person is devoid of wanting because he is devoid of "reasons" (rationalizing justifications for wanting them), that still doesn't have to be a problem.

If he wasn't wanting to protect his life any more than he wanted to not protect it, what would he do? If protection and carelessness were of equal lack of concern, what would he do? Toss a coin? In order to do that, he would have to want a solution more than he didn't! What would he do? Sit on a log and watch himself rot? He would have to want that more than he wanted to move! If he would indeed be not wanting, then he would do what he would do and be glad for what he was doing while he was doing or not doing it.

If you fear that perfect happiness means unrationalized, blissful doing and being, you may be right. But if you think that means it would be something where you would not be the real you, the most beautiful, most truthful, the most effective, most powerful, most living and most good for you, you would have to be wrong. Whatever is the mechanism in us that wants us to be happy would have to want to stay alive to be able to continue to want us to be happy.

For example, say that what we call the experience of feeling happy is the physical phenomenon of the body functioning undisturbed by our beliefs in unhappiness. Then whatever causes us to desire happiness would of necessity cause also the desire to sustain whatever function is the feeling of happiness. Certainly, life, in some sense, is part of our experience of happiness. When happy, we feel alive.

Fearing Perfect Happiness as Bad for Safety

The image of perfect happiness leading to uncaring death is a description of a depressive person. Again, however perfect happiness is described by a person who is not perfectly happy, it always contains an element of perfect misery.

Unhappy people are just not able or willing to imagine perfect happiness as happy. It is always something that it could not be. Perhaps perfect happiness is the total absence of whatever does not belong there.

Perhaps perfect happiness is nothing to fear, since it would be real perfect happiness as experienced by a perfectly happy person.

Perhaps we don't have to worry about experiencing perfect happiness, because with our fears we never would. So, if I said to a patient, "Don't worry! You'll never be perfectly happy with your attitude," I wonder what he would say! Perhaps, "Thank Goodness!" Then I would warn him to watch out because he just became happier and thereby closer to the misery of "too happy." Or if he became unhappy at my first warning, I would congratulate him on becoming further away from perfect happiness and therefore more safe. Then he would receive my warning by being more happy about being safe.

Since anyone who refuses to believe that they really want perfect happiness must find themselves on a teeter-totter balancing between "too happy that makes you unsafe" and "too safe that makes you miserable," they must believe that their desire for happiness is their greatest enemy to the safety they desire.

Except that as they see themselves safer, they find themselves happier with their self-protectiveness and unhappy about being an angry, vicious, unloving, unloved, depressed jail of safety. This, of course, scares them and back they go to balancing. A life of endless ups and downs. Anyone who does not admit to the desire for perfect happiness is one kind of manic-depressive or another, and there are only two kinds of manic-depressives: hysterics and paranoiacs. These are the only way to really balance. Manic-depressives who do not balance well as paranoiacs or hysterics (and who does?) try to balance both those attitudes because they also don't want to be "too paranoid" or "too hysterical." For this they must balance their environment, indeed, their whole world. Anyone not powerful or successful enough at this cosmic balancing act has to tip toward the side that they most succeed with. A well-balanced environment will now allow them to return to their manic-depressive balancing act.

What I'm trying to say is simply this: trying to balance yourself is manic-depressive. Trying to balance others and your environment in order to balance yourself is paranoiac-hysteria.

The predicament of all these positions is that no matter what solution you come to, whenever you engage in a balancing act you find that your balance is ultimately affected by events you have no control over, either because you were truly powerless or because you weakened yourself by tipping "too far" one way or the other.

Your happiness and your safety are both dependent on things around you. The solution, of course, would then seem to be power properly gained, i.e., control over other people who in turn will assist in controlling your environment. This is the financial or political solution. Both have power as their ends, and the promise of shared power as their means. The president (or tyrant) of either organization offers the reward of your being better able to control your environment if you work to help in his efforts to control his own.

This, of course, is no solution for one simple reason. Since all who are involved in balancing in the first place believe that they are balancing against an imbalance that is already present. The president is aware that the greed of the worker or the citizen is the same as his own and vice versa. All the participants in the same solution are also presupposed to be the cause of the problem.

What did the fear of perfect happiness consist of anyway, except that either everyone else was out to take advantage of you or that without unhappiness to goad people, they would not work for what they wanted or wouldn't even want anything?

So all endeavors to achieve the balance must consist in working with the ambitious and dangerous enemy who needs to be held back or the harmless slacker who needs to be goaded. Witness all revolutionary movements and any corporate or parliamentary government or any hierarchy or any human organization.

All the solutions are based on the "fact" that all the problems are caused by wanting which is caused only by unhappiness. All the solutions are believed to be able to be achieved only by wanting which is only able to be motivated and achieved by fearing unhappiness.

Again, concisely, the fearful belief is that one can only be safe and get what one wants, and can only want at all, by being unhappy in order to motivate oneself.

The Absurdity of Unhappiness

The fact of the matter is that what people mean by unhappiness is not feeling the way they want (in fact, feeling a little or a lot sick).

The dilemma of this whole crazy belief system is that I can get a lot of what I want by not having the feelings from myself that I want.

The belief is that I am some kind of absurd animal, who must give up my good feelings in order to be good enough to myself to get what I want for my own good. For my own good I must not feel all the good I want to feel.

The fact is that unhappy people are the most destructive of themselves and never achieve what they want.

Since I succeed at getting what I want by fearing, then each time I succeed that way I learn and re-believe that I can get more. The more unhappy I get, the more I want something in order to be happy.

The fact is that unhappy people do want. They want desperately. But they want very few things and need those few things very much. They will disregard everything for affection, or money, or a drink, etc.

What has happened is that because they hooked their happiness onto something, they have to have it before they can do anything else that only happiness can do.

Only happiness can love, think clearly, sleep well, do things freely and stop doing things freely.

Unhappiness means needing something in order to be happy. Not wanting it in order to be happier, but needing it to be happy again. There is compulsion because there can be no freedom to forget what one needs to be happy.

Only in happiness can a person freely want without needing and attend to many wants.

If I could somehow distill the whole problem of human existence into words, it would sound like this belief:

"Perfect happiness is not good for me." That belief can be made self-proving by manipulating the meanings and loading the words so that the terms are mutually exclusive. The belief itself is phrased by believers who believe that in their stating of this belief, they have somehow uttered a true fact of existence and they themselves are the holders of absolute knowledge as if they had experienced perfect happiness and returned.

Others may admit that they are guessing and are not taking any chances that the statement is not true, because there may not be any return from perfect happiness if they dared it.

They all assume they might achieve it if they dared.

One thing is clear: by believing this they are still able to believe in perfect happiness as possible, but account for not achieving it by a "sour grapes" saying like "I don't really want it."

They all allow it as a future possibility once they admit it is a state of believing.

By saying it is bad, they say it would be something they would not want.

Why is anything bad? What do humans mean by badness? All mean "unhappy-making"! When they are pressed into seeing the contradiction, they rejoin with "unhealthy-making" because we would not desire safety. This, to them, appears like a definition one could not refute. They gloat at their intelligence in being able to come up with the perfect "reason" for fearing perfect happiness. It will kill them. The "it," of course, is themselves. They, as perfectly happy, will consent to death and do nothing to prevent it. They practically promise to do so. It's as if they said to me, "Make me perfectly happy and I'll kill myself by not caring."

There is total disbelief that their natures, unimpeded by "reasons" for wanting to live, would not let them know what to do to live.

There is a total disbelief that the life instinct they attribute to amoeba and grass and jackasses is not present in them.

There is a total disbelief that their reasoning ability could be used in figuring out how to stay alive instead of always trying to figure out a reason for wanting to stay alive.

The question it boils down to is: if it is not in their nature to try to stay alive, what is prompting their reasoning into always coming up with an answer like "I'm alive because I am wanting to be safe"? If the tendency toward safety was not in them, what is prompting them to wanting to use unhappiness as a motivation to watch out?

What motivates us to try to motivate ourselves by unhappiness to get what we want if it is not the wanting, pure and simple, before reason?

I do not suggest we want without cause or without reason, but only that cause and reason are not the same. The cause of wanting is before reason. I come up with reasons after I notice that I am wanting, or else why bother wanting to reason?

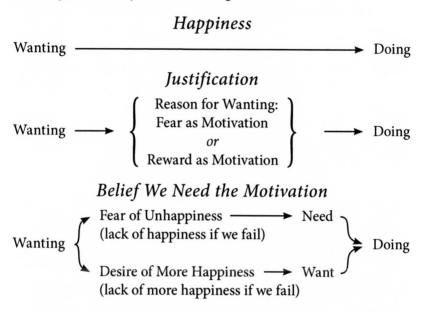

Happiness

Wanting ⟶ Doing

Justification

Wanting ⟶ { Reason for Wanting: Fear as Motivation *or* Reward as Motivation } ⟶ Doing

Belief We Need the Motivation

Wanting { Fear of Unhappiness ⟶ Need (lack of happiness if we fail) / Desire of More Happiness ⟶ Want (lack of more happiness if we fail) } Doing

If we get what we want, we attribute it to our motivation and its rationale.

"I would not have gotten what I wanted if I thought I could be happy without it, or I would not work towards what I wanted if I didn't believe it would make me happier. So with life."

Belief in the Need for Motivation

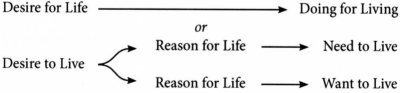

Desire for Life ⟶ Doing for Living

or

Desire to Live < Reason for Life ⟶ Need to Live / Reason for Life ⟶ Want to Live

"If I am perfectly happy, I will not have any reason to want to live." This is what is really meant by the fear of perfect happiness, since we believe we only want for reasons.

The wanting to live must be a powerful wanting, since it is the cause of seeking reasons for wanting to live. The only reason the desire to live constantly seeks reasons to live is that unhappiness constantly makes living seem less desirable.

It is because we use unhappiness to stay alive that we need reasons to want to live.

We don't fear perfect happiness. We fear that we have already killed our instinct for survival with our life of unhappiness. But it could only be our instinct for survival that is prompting us to be concerned that we may have killed it.

What we recognize is that if we were perfectly happy, we would (or might) want that more than we would want to live.

That is the predicament that we are in now.

It is now that we are wanting perfect happiness more than we want to live because we have made living less than perfectly happy. It is precisely because we make living so unhappy that we are scared that we will prefer one to the other. We are scared of perfect happiness because we desire it more than life. This is precisely because we always play one against the other in order to motivate ourselves. We fear blissful oblivion because we constantly play bliss against being and still desire happiness more. We desire happiness more simply because "happiness" is our word for that which we desire more than everything else when we make our desire for everything tinged with threat of unhappiness or danger. Everything we do or get has fear as an ingredient to its accomplishment. We need to justify our every wanting for fear that we will wind up unhappy or dead or both.

If we saw wanting as wanting and happiness as happiness and didn't threaten one with the other, would we believe that happiness is a threat to life?

If man is vulnerable and must suffer physical pain and death, all unhappiness can do is add unhappiness to the experience.

If pain and death do not have the ability to magically cause unhappiness and cannot rob us of bliss (unless we believe we have to hate ourselves not to prevent these events), then can we be sure that the perfectly happy person would not do anything that could even allow the slightest approach of whatever is not desired in life except for that which is more greatly desired?

If a perfectly happy person did not want safety that would only be because he was perfectly safe.

Just because we may believe that perfect happiness is more desirable than safety, that doesn't in any sense imply that safety is not also desired (no matter how much less) more than anything else that could come second to happiness.

If a person were perfectly happy, he would not want to be perfectly happy, so the only wanting would be for what he was not being. If he were not safe, he would want safety. If he were safe, he would not need to want safety, etc.

A perfectly happy person would not need reasons in order to want because all wanting would be good (in the sense that no wanting could be unhappiness-producing) and all doing would be good (because he would do nothing that could make him unhappy).

Happiness is the word we give to our cause for wanting anything. We always want for this reason or that, and that comes to happiness.

Life can never "mean" more than happiness. Anyone who believed that they could never be happy again would kill themselves.

Even the reason we want to live is connected to the desire for "happiness." When there is no hope for happiness, people will refuse to live. For some, getting what they want is so inextricably bound to being happy that they refuse to live if a lover leaves or they fail a test, etc. They see the endless fruitlessness of the game they have set up by using unhappiness as a way to everything (even happiness) that they seem to have no choice.

It is only because we believe we have to have reasons to justify everything we want that we fear perfect happiness is a place devoid of wanting.

Wanting means having reasons to move. We have cause and reason so mixed up that we even say that gravity is the "reason" that things fall.

Scientists start out searching for a cause and wind up finding "reasons." Psychologists and theologians especially are always giving us the causes why people act the way they do, but all they have really discovered is the reasons people use.

The parent's unhappiness (or neurosis/sin) could hardly be the cause of the child's unhappiness (neurosis/sin) but it surely will serve everybody as a good reason, including the child.

When we have no reasons for wanting to live or die, we will either want to live or not want to. But remember, there will be no unhappiness prompting us to give up life. Since life will be perfectly happy, it will not be played against happiness in order to stay alive. We will live if (we do what it takes) we consent to living and being, and do not consent to dying and unbeing.

When we consent to perfect happiness, we are consenting to feeling and being all that up to then we have wanted most to be.

Perfect happiness means knowing that nothing could make you unhappy. Nothing. Not you, not the universe of people, things or events. Nothing of non-being can make you unhappy either, not lies, not fantasies, not others' fears, not disease, not death.

Since perfect happiness means knowing being, it cannot imply the cessation of knowing or being. A perfectly happy being cannot "know" that he will stop knowing or being.

We may be able to be happy while poor, or in pain, or hungry, but we cannot be happy without knowing that we are happy.

Perfect happiness means knowing and believing that perfect happiness cannot be taken away or ended by anything being, myself included.

Fearing That We Could Turn
Away from Happiness

August 4, 1974

Any time anyone turns away from happiness (chooses unhappiness), it is because they are believing happiness to be something unhappy. No one would, it would seem, turn away from happiness that is truly Happiness. Why do we distort the only truly sought future: happiness? It is precisely because we fear that if we admitted the truth, i.e., that happiness is truly Happy, we may still turn away from it or not choose it.

We trick ourselves into believing happy is something to fear so that we do not have to believe something worse; that we would turn away or not choose happiness if we saw it purely as happiness, our heart's desire. And so, we condemn ourselves to what we most fear; that we would turn away from happiness.

If we believe that we might not choose happiness, we are in a state of fear of ourselves. We believe we are no good for ourselves. A person in fear sees even happiness as fearful; it is something like a horrible test of our true selves which we might fail. So rather than face the eventuality that I might find myself choosing against the only good, the only object of my life, the only desire of my heart, I forestall the choice by believing that I don't yet face that choice. I say that I am not yet seeing pure happiness and so I do not have to believe I might reject it if I saw it. I say "If I saw happiness purely, I would never reject it, but it's a shame that it doesn't show itself purely to me."

The truth is that we would not, of course, reject pure happiness, but we don't believe that, so we distort; we do not see it, and then say happiness is not showing itself clearly. It is as clear and as visible as nothing else could be. Nothing could be more visible. Happiness is happiness. We are just afraid to see it for fear that we would see ourselves rejecting it. Happiness is not hiding, nor is it elusive; it is the most present, most obvious reality. We shy our eyes away constantly. When it comes to us directly, unabashedly, decidedly, unequivocally and stirs our hearts and bodies, we distort our mind's eye and say that it is not here yet. We say "It is not clear. I need a more visible manifestation, bigger, more dramatic, more mind-blowing." All we are saying is "I have tightened my mind and closed my heart; happiness has to blow my mind and grab my heart so that I can be free to see what I want to see." But do you really mean that you *want* to see it? The truth is that you are afraid to see, afraid to see that in the face of the undeniable, you will still deny. So that is what you do.

What you have seen and known is undeniable. Yet you deny. You really are denying nothing. What you are saying is that you need to believe it hasn't happened yet so you can believe that by your denying, you are not *really* denying the Big Thing.

You will not deny happiness. If you know that, then you are now not denying it. You just only have to know who you are. You do not deny happiness.

If you don't do what you want, it is for similar reasons as denying happiness: you are not believing that your wanting is good and perfect and comes from the best of who you really are. You will not believe it comes from your best intentions. You will not believe that it comes from your knowing yourself, from what you want for your future, from Happiness itself, from God.

You are afraid to admit that. You say that if you saw that, then you would do what you want. That is true; but you don't believe it. You are afraid that even if you perfectly saw God wanting *as* you, as your form, you still might not do what you wanted, because you are afraid that you would go against your perfect knowing, which you say that you know only imperfectly.

Because you fear, for no reason, that you may go against your wanting, you condemn yourselves to do just that.

Acknowledgments

MY DEEPEST THANKS AND GRATITUDE TO THE MANY HANDS THAT helped birth this book. Aryeh Nielsen had the vision for this project; without his ideas, archival preservation work and enthusiasm, this book would still exist only in our imaginations. Richard Banton caught all of the big mistakes as we began to work with the raw material. Wendy Dolber, Bruce's student and friend, spent months reviewing; her watchful eye, editing skills and comprehensive understanding of Option was essential in making sure we "got it right." Frank Mosca's further review, editing and feedback was invaluable and put me at ease, knowing we had not missed anything important. I'd also like to thank Frank for his Foreword for this book as he so eloquently captured how so many of us feel about Bruce's work. Finally I would like to thank all of The Option Method students the world over who have patiently supported our efforts.

Deborah Mendel

The Editing Process

Bruce Di Marsico primarily taught in a group context. He often wrote short essays as seeds for group discussion, and would read the essay at the start of gatherings, followed by interactive discussion and commentary.

These essays sometimes were descriptive, and sometimes were poetic meditations. Bruce also wrote some essays for personal use, working out how best to convey an idea or to communicate to a particular person about a particular issue.

Bruce primarily worked through the spoken word, not the written. He recorded tapes of group gatherings from the 1970s through the 1990s, and over 500 hours of tapes exist. This represents an overwhelming amount of material, and so this work contains only a selection of materials from these tapes.

Both written and verbal works have sometimes been edited quite a bit for presentation here. While some pieces are exactly as written, others may have been modified by removing secondary themes to create a more focused essay, by weaving together two essays or talks on the same subject, by cutting whole sections of interactive discussions, or by adding a few extra words to clarify what did not need to be clarified in the context of an ongoing discussion. The principle was to only do what could be done with the confidence of maintaining the integrity of his authorial intent, as judged by some of Bruce's closest students.

The commentary sections in these volumes are to bring forth points that are felt to represent Bruce's ideas but for which good source material could not be found for using Bruce's own words. Some commentary is a synopsis of ideas that Bruce Di Marsico expressed in many writings or talks but did not express summarily in a single writing or talk. For example, a wide-ranging discussion about a topic over six hours of tapes might leave a very clear impression of Bruce's teachings on a subject, but present a great difficulty in extracting his words directly into a short, relatively linear essay.

Other commentary represents the editor's synthesis of ideas Bruce Di Marsico expressed only in fragments, such as intriguing short asides. In this case, there is more editorial extrapolation.

Finally, some commentaries are based on the editor's understanding of Bruce Di Marsico's teachings, often created in response to common misunderstandings of Option. These commentaries are not directly traceable to Bruce's words but may be edifying nonetheless.

The relationship of a given commentary to Bruce's work is stated at the opening of the commentary. Additionally, whenever an essay or talk can be traced to a particular date (and the vast majority can be so traced), the date is included so that future researchers of the archives of Bruce's material can easily check the edited version against the original.

The archives contain great quantities of materials that are wonderful and valuable, but were not presented here both for the sake of limiting the size of the volumes and not delaying their release by a period of decades! What is *not* here is the complete history of Bruce's playing out of Option in all the lived situations that actual people brought to him.

On that point, since Bruce often used a questioner's own language, a given talk might use a given term very differently than another talk, because the talk was in response to a different person. The context will make this clear.

As we continue to research the archives, and respond to questions for clarification, subsequent editions will invariably be created. Yet what is collected here is unquestionably more than sufficient for a complete understanding of Option. Enjoy!

About Bruce Di Marsico

Bruce Michael Di Marsico was born in 1942 in Weehawken, New Jersey. He was the first child born to Onofrio (Alfred) Di Marsico and Elizabeth (Bette) Bauer. In their first child they found an exceptionally bright and precocious boy. While Alfred tried disciplinarian methods, Bette turned to Dr. Spock in raising him. As Bruce grew older he became so adept at reasoning with his mother when he wanted something that it became obvious it was she who was learning from him.

Bruce was a restless child in school and was advanced a grade in elementary school after being tested by a psychologist. When it came time to attend high school he requested that he attend a Catholic school. He was drawn to a spiritual quest at a very young age. Upon graduating high school he was still seeking an immersion in theological study and chose to pursue a monastic life. He entered the Trappist order. After spending some time there as a novice he realized it was not the right path for him.

He decided to attend university and explore psychology and philosophy. He was fascinated by mankind's eternal pursuit of happiness. He thoroughly enjoyed the spiritual passions of the heart and soul. He always kept a volume or two of Butler's *The Lives of the Saints* at his bedside, loving the mysteries of the mystics. It was his own quest for happiness—the same desire that drew him to Catholic school, the monastery and the study of the works and teachings of many, from Buddha to Freud, that he came to create the Option teachings and Attitude. However, it was because of the joy he derived from helping others that he naturally came to develop The Option Method.

Bruce drew upon the wisdom of ancient philosophers. It was the Greek philosopher Epictetus who said, "Men are not worried by things, but by their ideas about things. When we meet with difficulties, become anxious or troubled, let us not blame others, but rather ourselves, that is, our ideas about things." Bruce realized it was not what was happening that made people unhappy, but their beliefs about what was happening that created their emotional responses. He developed his Option Method Questions based on the Socratic Method of teaching using non-judgmental questions. The theory of recollection, according to Socrates, means that before we are born we possess all knowledge. We are never taught anything new, but instead are reminded of things we already know. Bruce felt this was true about our happiness. He believed that every one of us already possesses everything we need to be happy.

Bruce became a psychotherapist, and around 1970 introduced Option at a paraprofessional school called Group Relations Ongo-ing Workshops (GROW) in New York City. Bruce's classes became "standing room only" as he taught laymen and practitioners from a variety of backgrounds his Option Method. Over the years Bruce offered various workshops and groups in and around New York City, Long Island and New Jersey. When GROW closed, a group of students asked him to continue teaching them. He created what came to be known as the "Monday night group" at his home in Montclair, New Jersey. A closeness and camaraderie developed among them and oftentimes discussions would carry on into dawn, with breaks for fettuccini alfredo, family style, in the large eat-in kitchen. You will find transcripts of recordings of these groups throughout this book.

In the 1980s and 1990s Bruce continued to conduct workshops and groups from his home in Montclair as well as seeing private clients in his office in Greenwich Village, New York City. You will also find material from these workshops within these pages. It was during this time that Bruce was diagnosed with heart disease and later diabetes. Through years of physical pain and suffering, he con-tinued to teach as he did in his last recorded lecture on November 11, 1995, transcribed in these volumes. Bruce was a testament to his own Option realization that pain itself cannot cause us to be unhappy. Bruce passed away on December 4th, 1995, with several of his last students at his side.

Deborah Mendel

Index

A

Anger 315
Anxiety 312
Appreciation 323
Asking 257
Attraction 39, 163

B

Behavior
    Option Method model of 65
Beliefs
    and causality 27
    as biological 25
    as not a problem 10
    as not verbal 8
    as personal 15
    biological definition 53
    defined 55
    known as the truth 174
    testing 16, 51
Body
    as happy 6
    believing with 5
Boredom 37, 325

C

Commitment 234
Consequences 277

D

Debts. *See* Obligation
Depression 322, 347
Desire
    and causality 27
Desiring. *See* Wanting
Despair 313
Doing
    as sign of self 187
    happiness and 182
    not knowing what to do 185
    possible 184
    what you want 197

E

Emotions 131
    and wanting 59
    in relation to Stimulus-
        Organism-Response 66
    negative 135

F

Fear 307, 309
    of changing desires 168
Feelings
    bad 289
Future
    and believing 18

CPSIA information can be obtained at www.ICGtesting.com
Printed in the USA
BVOW020135101111

275681BV00002B/16/P